THE NÜRNBERG CASE

MR. JUSTICE JACKSON CLOSES THE CASE FOR
THE UNITED STATES

"If you were to say of these men that they are not guilty, it would be as true to say there has been no war, there are no slain, there has been no crime."

THE
NÜRNBERG CASE

AS PRESENTED BY

ROBERT H. JACKSON

CHIEF OF COUNSEL FOR THE UNITED STATES

TOGETHER WITH
OTHER DOCUMENTS

NEW YORK
COOPER SQUARE PUBLISHERS, INC.
1971

Originally Published and Copyright © 1947 by
Alfred A. Knopf, Inc.
Reprinted by Permission of Alfred A. Knopf, Inc.
Published 1971 by Cooper Square Publishers, Inc.
59 Fourth Avenue, New York, N. Y. 10003
International Standard Book No. 0-8154-0403-4
Library of Congress Catalog Card No. 73-166584

Printed in the United States of America, by
Noble Offset Printers, Inc. New York, N.Y. 10003

PREFACE

THE mission of this book is to make conveniently available fundamental information about the world's first international criminal assizes. Although the Nürnberg trials of the Nazi war criminals may profoundly influence their lives, few people will have the inclination and fewer will find time to read the transcript of the testimony running to some seventeen thousand pages, or the four thousand documentary exhibits which make up several volumes. To condense the evidence and to relate it to the doctrine of the case in a series of addresses to the Tribunal was my duty as Chief of Counsel for the United States. These speeches were addressed to a bench which had heard all of the evidence with notable patience and close attention and may sometimes assume background knowledge not possessed by the average reader. But they are not in technical terms and perhaps present as comprehensive a statement of the contentions of the prosecution as most readers will find time to study. I am grateful for the offer of the house of Knopf to publish them as a means to inform my countrymen, laymen as well as lawyers, what was being done in their name abroad and to invite support for the principles on which the case was founded.

The idea of bringing the top Nazi leaders and organizations to trial as criminals had originated and had been the subject of extensive study in the War, State, and Justice Departments long before I was enlisted in the case. It was discussed in general terms at the Yalta Conference. At the time of President Roosevelt's death Judge Samuel I. Rosenman was representing him abroad to obtain an agreement among the nations on a plan of trial. He later presented a program to the Soviet, French, and British Foreign Ministers at San Francisco. Extensive consideration, however, was deferred and the task of negotiation ultimately was delegated to me.

Meanwhile, the first authoritative and definitive public announcement of the program of the United States was made when President Truman approved and released my Report of June 7, 1945. This was widely published in Europe and, because of

v

the President's approval, became a sort of bench mark by which all subsequent proposals were surveyed. For that reason it is included in this book.

The negotiations between the United Kingdom, the Soviet Union, France, and the United States resulted in the Agreement of London, signed on August 8, 1945, which adopted a Charter for an International Military Tribunal. It is significant for two features—the definition of international crimes, contained in Article 6 thereof, and the procedure which it establishes for the trial of the accused. The importance to International Law of this definition, particularly as to Crimes against Peace, was a theme of the Opening Speech.

The procedure prescribed was designed to be workable and efficient, to not offend the sense of fairness of any of the peoples involved, and to reconcile the conflicting legal philosophies of the four signatory nations. This was not easy. Some concepts basic in Anglo-American legal thinking are not accepted by Continental peoples and some of our phrases which embody assumptions are not even translatable for want of equivalent terms. Cross-examination, considered by us the best way of testing the truthfulness of testimony, is little used in Continental practice because witnesses are usually interrogated by the judges instead of by first one and then the other of adversary counsel. Indictment also carries different implications in different systems of law. It was something of a shock to me to hear the Russian delegation object to our Anglo-American practice as not fair to a defendant. The point of the observation was this: We indict merely by charging the crime in general terms and then we produce the evidence at the trial. Their method requires that the defendant be given, as part of the indictment, all evidence to be used against him—both documents and the statements of witnesses. An indictment in this form is a sort of self-proving document. The trial therefore becomes less a matter of hearing proof of the indictment than of hearing what the defendant can show to overcome the evidence contained in the indictment. So, while we may think that Continental procedure puts too much burden of proof on the defendant, the Anglo-American method seems unfair to them because it does not inform a defendant of the whole evidence against him. When we produce it at the trial it may cause surprise and become known too late to be answered adequately. Our method, it is said, makes a criminal trial something of a game. This criticism is certainly not irrational.

Some differences in legal philosophy between the signatory powers have resulted in advantage to the defendants. For example, under most Continental practices a defendant may not testify under oath in his own defense, but at the end of the trial may make an unsworn statement. While this once was the law in England, it has been abandoned there and in most American jurisdictions. Few Anglo-American lawyers would think it just if a defendant could not testify for himself. On the other hand, few Continental lawyers would think it just if a defendant were not allowed to close the case with an unsworn statement of his own. So we settled the conflict by allowing these defendants to do both.

While the Charter is not a long document and necessarily left much to the discretion of the Tribunal, it proved to be a very workable instrument. It required counsel for defendants and carefully laid down the conditions of fair hearing. It simplified rules of evidence by requiring that any evidence deemed to have probative value be heard. The effort was to shift the trial controversy away from preliminary argument about technical rules of admissibility of evidence to ultimate questions of its value. Judges trained in four different legal systems were obliged to exercise their judgments on the many problems that arose in course of a trial. It is notable that while there were differences of opinion among them at times, solutions were found always sufficiently acceptable from the viewpoint of all systems of law so that no member ever publicly dissented in a matter of procedure or evidence.

The Indictment was presented at the first public session of the Tribunal, held October 18, 1945, at Berlin. It had organized by choosing the Right Honourable Lord Justice Geoffrey Lawrence of Great Britain as its President. His patience and Britannic calm did much to impress defendants, their counsel, and spectators with the fairness and dignity of the proceedings. The other members, Honorable Francis Biddle, with Judge John J. Parker as alternate for the United States, Monsieur le Professeur Donnedieu de Vabres, with Monsieur le Conseiller Robert Falco for the

PREFACE

French Republic, Major General Jurisprudence I. T. Nikitchenko with Lieutenant Colonel A. F. Volchkov as alternate for the Union of Soviet Socialist Republics, and the Honorable Mr. Justice Birkett as alternate for the presiding member, constituted a court of broad experience and conspicuous ability.

The trial opened in the bomb-damaged Palace of Justice at Nürnberg on November 20, 1945. This was only some six months after the surrender of Germany. The imperative public demand for getting on with the trial was met at some cost in preparation and organization of the case. I am sure that a longer period of preparation would have saved trial time and would have enabled us to present a more compact case in a more workmanlike manner. As the United States had the largest part of the case to present, that is, the conspiracy count, and had to do it at the opening, we more than others felt the disadvantages of the public pressure for haste.

On two basic decisions of trial policy there was disagreement among members of the United States staff. The first was whether primarily to rely on documents or an oral testimony of witnesses. Our staff had hurriedly screened over 100,000 captured documents, about 4,000 of which were translated and ultimately used as evidence. One view was that the appearance of witnesses would afford greater news interest than the documents, which should be used only incidentally. I decided, however, and with the concurrence of most of our staff, to make captured documents the foundation of the American case, using witnesses sparingly. We called less than a half-dozen. This reliance chiefly on documents admittedly made a drab case from a news point of view and a difficult one to report. However, the disinterestedness and unquestioned authenticity of documents settle doubts which always would linger if the same story were told by witnesses, the best of whom always are open to suspicion of bias, bad memory, and influence. While no doubt we sacrificed something of contemporary interest, I am confident that the strategy laid a more solid foundation for the case in history, particularly and importantly in German history. In its judgment the Court said: "The case, therefore, against the defendants rests in large measure on documents of their own making, the authenticity of which has not been challenged except in one or two cases."

PREFACE

Another issue was whether to call certain of the defendants as prosecution witnesses against other defendants. This, of course, would have made a dramatic performance. Some possessed damaging information about their fellow defendants and probably could have been induced to testify. One defendant, in fact, intimated through counsel a willingness to co-operate with the prosecution if he could be assured that he would be shot rather than hanged. He assumed he would be convicted and in this was not disappointed. The concession would seem rather trivial to me but, under the German code, to be shot is to die an honorable soldier's death, to be hanged is to die as a culprit, unworthily. My primary objection to using testimony of some defendants to convict others was that such testimony always would carry the odor of a bargain. It always would be suspect. Instead, the strategy adopted was to try to make a case on the documents so strong that each defendant would feel obliged to take the stand in his own defense, then to bring out by cross-examination such damaging information as he had about others. This was successful with all defendants except Frick and Hess who did not take the witness box, but both nevertheless were convicted. This did not put us in the position of asking favors from those we were prosecuting. I am convinced that we obtained substantially all of the information in this way that we could have obtained by a bargain. The testimony thus obtained is not discredited by the suspicion that it was influenced by promises or expectations of leniency.

The Opening Statement and the Closing Speech for the United States, one anticipating, the other reviewing the evidence, state the substance of the conspiracy case against the individual defendants. Both speeches refer by citation or by footnotes to documents which support the text. These documents are published in English translation, under these designations, in eight volumes by the Government Printing Office. They can be made available by the War or the State Department and by libraries generally to those who desire to pursue the subject to sources.

The Tribunal asked the prosecution to expound in a separate argument the theory of the Charter provisions which authorize it to declare the accused Nazi organizations to have been criminal ones. The argument for the United States on that much misunderstood and somewhat difficult subject is also included in this volume. The evidence against particular organizations is not presented in the argument which deals only with the principles by which the evidence should be weighed and the organization cases decided.

Some excerpts from cross-examinations of defendants are also included in this volume. The case derived much strength from defendants' admissions and assertions in response to cross-examination. No attempt is made to cover all the issues tried or to collect all of the testimony on any particular subject. The object is not to convince the reader, but to let him learn something of the Nazi philosophy which has made so much trouble for the world from the lips of its champions, and to catch some of the atmosphere of the trial. A free citizen could learn few more useful lessons than Göring's Machiavellian exposition of the measures which every dictatorship finds necessary to consolidate and maintain its power. Americans ought to be taught to recognize the early symptoms of such trends, for they can be checked only in their incipient stages. And the underlying philosophy of the whole Nazi movement—that the end justified the means—is nowhere better exposed than by Schacht, whose acquittal was one of the disappontments of the judgment. Confronted with one deception after another, he finally declared to the judges, whom he was asking to believe his words against his acts, "I think you can score many more successes when you want to lead someone if you don't tell them the truth than if you tell them the truth."

The cross-examinations as here presented are taken from the official transcript before revision. All answers were interpreted from the German. The difference in sentence structures of the two languages makes instantaneous interpreting difficult. Some corrections have been made herein, but the form of expression is not unlikely to be altered in the final verified official text. Repetitions and irrelevancies have been eliminated. The effort has been to present fairly the position of the witnesses on the subjects treated. All defendants were interrogated by the American staff before trial, and most of them before indictment. In cross-examination it is these prior interrogations which are so frequently quoted.

It is unfortunate that the pretrial interrogations of these men will probably remain unpublished. There was a candor and absence of posing while being privately examined that did not always prevail at the trial when they were aware that they had the world as an audience. I cannot forbear to quote a sample of such unconscious candor from an interrogation of Ribbentrop which is both amusing and illuminating as to the German mentality. In answering some questions, he referred to the war as "so terrible," and I asked: "When did the war become terrible, Ribbentrop? When did this war impress you as terrible?" Without the twinkle of an eye or trace of a smile he replied in deadly seriousness, "It became to me terrible—I can tell you the exact moment. From the moment of the African landing—I mean of the English-American forces." And this seemed a fair statement of the attitude almost universal among the Nazis—it was a terrible war when it became a losing one. So long as it was winning few of them saw anything terrible about it.

A word should be said about the defendants' counsel. Two of the defendants—two of the most blood-stained men in the dock, both of whom were sentenced to death by hanging—were lawyers. Kaltenbrunner, head of the dreaded Gestapo and overseer of the system of concentration camps, was a disbarred Austrian advocate. Hans Frank, Governor-General of Poland, was titular head of the German legal profession under the Nazi regime. The dock was not lacking in legal acumen and it knew the German legal profession well. Each defendant was allowed to choose his counsel, and if he could not get counsel of his choice counsel was assigned by the Tribunal. Several of these counsel, both chosen and assigned, had been ardent Nazis and more than one was unrepentant.

The defendants' counsel were men of learning. They were not unprofessionally obstructionist or disrespectful towards the Tribunal. Many of them were sincerely amazed at the trial's disclosures. Several of them had sharp differences with their own clients. Trained in a legal system where the judge conducts the examination of witnesses, their own examination of witnesses seemed clumsy and their cross-examinations somewhat inept. But they did their duty to their clients in the best tradition of the profession.

The chasm that separates the thinking of the German legal profession from that of the Anglo-American profession today certainly is greater than that between us and the French. I am convinced it is as great as that between us and the Russians. This was not always so. The summations of most of the German counsel were extremely abstract and philosophical with relatively little attention to questions of fact. But perhaps it is not fair to generalize too much on an experience in one case in which most of the facts were capable neither of denial nor of defense, and in which refuge in abstract philosophy may have been the most hopeful course. At all events, the German judges and the legal profession as a whole were among the last of the groups to stand out against the Nazi regime. For this they are entitled to great credit. But the long, absolute, and terrifying Nazi control did much to demoralize the legal profession of Germany, as it did all decent elements of German life.

The trial occupied 216 days of trial time. The 4 prosecutors together called 33 witnesses in addition to the documentary, photographic, and motion picture exhibits. The defendants called 61 witnesses, used interrogatories answered by 143 witnesses, and 19 of them took the stand. The proceedings were conducted and recorded simultaneously in English, German, French, and Russian languages, and all proceedings were sound-recorded in the original language.

The Tribunal on September 30 and October 1, 1946, rendered judgment in the first international criminal assizes in history. It found 19 of the 22 defendants guilty on one or more of the counts of the Indictment and acquitted 3—Schacht, Von Papen, and Fritzsche. It sentenced 12 to death by hanging, 3 to imprisonment for life, and the 4 others to terms of 10 to 20 years imprisonment. The convictions and sentences were as follows:

	Count 1	Count 2	Count 3	Count 4	Fate
Hermann Göring	G	G	G	G	Hanging †
Rudolf Hess	G	G	I	I	Life
Martin Bormann	I		G	G	Hanging *
Joachim von Ribbentrop	G	G	G	G	Hanging *
Wilhelm Keitel	G	G	G	G	Hanging *
Ernst Kaltenbrünner	I		G	G	Hanging *
Alfred Rosenberg	G	G	G	G	Hanging *
Hans Frank	I		G	G	Hanging *

Wilhelm Frick	I	G	G	G	Hanging *
Julius Streicher	I			G	Hanging *
Walther Funk	I	G	G	G	Life
Hjalmar Schacht	I	I			Acquitted
Karl Dönitz	I	G	G		10 years
Erich Raeder	G	G	G		Life
Baldur von Schirach	I			G	20 years
Fritz Sauckel	I	I	G	G	Hanging *
Alfred Jodl	G	G	G	G	Hanging *
Franz von Papen	I	I			Acquitted
Artur Seyss-Inquart	I	G	G	G	Hanging *
Albert Speer	I	I	G	G	20 years
Constantin von Neurath	G	G	G	G	15 years
Hans Fritzsche	I	G	I	I	Acquitted

(G—guilty; I—innocent; Blank—not accused)
* Sentences carried out October 16, 1946 at Nürnberg.
† Suicide by poison.

The indictment is not printed here. It was published in *The Case Against the Nazi War Criminals* (Knopf, 1945). But it may be helpful to know that generally Count One charged the common plan or conspiracy to seize power, establish a totalitarian regime, prepare and wage a war of aggression. Count Two charged the waging of wars of aggression. Count Three charged the violation of the laws of war, and Count Four charged the crimes against humanity, the persecution and extermination.

The Tribunal also declared four Nazi organizations to have been criminal in character. These are: The Leadership Corps of the Nazi Party; *Die Schutzstaffeln,* known as the SS; *Der Sicherheitsdienst,* known as the SD; and *Die Geheime Staatspolizei,* known as the Gestapo, or Secret State Police. It declined to make that finding as to *Die Sturmabteilungen,* known as the SA; the Reichscabinet, and the General Staff and High Command. The latter was solely because the structure of the particular group was considered by the Tribunal to be too loose to constitute a coherent "group" or "organization," and was not because of any doubt of its criminality in war plotting. In its judgment the Tribunal condemned the officers who performed General Staff and High Command functions as "a ruthless military caste" and said they were "responsible in large measure for the miseries and suffering that have fallen on millions of men, women and children. They have been a disgrace to the honorable profession of arms." This finding should dispose of any fear that we were prosecuting soldiers just because they fought for their country and lost, but otherwise the failure to declare the criminality of the "caste" is regrettable.

The judgment of the Tribunal, which took the better part of two days to pronounce, was a painstaking one reviewing the law of the case and reciting the facts with meticulous care. The Soviet member's dissent from the acquittal of Schacht, Von Papen and Fritzsche and the failure to declare the General Staff and High Command criminal, is a temperate but powerful opinion which does not weaken but confirms the legal principles involved in the Tribunal's judgment. The judgment becomes one of the landmarks in International Law.

I can give no better summary of the results of this great trial, as I see them, than my final report to the President, filed on October 7, 1946, exactly seventeen months after my first report, the concluding paragraphs of which I quote:

> The vital question in which you and the country are interested is whether the results of this trial justify this heavy expenditure of effort. While the sentences imposed upon individuals hold dramatic interest, and while the acquittals, especially of Schacht and Von Papen, are regrettable, the importance of this case is not measurable in terms of the personal fate of any of the defendants who were already broken and discredited men. We are too close to the trial to appraise its long-range effects. The only criterion of success presently applicable is the short-range test as to whether we have done what we set out to do. This was outlined in my report to you on June 7, 1945. By this standard we have succeeded.
>
> The importance of the trial lies in the principles to which the Four Powers became committed by the Agreement, by their participation in the prosecution, and by the judgment rendered by the Tribunal. What has been accomplished may be summarized as follows:
>
> 1. We negotiated and concluded an Agreement with the four dominant powers of the earth, signed at London on August 8, 1945, which for the first time made explicit and unambiguous what was theretofore, as the Tribunal has declared, implicit in International

Law, namely, that to prepare, incite, or wage a war of aggression, or to conspire with others to do so, is a crime against international society, and that to persecute, oppress, or do violence to individuals or minorities on political, racial, or religious grounds in connection with such a war, or to exterminate, enslave, or deport civilian populations, is an international crime, and that for the commission of such crimes individuals are responsible. This Agreement also won the adherence of nineteen additional nations and represents the combined judgments of the overwhelming majority of civilized people. It is a basic charter in the International Law of the future.

2. We have also incorporated its principles into a judicial precedent. "The power of the precedent," Mr. Justice Cardozo said, "is the power of the beaten path." One of the chief obstacles to this trial was the lack of a beaten path. A judgment such as has been rendered shifts the power of the precedent to the support of these rules of law. No one can hereafter deny or fail to know that the principles on which the Nazi leaders are adjudged to forfeit their lives constitute law—and law with a sanction.

3. The Agreement devised a workable procedure for the trial of crimes which reconciled the basic conflicts in Anglo-American, French, and Soviet procedures. In matters of procedure, legal systems differ more than in substantive law. But the Charter set up a few simple rules which assured all of the elements of fair and full hearing, including counsel for the defense. Representatives of the Four Powers, both on the Bench and at the Prosecutors' table, have had to carry out that Agreement in day-to-day co-operation for more than a year. The law is a contentious profession and a litigation offers countless occasions for differences even among lawyers who represent the same clients and are trained in a single system of law. When we add the diversities of interests that exist among our four nations, and the differences in tradition, viewpoint, and language, it will be seen that our co-operation was beset with real difficulties. My colleagues, representing the United Kingdom, France, and the Soviet Union, exemplified the best professional tradition of their countries and have earned our gratitude for the patience, generosity, good will, and professional ability which they brought to the task. It would be idle to pretend that we have not had moments of difference and vexation, but the steadfast purpose of all delegations, that this first international trial should prove the possibility of successful international co-operation in use of the litigation process, always overcame transient irritations.

PREFACE

4. In a world torn with hatreds and suspicions where passions are stirred by the "frantic boast and foolish word," the Four Powers have given the example of submitting their grievances against these men to a dispassionate inquiry on legal evidence. The atmosphere of the Tribunal never failed to make a strong and favorable impression on visitors from all parts of the world because of its calmness and the patience and attentiveness of every Member and Alternate on the Tribunal. The nations have given the example of leaving punishment of individuals to the determination of independent judges, guided by principles of law, after hearing all of the evidence for the defense as well as the prosecution. It is not too much to hope that this example of full and fair hearing, and tranquil and discriminating judgment will do something toward strengthening the processes of justice in many countries.

5. We have documented from German sources the Nazi aggressions, persecutions, and atrocities with such authenticity and in such detail that there can be no responsible denial of these crimes in the future and no tradition of martyrdom of the Nazi leaders can arise among informed people. No history of this era can be entitled to authority which fails to take into account the record of Nürnberg. While an effort was made by Göring and others to portray themselves as "glowing patriots," their admitted crimes of violence and meanness, of greed and graft, leave no ground for future admiration of their characters and their fate leaves no incentive to emulation of their examples.

6. It has been well said that this trial is the world's first post mortem examination of a totalitarian regime. In this trial, the Nazis themselves with Machiavellian shamelessness exposed their methods of subverting people's liberties and establishing their dictatorship. The record is a merciless exposé of the cruel and sodrid methods by which a militant minority seized power, suppressed opposition, set up secret political police and concentration camps. They resorted to legal devices such as "protective custody," which Göring frankly said meant the arrest of people not because they had committed any crime but because of acts it was suspected they might commit if left at liberty. They destroyed all judicial remedies for the citizen and all protections against terrorism. The record discloses the early symptoms of dictatorship and shows that it is only in its incipient stages that it can be brought under control. And the testimony records the German example that the destruction of opposition produces eventual deterioration in the government

that does it. By progressive intolerance a dictatorship by its very nature becomes so arbitrary that it cannot tolerate opposition, even when it consists merely of the correction of misinformation or the communication to its highest officers of unwelcome intelligence. It was really the recoil of the Nazi blows at liberty that destroyed the Nazi regime. They struck down freedom of speech and press and other freedoms which pass as ordinary civil rights with us so thoroughly that not even its highest officers dared to warn the people or the Führer that they were taking the road to destruction. The Nürnberg trial has put that handwriting on the wall for the oppressor as well as the oppressed to read.

Of course, it would be extravagant to claim that agreements or trials of this character can make aggressive war or persecution of minorities impossible, just as it would be extravagant to claim that our federal laws make federal crime impossible. But we cannot doubt that they strengthen the bulwarks of peace and tolerance. The four nations through their prosecutors and through their representatives on the Tribunal, have enunciated standards of conduct which bring new hope to men of good will and from which future statesmen will not lightly depart. These standards by which the Germans have been condemned will become the condemnation of any nation that is faithless to them.

By the Agreement and this trial we have put International Law squarely on the side of peace as against aggressive warfare, and on the side of humanity as against persecution. In the present depressing world outlook it is possible that the Nürnberg trial may constitute the most important moral advance to grow out of this war. The trial and decision by which the four nations have forfeited the lives of some of the most powerful political and military leaders of Germany because they have violated fundamental International Law, do more than anything in our time to give to International Law what Woodrow Wilson described as "the kind of vitality it can only have if it is a real expression of our moral judgment."

I hereby resign my commission as your representative and Chief of Counsel for the United States. In its execution I have had the help of many able men and women, too many to mention individually, who have made personal sacrifice to carry on a work in which they earnestly believed. I also want to express deep personal appreciation for this opportunity to do what I believe to be a constructive work for the peace of the world and for the better protection of persecuted peoples. It was, perhaps, the greatest

PREFACE

opportunity ever presented to an American lawyer. In pursuit of it many mistakes have been made and many inadequacies must be confessed. I am consoled by the fact that in proceedings of this novelty, errors and missteps may also be instructive to the future.

The list of those who as members of the American staff contributed importantly to the trial of this case is too long to recite. The responsibilities of the prosecution were shared by able, conscientious, and co-operative representatives from each of the signatory powers. Attorneys General, Sir Hartley Shawcross and Sir David Maxwell Fyfe, for Great Britain, François de Menthon and Donnedieu Champetier de Ribes and M. Charles Dubost for the Republic of France, and General R. A. Rudenko of the Soviet Union, made contributions to the prosecution which paralleled my own. It is a pity that there is not space to include at least excerpts from their notable speeches and cross-examinations.

My special personal debt is to Lieutenant William E. Jackson who has been tireless in research and in editing his father's efforts and in preparing the documentary evidence for publication, and to my secretary, Mrs. Elsie L. Douglas, who often literally by candlelight, when the lighting in Nürnberg failed, transcribed notes for these speeches and cross-examinations which had been dictated at odd intervals in air and on land and carried many burdens of detail besides. They, together with many of the staff, have labored gladly, inspired by a confidence that what we were doing was worth the pain, for while it would not make another world war impossible, it would at least make statesmen individually accountable for their aggressive breaches of the peace.

ROBERT H. JACKSON

Washington, D. C.
October 10, 1946

CONTENTS

I   *Report to the President of the United States, June 7, 1945.*   **3**

II   *Four-Power Agreement for Trials and Charter of International Military Tribunal, August 8, 1945.*   **19**

III   *Opening Statement for the United States, November 21, 1945*   **30**

IV   *The Law Under Which Nazi Organizations Are Accused of Being Criminal, Argument by Robert H. Jackson, February 28, 1946.*   **95**

V   *Closing Address, July 26, 1946.*   **120**

VI   *Excerpts from Cross-Examination of Defendants:*   **184**
     1. Hermann Göring
     2. Hjalmar Schacht
     3. Albert Speer
     4. Erhard Milch

ILLUSTRATIONS

Justice Jackson closing the case for the United States

FRONTISPIECE

Signing the Agreement of London   FACING PAGE 20

Nürnberg ruins   30

The Warsaw Ghetto (German photographs)   52

The United States asking that Nazi organizations be declared criminal   96

Hermann Göring on the witness stand   184

Hjalmar Schacht testifying   226

Albert Speer testifying   254

THE NÜRNBERG CASE

I

REPORT TO THE PRESIDENT OF THE UNITED STATES BY ROBERT H. JACKSON, CHIEF OF COUNSEL FOR THE UNITED STATES. RELEASED FOR PUBLICATION BY PRESIDENT TRUMAN WITH HIS APPROVAL ON JUNE 7, 1945.

June 7, 1945

MY DEAR MR. PRESIDENT:

I have the honor to report accomplishments during the month since you named me as Chief of Counsel for the United States in prosecuting the principal Axis War Criminals. In brief, I have selected staffs from the several services, departments, and agencies concerned; worked out a plan for preparation, briefing, and trial of the cases; allocated the work among the several agencies; instructed those engaged in collecting or processing evidence; visited the European Theater to expedite the examination of captured documents, and the interrogation of witnesses and prisoners; co-ordinated our preparation of the main case with preparation by Judge Advocates of many cases not included in my responsibilities; and arranged co-operation and mutual assistance with the United Nations War Crimes Commission and with Counsel appointed to represent the United Kingdom in the joint prosecution.

I.

The responsibilities you have conferred on me extend only to "the case of major criminals whose offenses have no particular geographical localization and who will be punished by joint decision of the governments of the Allies," as provided in the Moscow Declaration of November 1, 1943, by President Roosevelt, Prime Minister Churchill, and Premier Stalin. It does not include localized cases of any kind. Accordingly, in visiting the European Theater, I attempted to establish standards to segregate from our case against the principal offenders, cases against many other offenders and to expedite their trial. These cases fall into three principal classes:

1. The first class comprises offenses against military personnel

of the United States—such, for example, as the killing of American airmen who crash-landed, and other Americans who become prisoners of war. In order to insure effective military operation, the field forces from time immemorial have dealt with such offenses on the spot. Authorization of this prompt procedure, however, had been withdrawn because of the fear of stimulating retaliation through execution of captured Americans on trumped-up charges. The surrender of Germany and liberation of our prisoners has ended that danger. The morale and safety of our own troops and effective government of the control area seemed to require prompt resumption of summary dealing with this type of case. Such proceedings are likely to disclose evidence helpful to the case against the major criminals and will not prejudice it in view of the measures I have suggested to preserve evidence and to prevent premature execution of those who are potential defendants or witnesses in the major case.

I flew to Paris and Frankfurt and conferred with Generals Eisenhower, Smith, Clay, and Betts, among others, and arranged to have a representative on hand to clear questions of conflict in any particular case. We also arranged an exchange of evidence between my staff and the Theater Judge Advocate's staff. The officials of other countries were most anxious to help. For example, the French brought to General Donovan and me in Paris evidence that civilians in Germany had beaten to death with wrenches three American airmen. They had obtained from the German Burgermeister identification of the killers, had taken them into custody, and offered to deliver them to our forces. Cases such as this are not infrequent. Under the arrangements perfected, the military authorities are enabled to move in cases of this class without delay. Some are already under way; some by now have been tried and verdicts rendered. Some concentration camp cases are also soon to go on trial.

2. A second class of offenders, the prosecution of which will not interfere with the major case, consists of those who, under the Moscow Declaration, are to be sent back to the scene of their crimes for trial by local authorities. These comprise localized offenses or atrocities against persons or property, usually of civilians of countries formerly occupied by Germany. The part of the United States in these cases consists of the identification of

offenders and the surrender on demand of those who are within our control.

The United Nations War Crimes Commission is especially concerned with cases of this kind. It represents many of the United Nations, with the exception of Russia. It has been usefully engaged as a body with which the aggrieved of all the United Nations have recorded their accusations and evidence. Lord Wright, representing Australia, is the Chairman of this Commission, and Lieutenant Colonel Joseph V. Hodgson is the United States representative.

In London, I conferred with Lord Wright and Colonel Hodgson in an effort to co-ordinate our work with that of the Commission wherever there might be danger of conflict or duplication. There was no difficulty in arriving at an understanding for mutual exchange of information. We undertook to respond to requests for any evidence in our possession against those listed with the Commission as criminals and to co-operate with each of the United Nations in efforts to bring this class of offenders to justice.

Requests for the surrender of persons held by American forces may present diplomatic or political problems which are not my responsibility. But so far as my work is concerned, I advised the Commission, as well as the appropriate American authorities, that there is no objection to the surrender of any person except on grounds that we want him as a defendant or as a witness in the major case.

3. In a third class of cases, each country, of course, is free to prosecute treason charges in its own tribunals and under its own laws against its own traitorous nationals—Quislings, Lavals, "Lord Haw-Haws," and the like.

The consequence of these arrangements is that preparations for the prosecution of major war criminals will not impede prosecution of other offenders. In these latter cases, however, the number of known offenses is likely to exceed greatly the number of prosecutions, because witnesses are rarely able satisfactorily to identify particular soldiers in uniform whose acts they have witnessed. This difficulty of adequately identifying individual perpetrators of atrocities and crimes makes it the more important that we proceed against the top officials and organizations responsible for originating the criminal policies, for only by so doing can there be just retribution for many of the most brutal acts.

II.

Over a month ago the United States proposed to the United Kingdom, Soviet Russia, and France a specific plan, in writing, that these four powers join in a protocol establishing an International Military Tribunal, defining the jurisdiction and powers of the tribunal, naming the categories of acts declared to be crimes, and describing those individuals and organizations to be placed on trial. Negotiation of such an agreement between the four powers is not yet completed.

In view of the immensity of our task, it did not seem wise to await consummation of international arrangements before proceeding with preparation of the American case. Accordingly, I went to Paris, to American Army Headquarters at Frankfurt and Wiesbaden, and to London, for the purpose of assembling, organizing, and instructing personnel from the existing services and agencies and getting the different organizations co-ordinated and at work on the evidence. I uniformly met with eager cooperation.

The custody and treatment of war criminals and suspects appeared to require immediate attention. I asked the War Department to deny those prisoners who are suspected war criminals the privileges which would appertain to their rank if they were merely prisoners of war; to assemble them at convenient and secure locations for interrogation by our staff; to deny them access to the press; and to hold them in the close confinement ordinarily given suspected criminals. The War Department has been subjected to some criticism from the press for these measures, for which it is fair that I should acknowledge responsibility. The most elementary considerations for insuring a fair trial and for the success of our case suggest the imprudence of permitting these prisoners to be interviewed indiscriminately or to use the facilities of the press to convey information to each other and to criminals yet uncaptured. Our choice is between treating them as honorable prisoners of war with the privileges of their ranks, or to classify them as war criminals, in which case they should be treated as such. I have assurances from the War Department that those likely to be accused as war criminals will be kept in close confinement and stern control.

Since a considerable part of our evidence has been assembled in London, I went there on May 28 with General Donovan to arrange for its examination, and to confer with the United Nations War Crimes Commission and with officials of the British Government responsible for the prosecution of war criminals. We had extended conferences with the newly appointed Attorney General, the Lord Chancellor, the Foreign Secretary, the Treasury Solicitor, and others. On May 29, Prime Minister Churchill announced in the House of Commons that Attorney General Sir David Maxwell Fyfe had been appointed to represent the United Kingdom in the prosecution. Following this announcement, members of my staff and I held extended conferences with the Attorney General and his staff. The sum of these conferences is that the British are taking steps parallel with our own to clear the military and localized cases for immediate trial, and to effect a complete interchange of evidence and a co-ordination of planning and preparation of the case by the British and American representatives. Despite the fact that the prosecution of the major war criminals involves problems of no mean dimensions, I am able to report that no substantial differences exist between the United Kingdom representatives and ourselves, and that minor differences have adjusted easily as one or the other of us advanced the better reasons for his view.

The Provisional Government of the French Republic has advised that it accepts in principle the American proposals for trials before an International Military Tribunal. It is expected to designate its representative shortly. The government of the Union of Soviet Socialist Republics, while not yet committed, has been kept informed of our steps and there is no reason to doubt that it will unite in the prosecution. We propose to make provision for others of the United Nations to become adherents to the agreement.

III.

The time, I think, has come when it is appropriate to outline the basic features of the plan of prosecution on which we are tentatively proceeding in preparing the case of the United States.

1. The American case is being prepared on the assumption

that an inescapable responsibility rests upon this country to conduct an inquiry, preferably in association with others, but alone
if necessary, into the culpability of those whom there is probable
cause to accuse of atrocities and other crimes. We have many
such men in our possession. What shall we do with them? We
could, of course, set them at large without a hearing. But it has
cost unmeasured thousands of American lives to beat and bind
these men. To free them without a trial would mock the dead
and make cynics of the living. On the other hand, we could
execute or otherwise punish them without a hearing. But undis-
criminating executions or punishments without definite findings
of guilt, fairly arrived at, would violate pledges repeatedly given,
and would not set easily on the American conscience or be remembered by our children with pride. The only other course is
to determine the innocence or guilt of the accused after a hearing
as dispassionate as the times and horrors we deal with will permit, and upon a record that will leave our reasons and motives
clear.

2. These hearings, however, must not be regarded in the same
light as a trial under our system, where defense is a matter of
constitutional right. Fair hearings for the accused are, of course,
required to make sure that we punish only the right men and for
the right reasons. But the procedure of these hearings may
properly bar obstructive and dilatory tactics resorted to by defendants in our ordinary criminal trials.

Nor should such a defense be recognized as the obsolete doctrine that a head of state is immune from legal liability. There is
more than a suspicion that this idea is a relic of the doctrine of
the divine right of kings. It is, in any event, inconsistent with
the position we take toward our own officials, who are frequently
brought to court at the suit of citizens who allege their rights to
have been invaded. We do not accept the paradox that legal
responsibility should be the least where power is the greatest.
We stand on the principle of responsible government declared
some three centuries ago to King James by Lord Chief Justice
Coke, who proclaimed that even a King is still "under God and
the law."

With the doctrine of immunity of a head of state usually is
coupled another, that orders from an official superior protect one

who obeys them. It will be noticed that the combination of these two doctrines means that nobody is responsible. Society as modernly organized cannot tolerate so broad an area of official irresponsibility. There is doubtless a sphere in which the defense of obedience to superior orders should prevail. If a conscripted or enlisted soldier is put on a firing squad, he should not be held responsible for the validity of the sentence he carries out. But the case may be greatly altered where one has discretion because of rank or the latitude of his orders. And of course, the defense of superior orders cannot apply in the case of voluntary participation in a criminal or conspiratorial organization, such as the Gestapo or the SS. An accused should be allowed to show the facts about superior orders. The Tribunal can then determine whether they constitute a defense or merely extenuating circumstances, or perhaps carry no weight at all.

3. Whom will we accuse and put to their defense? We will accuse a large number of individuals and officials who were in authority in the government, in the military establishment, including the General Staff, and in the financial, industrial, and economic life of Germany who by all civilized standards are provable to be common criminals. We also propose to establish the criminal character of several voluntary organizations which have played a cruel and controlling part in subjugating first the German people and then their neighbors. It is not, of course, suggested that a person should be judged a criminal merely because he voted for certain candidates or maintained political affiliations in the sense that we in America support political parties. The organizations which we will accuse have no resemblance to our political parties. Organizations such as the Gestapo and the SS were direct action units, and were recruited from volunteers accepted only because of aptitude for, and fanatical devotion to, their violent purposes.

In examining the accused organizations in the trial, it is our proposal to demonstrate their declared and covert objectives, methods of recruitment, structure, lines of responsibility, and methods of effectuating their programs. In this trial, important representative members will be allowed to defend their organizations as well as themselves. The best practicable notice will be given, that named organizations stand accused and that any member is privileged to appear and join in their defense. If in the main trial an organization is found to be criminal, the second stage will be to identify and try before regular military tribunals individual members not already personally convicted in the principal case. Findings in the main trial that an organization is criminal in nature will be conclusive in any subsequent proceedings against individual members. The individual member will thereafter be allowed to plead only personal defenses or extenuating circumstances, such as that he joined under duress, and as to those defenses he should have the burden of proof. There is nothing novel in the idea that one may lose a part of or all his defense if he fails to assert it in an appointed forum at an earlier time. In United States war-time legislation, this principle has been utilized and sustained as consistent with our concept of due process of law.

4. Our case against the major defendants is concerned with the Nazi master plan, not with individual barbarities and perversions which occurred independently of any central plan. The groundwork of our case must be factually authentic and constitute a well-documented history of what we are convinced was a grand, concerted pattern to incite and commit the aggressions and barbarities which have shocked the world. We must not forget that when the Nazi plans were boldly proclaimed they were so extravagant that the world refused to take them seriously. Unless we write the record of this movement with clarity and precision, we cannot blame the future if in days of peace it finds incredible the accusatory generalities uttered during the war. We must establish incredible events by credible evidence.

5. What specifically are the crimes with which these individuals and organizations should be charged, and what marks their conduct as criminal?

There is, of course, real danger that trials of this character will become enmeshed in voluminous particulars of wrongs committed by individual Germans throughout the course of the war, and in the multitude of doctrinal disputes which are part of a lawyer's paraphernalia. We can save ourselves from those pitfalls if our test of what legally is crime gives recognition to those things which fundamentally outraged the conscience of the American people and brought them finally to the conviction that their own liberty and civilization could not persist in the same world with the Nazi power.

Those acts which offended the conscience of our people were criminal by standards generally accepted in all civilized countries, and I believe that we may proceed to punish those responsible in full accord with both our own traditions of fairness and with standards of just conduct which have been internationally accepted. I think also that through these trials we should be able to establish that a process of retribution by law awaits those who in the future similarly attack civilization. Before stating these offenses in legal terms and concepts, let me recall what it was that affronted the sense of justice of our people.

Early in the Nazi regime, people of this country came to look upon the Nazi government as not constituting a legitimate state pursuing the legitimate objectives of a member of the international community. They came to view the Nazis as a band of brigands, set on subverting within Germany every vestige of a rule of law which would entitle an aggregation of people to be looked upon collectively as a member of the family of nations. Our people were outraged by the oppressions, the cruelest forms of torture, the large-scale murder, and the wholesale confiscation of property which initiated the Nazi regime within Germany. They witnessed persecution of the greatest enormity on religious, political, and racial grounds, the breakdown of trade unions, and the liquidation of all religious and moral influences. This was not the legitimate activity of a state within its own boundaries, but was preparatory to the launching of an international course of aggression and was with the evil intention, openly expressed by the Nazis, of capturing the form of the German state as an instrumentality for spreading their rule to other countries. Our people felt that these were the deepest offenses against that International Law described in the Fourth Hague Convention of 1907 as including the "laws of humanity and the dictates of the public conscience."

Once these international brigands, the top leaders of the Nazi Party, the SS, and the Gestapo, had firmly established themselves within Germany by terrorism and crime, they immediately set out on a course of international pillage. They bribed, debased, and incited to treason the citizens and subjects of other nations for the purpose of establishing their fifth columns of corruption and sabotage within those nations. They ignored the commonest obligations of one state respecting the internal affairs of another. They lightly made and promptly broke international engagements as a part of their settled policy to deceive, corrupt, and overwhelm. They made, and made only to violate, pledges respecting the demilitarized Rhineland, and Czechoslovakia, and Poland, and Russia. They did not hesitate to instigate the Japanese to treacherous attack on the United States. Our people saw in this succession of events the destruction of the minimum elements of trust which can hold the community of nations together in peace and progress. Then, in consummation of their plan, the Nazis swooped down upon the nations they had deceived and ruthlessly conquered them. They flagrantly violated the obligations which states, including their own, have undertaken by convention or tradition as a part of the rules of land warfare, and of the law of the sea. They wantonly destroyed cities like Rotterdam for no military purpose. They wiped out whole populations, as at Lidice, where no military purposes were to be served. They confiscated property of the Poles and gave it to party members. They transported in labor battalions great sectors of the civilian populations of the conquered countries. They refused the ordinary protections of law to the populations which they enslaved. The feeling of outrage grew in this country, and it became more and more felt that these were crimes committed against us and against the whole society of civilized nations by a band of brigands who had seized the instrumentality of a state.

I believe that those instincts of our people were right and that they should guide us as the fundamental tests of criminality. We propose to punish acts which have been regarded as criminal since the time of Cain and have been so written in every civilized code.

In arranging these trials we must also bear in mind the aspirations with which our people have faced the sacrifices of war. After we entered the war, and as we expended our men and our wealth to stamp out these wrongs, it was the universal feeling of our people that out of this war should come unmistakable rules and workable machinery from which any who might contemplate another era of brigandage would know that they would be held personally responsible and would be personally punished. Our people have been waiting for these trials in the spirit of Woodrow Wilson, who hoped to "give to international law the kind of vitality which it can only have if it is a real expression of our moral judgment."

Against this background it may be useful to restate in more technical lawyer's terms the legal charges against the top Nazi leaders and those voluntary associations such as the SS and Gestapo which clustered about them and were ever the prime instrumentalities, first, in capturing the German state, and then, in directing the German state to its spoliations against the rest of the world.

(a) Atrocities and offenses against persons or property constituting violations of International Law, including the laws, rules, and customs of land and naval warfare. The rules of warfare are well established and generally accepted by the nations. They make offenses of such conduct as killing of the wounded, refusal of quarter, ill-treatment of prisoners of war, firing on undefended localities, poisoning of wells and streams, pillage and wanton destruction, and ill-treatment of inhabitants in occupied territory.

(b) Atrocities and offenses, including atrocities and persecutions on racial or religious grounds, committed since 1933. This is only to recognize the principles of criminal law as they are generally observed in civilized states. These principles have been assimilated as a part of International Law at least since 1907. The Fourth Hague Convention provided that inhabitants and belligerents shall remain under the protection and the rule of "the principles of the law of nations, as they result from the usage established among civilized peoples, from the laws of humanity and the dictates of the public conscience."

(c) Invasions of other countries and initiation of wars of aggression in violation of International Law or treaties.

The persons to be reached by these charges will be determined by the rule of liability, common to all legal systems, that all who participate in the formulation or execution of a criminal plan involving multiple crimes are liable for each of the offenses committed and responsible for the acts of each other. All are liable who have incited, ordered, procured, or counseled the commission of such acts, or who have taken what the Moscow Declaration describes as "a consenting part" therein.

IV.

The legal position which the United States will maintain, being thus based on the common sense of justice, is relatively simple and nontechnical. We must not permit it to be complicated or obscured by sterile legalisms developed in the age of imperialism to make war respectable.

Doubtless what appeals to men of good will and common sense as the crime which comprehends all lesser crimes is the crime of making unjustifiable war. War necessarily is a calculated series of killings, of destructions of property, of oppressions. Such acts unquestionably would be criminal except that International Law throws a mantle of protection around acts which otherwise would be crimes, when committed in pursuit of legitimate warfare. In this they are distinguished from the same acts in pursuit of piracy or brigandage which have been considered punishable wherever and by whomever the guilty are caught. But International Law as taught in the nineteenth and the early part of the twentieth century generally declared that war-making was not illegal and is no crime at law. Summarized by a standard authority, its attitude was that "both parties to every war are regarded as being in an identical legal position, and consequently as being possessed of equal rights." This, however, was a departure from the doctrine taught by Grotius, the father of International Law, that there is a distinction between the just and the unjust war—the war of defense and the war of aggression.

International Law is more than a scholarly collection of abstract and immutable principles. It is an outgrowth of treaties or agreements between nations and of accepted customs. But every custom has its origin in some single act, and every agreement has to be initiated by the action of some state. Unless we are prepared to abandon every principle of growth for International Law, we cannot deny that our own day has its right to institute customs and to conclude agreements that will themselves become sources of a newer and strengthened International Law. International Law is not capable of development by legislation, for there is no continuously sitting international legislature. Innovations and revisions in International Law are brought about by the action of governments designed to meet a change in circumstances. It grows, as did the Common Law, through decisions reached from time to time in adapting settled principles to new situations. Hence, I am not disturbed by the lack of precedent for the inquiry we propose to conduct. After the shock to civilization of the last World War, however, a marked reversion to the earlier and sounder doctrines of International Law took place. By the time the Nazis came to power it was thoroughly established that launching an aggressive war or the institution of war by treachery was illegal and that the defense of legitimate warfare was no longer available to those who engaged in such an enterprise. It is high time that we act on the juridical principle that aggressive war-making is illegal and criminal.

The re-establishment of the principle of unjustifiable war is traceable in many steps. One of the most significant is the Briand-Kellogg Pact of 1928, by which Germany, Italy, and Japan, in common with ourselves and practically all the nations of the world, renounced war as an instrument of national policy, bound themselves to seek the settlement of disputes only by pacific means, and condemned recourse to war for the solution of international controversies. Unless this Pact altered the legal status of wars of aggression, it has no meaning at all and comes close to being an act of deception. In 1932, Mr. Stimson, as Secretary of State, gave voice to the American concept of its effect. He said, "War between nations was renounced by the signatories of the Briand-Kellogg Treaty. This means that it has become illegal throughout practically the entire world. It is no longer to be the source and subject of rights. It is no longer to be the principle around which the duties, the conduct, and the rights of nations revolve. It is an illegal thing. . . . By that very act, we have made obsolete many legal precedents and have given the legal profession the task of re-examining many of its codes and treaties."

This Pact constitutes only one in a series of acts which have reversed the viewpoint that all war is legal and have brought International Law into harmony with the common sense of mankind, that unjustifiable war is a crime. Without attempting an exhaustive catalogue, we may mention the Geneva Protocol of 1924 for the Pacific Settlement of International Disputes, signed by the representatives of forty-eight governments, which declared that "a war of aggression constitutes . . . an international crime." The Eighth Assembly of the League of Nations in 1927, on unanimous resolution of the representatives of forty-eight member nations, including Germany, declared that a war of aggression constitutes an international crime. At the Sixth Pan-American Conference of 1928, the twenty-one American republics unanimously adopted a resolution stating that "war of aggression constitutes an international crime against the human species."

The United States is vitally interested in recognizing the principle that treaties renouncing war have juridical as well as political meaning. We relied upon the Briand-Kellogg Pact and made it the cornerstone of our national policy. We neglected our armaments and our war machine in reliance upon it. All violations of it, wherever started, menace our peace as we now have good reason to know. An attack on the foundations of international relations cannot be regarded as anything less than a crime against the international community, which may properly vindicate the integrity of its fundamental compacts by punishing aggressors. We therefore propose to charge that a war of aggression is a crime, and that modern International Law has abolished the defense that those who incite or wage it are engaged in legitimate business. Thus may the forces of the law be mobilized on the side of peace.

Any legal position asserted on behalf of the United States will have considerable significance in the future evolution of International Law. In untroubled times progress toward an effective rule of law in the international community is slow indeed. Inertia rests more heavily upon the society of nations than upon any other society. Now we stand at one of those rare moments when the thought and institutions and habits of the world have been shaken by the impact of world war on the lives of countless millions. Such occasions rarely come and quickly pass. We are put under a heavy responsibility to see that our behavior during this unsettled period will direct the world's thought toward a firmer enforcement of the laws of international conduct, so as to make war less attractive to those who have governments and the destinies of peoples in their power.

V.

I have left until last the first question which you and the American people are asking—when can this trial start and how long will it take? I should be glad to answer if the answer were within my control. But it would be foolhardy to name dates which depend upon the action of other governments and of many agencies. Inability to fix definite dates, however, would not excuse failure to state my attitude toward the time and duration of trial.

I know that the public has a deep sense of urgency about these trials. Because I, too, feel a sense of urgency, I have proceeded with the preparations of the American case before completion of the diplomatic exchanges concerning the Tribunal to hear it and the agreement under which we are to work. We must, however, recognize the existence of serious difficulties to be overcome in preparation of the case. It is no criticism to say that until the surrender of Germany the primary objective of the military intelligence services was naturally to gather military information rather than to prepare a legal case for trial. We must now sift and compress within a workable scope voluminous evidence relating to a multitude of crimes committed in several countries and participated in by thousands of actors over a decade of time. The preparation must cover military, naval, diplomatic, political, and commercial aggressions. The evidence is scattered among various agencies and in the hands of several armies. The captured documentary evidence—literally tons of orders, records, and reports—is largely in foreign languages. Every document and the trial itself must be rendered into several languages. An immense amount of work is necessary to bring this evidence together physically, to select what is useful, to integrate it into a case, to overlook no relevant detail, and at the same time and at all costs to avoid becoming lost in a wilderness of single instances. Some sacrifice of perfection to speed can wisely be made and, of course, urgency overrides every personal convenience and comfort for all of us who are engaged in this work.

Beyond this I will not go in prophecy. The task of making this record complete and accurate, while memories are fresh, while witnesses are living, and while a tribunal is available, is too important to the future opinion of the world to be undertaken before

17

the case can be sufficiently prepared to make a creditable presentation. Intelligent, informed, and sober opinion will not be satisfied with less.

The trial must not be protracted in duration by anything that is obstructive or dilatory, but we must see that it is fair and deliberative and not discredited in times to come by any mob spirit. Those who have regard for the good name of the United States as a symbol of justice under law would not have me proceed otherwise.

May I add that your personal encouragement and support have been a source of strength and inspiration to every member of my staff, as well as to me, as we go forward with a task so immense that it can never be done completely or perfectly, but which we hope to do acceptably.

Respectfully yours,
ROBERT H. JACKSON

II

AGREEMENT BY THE GOVERNMENT OF THE
UNITED STATES OF AMERICA, THE PROVISIONAL
GOVERNMENT OF THE FRENCH REPUBLIC, THE
GOVERNMENT OF THE UNITED KINGDOM OF
GREAT BRITAIN AND NORTHERN IRELAND AND
THE GOVERNMENT OF THE UNION OF SOVIET
SOCIALIST REPUBLICS FOR THE PROSECUTION
AND PUNISHMENT OF THE MAJOR WAR CRIMI-
NALS OF THE EUROPEAN AXIS.

WHEREAS the United Nations have from time to time made
declarations of their intention that War Criminals shall be
brought to justice;

AND WHEREAS the Moscow Declaration of the 30th October
1943 on German atrocities in Occupied Europe stated that those
German Officers and men and members of the Nazi Party who
have been responsible for or have taken a consenting part in
atrocities and crimes will be sent back to the countries in which
their abominable deeds were done in order that they may be
judged and punished according to the laws of these liberated
countries and of the free Governments that will be created therein;

AND WHEREAS this Declaration was stated to be without prejudice to the case of major criminals whose offenses have no particular geographic location and who will be punished by the joint
decision of the Governments of the Allies;

NOW THEREFORE the Government of the United States of
America, the Provisional Government of the French Republic,
the Government of the United Kingdom of Great Britain and
Northern Ireland and the Government of the Union of Soviet
Socialist Republics (hereinafter called "the Signatories") acting
in the interests of all the United Nations and by their representatives duly authorized thereto have concluded this Agreement.

Article 1. There shall be established after consultation with
the Control Council for Germany an International Military Tri-

bunal for the trial of war criminals whose offenses have no particular geographical location whether they be accused individually or in their capacity as members of organizations or groups or in both capacities.

Article 2. The constitution, jurisdiction and functions of the International Military Tribunal shall be those set out in the Charter annexed to this Agreement, which Charter shall form an integral part of this Agreement.

Article 3. Each of the Signatories shall take the necessary steps to make available for the investigation of the charges and trial the major war criminals detained by them who are to be tried by the International Military Tribunal. The Signatories shall also use their best endeavors to make available for investigation of the charges against and the trial before the International Military Tribunal such of the major war criminals as are not in the territories of any of the Signatories.

Article 4. Nothing in this Agreement shall prejudice the provisions established by the Moscow Declaration concerning the return of war criminals to the countries where they committed their crimes.

Article 5. Any Government of the United Nations may adhere to this Agreement by notice given through the diplomatic channel to the Government of the United Kingdom, who shall inform the other Signatory and adhering Governments of each such adherence.

Article 6. Nothing in this Agreement shall prejudice the jurisdiction or the powers of any national or occupation court established or to be established in any allied territory or in Germany for the trial of war criminals.

Article 7. This Agreement shall come into force on the day of signature and shall remain in force for the period of one year and shall continue thereafter, subject to the right of any Signatory to give, through the diplomatic channel, one month's notice of intention to terminate it. Such termination shall not prejudice any proceedings already taken or any findings already made in pursuance of this Agreement.

IN WITNESS WHEREOF the Undersigned have signed the present Agreement.

DONE in quadruplicate in London this 8th day of August 1945

I. T. Nikitchenko   Lord Chancellor Jowitt   Mr. Justice Jackson   Judge Robert Falco
Soviet Russia   United Kingdom   United States   France

*IGNING THE AGREEMENT OF LONDON WHICH ESTABLISHED
THE TRIBUNAL*

*"The Agreement of London, whether it originates or merely records,
at all events marks a transition in International Law. . . ."*

CLOSING ADDRESS

each in English, French and Russian, and each text to have equal authenticity.

For the Government of the United States of America
ROBERT H. JACKSON

For the Provisional Government of the French Republic
ROBERT FALCO

For the Government of the United Kingdom of Great Britain and Northern Ireland

JOWITT

For the Government of the Union of Soviet Socialist Republics
I. T. NIKITCHENKO (*and*) A. N. TRAININ

CHARTER OF THE INTERNATIONAL MILITARY TRIBUNAL

I. CONSTITUTION OF THE TRIBUNAL

Article 1. In pursuance of the Agreement signed on the 8th day of August 1945 by the Government of the United States of America, the Provisional Government of the French Republic, the Government of the United Kingdom of Great Britain and Northern Ireland and the Government of the Union of Soviet Socialist Republics, there shall be established an International Military Tribunal (hereinafter called "the Tribunal") for the just and prompt trial and punishment of the major war criminals of the European Axis.

Article 2. The Tribunal shall consist of four members, each with an alternate. One member and one alternate shall be appointed by each of the Signatories. The alternates shall, so far as they are able, be present at all sessions of the Tribunal. In case of illness of any member of the Tribunal or his incapacity for some other reason to fulfill his functions, his alternate shall take his place.

Article 3. Neither the Tribunal, its members nor their alternates can be challenged by the prosecution, or by the Defendants or their Counsel. Each Signatory may replace its member of the Tribunal or his alternate for reasons of health or for other good reasons, except that no replacement may take place during a Trial, other than by an alternate.

Article 4.

(a) The presence of all four members of the Tribunal or the alternate for any absent member shall be necessary to constitute the quorum.

(b) The members of the Tribunal shall, before any trial begins, agree among themselves upon the selection from their number of a President, and the President shall hold office during that trial, or as may otherwise be agreed by a vote of not less than three members. The principle of rotation of presidency for successive trials is agreed. If, however, a session of the Tribunal takes place on the territory of one of the four Signatories, the representative of that Signatory on the Tribunal shall preside.

(c) Save as aforesaid the Tribunal shall take decisions by a majority vote and in case the votes are evenly divided, the vote of the President shall be decisive: provided always that convictions and sentences shall only be imposed by the affirmative votes of at least three members of the Tribunal.

Article 5. In case of need and depending on the number of the matters to be tried, other Tribunals may be set up; and the establishment, functions, and procedure of each Tribunal shall be identical, and shall be governed by this Charter.

II. JURISDICTION AND GENERAL PRINCIPLES

Article 6. The Tribunal established by the Agreement referred to in Article 1 hereof for the trial and punishment of the major war criminals of the European Axis countries shall have the power to try and punish persons who, acting in the interests of the European Axis countries, whether as individuals or as members of organizations, committed any of the following crimes.

The following acts, or any of them, are crimes coming within the jurisdiction of the Tribunal for which there shall be individual responsibility:

(a) *Crimes Against Peace:* namely, planning, preparation, initiation or waging of a war of aggression, or a war in violation of international treaties, agreements or assurances, or participation in a common plan or conspiracy for the accomplishment of any of the foregoing;

(b) *War Crimes:* namely, violations of the laws or customs of war. Such violations shall include, but not be limited to, murder, ill-treatment or deportation to slave labor or for any other purpose of civilian population of or in occupied territory, murder or ill-treatment of prisoners of war or persons on the seas, killing of hostages, plunder of public or private property, wanton destruction of cities, towns or villages, or devastation not justified by military necessity;

(c) *Crimes Against Humanity:* namely, murder, extermination, enslavement, deportation, and other inhumane acts committed against any civilian population, before or during the war; or persecutions on political, racial or religious grounds in execution of or in connection with any crime within the jurisdiction of the Tribunal, whether or not in violation of domestic law of the country where perpetrated.

Leaders, organizers, instigators and accomplices participating in the formulation or execution of a common plan or conspiracy to commit any of the foregoing crimes are responsible for all acts performed by any persons in execution of such plan.

Article 7. The official position of defendants, whether as Heads of State or responsible officials in Government Departments, shall not be considered as freeing them from responsibility or mitigating punishment.

Article 8. The fact that the Defendant acted pursuant to order of his Government or of a superior shall not free him from responsibility, but may be considered in mitigation of punishment if the Tribunal determine that justice so requires.

Article 9. At the trial of any individual member of any group or organization the Tribunal may declare (in connection with any act of which the individual may be convicted) that the group or organization of which the individual was a member was a criminal organization.

After receipt of the Indictment the Tribunal shall give such notice as it thinks fit that the prosecution intends to ask the Tribunal to make such declaration and any member of the organization will be entitled to apply to the Tribunal for leave to be heard by the Tribunal upon the question of the criminal character of the organization. The Tribunal shall have power to allow or reject the application. If the application is allowed, the Tribunal may direct in what manner the applicants shall be represented and heard.

Article 10. In cases where a group or organization is declared criminal by the Tribunal, the competent national authority of any Signatory shall have the right to bring individuals to trial for membership therein before national, military or occupation courts. In any such case the criminal nature of the group or organization is considered proved and shall not be questioned.

Article 11. Any person convicted by the Tribunal may be charged before a national, military or occupation court, referred to in Article 10 of this Charter, with a crime other than of membership in a criminal group or organization and such court may, after convicting him, impose upon him punishment independent of and additional to the punishment imposed by the Tribunal for participation in the criminal activities of such group or organization.

Article 12. The Tribunal shall have the right to take proceedings against a person charged with crimes set out in Article 6 of this Charter in his absence, if he has not been found or if the Tribunal, for any reason, finds it necessary, in the interests of justice, to conduct the hearing in his absence.

Article 13. The Tribunal shall draw up rules for its procedure. These rules shall not be inconsistent with the provisions of this Charter.

III. COMMITTEE FOR THE INVESTIGATION AND PROSECUTION OF MAJOR WAR CRIMINALS

Article 14. Each Signatory shall appoint a Chief Prosecutor for the investigation of the charges against and the prosecution of major war criminals.

The Chief Prosecutors shall act as a committee for the following purposes:

(a) to agree upon a plan of the individual work of each of the Chief Prosecutors and his staff,

(b) to settle the final designation of major war criminals to be tried by the Tribunal,

(c) to approve the Indictment and the documents to be submitted therewith,

(d) to lodge the Indictment and the accompanying documents with the Tribunal,

(e) to draw up and recommend to the Tribunal for its approval draft rules of procedure, contemplated by Article 13 of this Charter. The Tribunal shall have power to accept, with or without amendments, or to reject, the rules so recommended.

The Committee shall act in all the above matters by a majority vote and shall appoint a Chairman as may be convenient and in accordance with the principle of rotation: provided that if there is an equal division of vote concerning the designation of a Defendant to be tried by the Tribunal, or the crimes with which he shall be charged, that proposal will be adopted which was made by the party which proposed that the particular Defendant be tried, or the particular charges be preferred against him.

Article 15. The Chief Prosecutors shall individually, and acting in collaboration with one another, also undertake the following duties:

(a) investigation, collection and production before or at the Trial of all necessary evidence,

(b) the preparation of the Indictment for approval by the Committee in accordance with paragraph (c) of Article 14 hereof,

(c) the preliminary examination of all necessary witnesses and of the Defendants,

(d) to act as prosecutor at the Trial,

(e) to appoint representatives to carry out such duties as may be assigned to them,

(f) to undertake such other matters as may appear necessary to them for the purposes of the preparation for and conduct of the Trial.

It is understood that no witness or Defendant detained by any Signatory shall be taken out of the possession of that Signatory without its assent.

IV. FAIR TRIAL FOR DEFENDANTS

Article 16. In order to ensure fair trial for the Defendants, the following procedure shall be followed:

(a) The Indictment shall include full particulars specifying in detail the charges against the Defendants. A copy of the Indictment and of all the documents lodged with the Indictment, translated into a language which he understands, shall be furnished to the Defendant at a reasonable time before the Trial.

(b) During any preliminary examination or trial of a Defendant he shall have the right to give any explanation relevant to the charges made against him.

(c) A preliminary examination of a Defendant and his Trial shall be conducted in, or translated into, a language which the Defendant understands.

(d) A defendant shall have the right to conduct his own defense before the Tribunal or to have the assistance of Counsel.

(e) A defendant shall have the right through himself or through his Counsel to present evidence at the Trial in support of his defense, and to cross-examine any witness called by the Prosecution.

V. POWERS OF THE TRIBUNAL AND CONDUCT
OF THE TRIAL

Article 17. The Tribunal shall have the power

(a) to summon witnesses to the Trial and to require their attendance and testimony and to put questions to them,

(b) to interrogate any Defendant,

(c) to require the production of documents and other evidentiary material,

(d) to administer oaths to witnesses,

(e) to appoint officers for the carrying out of any task designated by the Tribunal including the power to have evidence taken on commission.

Article 18. The Tribunal shall

(a) confine the Trial strictly to an expeditious hearing of the issues raised by the charges,

(b) take strict measures to prevent any action which will cause unreasonable delay, and rule out irrelevant issues and statements of any kind whatsoever,

(c) deal summarily with any contumacy, imposing appropriate punishment, including exclusion of any Defendant or his Counsel from some or all further proceedings, but without prejudice to the determination of the charges.

Article 19. The Tribunal shall not be bound by technical rules of evidence. It shall adopt and apply to the greatest possible extent expeditious and nontechnical procedure, and shall admit any evidence which it deems to have probative value.

Article 20. The Tribunal may require to be informed of the nature of any evidence before it is offered so that it may rule upon the relevance thereof.

Article 21. The Tribunal shall not require proof of facts of common knowledge but shall take judicial notice thereof. It shall also take judicial notice of official governmental documents and reports of the United Nations, including the acts and documents of the committees set up in the various allied countries for the investigation of war crimes, and the records and findings of military or other Tribunals of any of the United Nations.

Article 22. The permanent seat of the Tribunal shall be in Berlin. The first meetings of the members of the Tribunal and of the Chief Prosecutors shall be held at Berlin in a place to be designated by the Control Council for Germany. The first trial shall be held at Nürnberg, and any subsequent trials shall be held at such places as the Tribunal may decide.

Article 23. One or more of the Chief Prosecutors may take part in the prosecution at each Trial. The function of any Chief Prosecutor may be discharged by him personally, or by any person or persons authorized by him.

The function of Counsel for a Defendant may be discharged at the Defendant's request by any Counsel professionally qualified to conduct cases before the Courts of his own country, or by any other person who may be specially authorized thereto by the Tribunal.

Article 24. The proceedings at the Trial shall take the following course:

(a) The Indictment shall be read in court.

(b) The Tribunal shall ask each Defendant whether he pleads "guilty" or "not guilty."

(c) The prosecution shall make an opening statement.

(d) The Tribunal shall ask the prosecution and the defense what evidence (if any) they wish to submit to the Tribunal, and the Tribunal shall rule upon the admissibility of any such evidence.

(e) The witnesses for the Prosecution shall be examined and after that the witnesses for the Defense. Thereafter such rebutting evidence as may be held by the Tribunal to be admissible shall be called by either the Prosecution or the Defense.

(f) The Tribunal may put any question to any witness and to any Defendant, at any time.

(g) The Prosecution and the Defense shall interrogate and may cross-examine any witnesses and any Defendant who gives testimony.

(h) The Defense shall address the court.

(i) The Prosecution shall address the court.

(j) Each Defendant may make a statement to the Tribunal.

(k) The Tribunal shall deliver judgment and pronounce sentence.

Article 25. All official documents shall be produced, and all court proceedings conducted, in English, French, and Russian, and in the language of the Defendant. So much of the record and of the proceedings may also be translated into the language of any country in which the Tribunal is sitting, as the Tribunal considers desirable in the interests of justice and public opinion.

VI. JUDGMENT AND SENTENCE

Article 26. The judgment of the Tribunal as to the guilt or the innocence of any Defendant shall give the reasons on which it is based, and shall be final and not subject to review.

Article 27. The Tribunal shall have the right to impose upon a Defendant on conviction, death or such other punishment as shall be determined by it to be just.

Article 28. In addition to any punishment imposed by it, the Tribunal shall have the right to deprive the convicted person of any stolen property and order its delivery to the Control Council for Germany.

Article 29. In case of guilt, sentences shall be carried out in accordance with the orders of the Control Council for Germany, which may at any time reduce or otherwise alter the sentences, but may not increase the severity thereof. If the Control Council for Germany, after any Defendant has been convicted and sentenced, discovers fresh evidence which, in its opinion, would found a fresh charge against him, the Council shall report accordingly to the Committee established under Article 14 hereof, for such action as they may consider proper, having regard to the interests of justice.

VII. EXPENSES

Article 30. The expenses of the Tribunal and of the Trials, shall be charged by the Signatories against the funds allotted for maintenance of the Control Council for Germany.

III

OPENING STATEMENT FOR THE UNITED STATES OF AMERICA BY ROBERT H. JACKSON, CHIEF OF COUNSEL FOR THE UNITED STATES AT THE PALACE OF JUSTICE, NÜRNBERG, GERMANY, NOVEMBER 21, 1945.

INTERNATIONAL MILITARY TRIBUNAL NO. I

The United States of America, the French Republic, the United Kingdom of Great Britain and Northern Ireland, and the Union of Soviet Socialist Republics

AGAINST

Hermann Wilhelm Göring, Rudolf Hess, Joachim von Ribbentrop, Robert Ley, Wilhelm Keitel, Ernst Kaltenbrunner, Alfred Rosenberg, Hans Frank, Wilhelm Frick, Julius Streicher, Walter Funk, Hjalmar Schacht, Gustav Krupp von Bohlen und Halbach, Karl Dönitz, Erich Raeder, Baldur von Schirach, Fritz Sauckel, Alfred Jodl, Martin Bormann, Franz von Papen, Artur Seyss-Inquart, Albert Speer, Constantin von Neurath, and Hans Fritzsche,

Individually and as Members of Any of the Following Groups or Organizations to which They Respectively Belonged Namely: Die Reichsregierung (Reich Cabinet); Das Korps der Politischen Leiter der Nationalsozialistischen Deutschen Arbeiterpartei (Leadership Corps of the Nazi Party); Die Schutzstaffeln der Nationalsozialistischen Deutschen Arbeiterpartei (commonly known as the "SS") and including Die Sicherheitsdienst (commonly known as the "SD"); Die Geheime Staatspolizei (Secret State Police, commonly known as the "Gestapo"); Die Sturmabteilungen der N.S.D.A.P. (commonly known as the "SA") and the General Staff and High Command of the German Armed Forces.

DEFENDANTS

MAY IT PLEASE YOUR HONORS:

The privilege of opening the first trial in history for crimes against the peace of the world imposes a grave responsibility. The wrongs which we seek to condemn and punish have been so calculated, so malignant and so devastating, that civilization

NÜRNBERG RUINS

"It is not necessary among the ruins of this ancient and beautiful city, with untold numbers of its civilian inhabitants still buried in its rubble, to argue the proposition that to start or wage a war of aggression has the moral qualities of the worst of crimes." **OPENING ADDRESS**

cannot tolerate their being ignored because it cannot survive their being repeated. That four great nations, flushed with victory and stung with injury stay the hand of vengeance and voluntarily submit their captive enemies to the judgment of the law is one of the most significant tributes that Power ever has paid to Reason.

This Tribunal, while it is novel and experimental, is not the product of abstract speculations nor is it created to vindicate legalistic theories. This inquest represents the practical effort of four of the most mighty of nations, with the support of seventeen more, to utilize International Law to meet the greatest menace of our times—aggressive war. The common sense of mankind demands that law shall not stop with the punishment of petty crimes by little people. It must also reach men who possess themselves of great power and make deliberate and concerted use of it to set in motion evils which leave no home in the world untouched. It is a cause of this magnitude that the United Nations will lay before Your Honors.

In the prisoners' dock sit twenty-odd broken men. Reproached by the humiliation of those they have led almost as bitterly as by the desolation of those they have attacked, their personal capacity for evil is forever past. It is hard now to perceive in these miserable men as captives the power by which as Nazi leaders they once dominated much of the world and terrified most of it. Merely as individuals, their fate is of little consequence to the world.

What makes this inquest significant is that these prisoners represent sinister influences that will lurk in the world long after their bodies have returned to dust. They are living symbols of racial hatreds, of terrorism and violence, and of the arrogance and cruelty of power. They are symbols of fierce nationalisms and of militarism, of intrigue and war-making which have embroiled Europe generation after generation, crushing its manhood, destroying its homes, and impoverishing its life. They have so identified themselves with the philosophies they conceived and with the forces they directed that any tenderness to them is a victory and an encouragement to all the evils which are attached to their names. Civilization can afford no compromise with the social forces which would gain renewed strength if we

31

deal ambiguously or indecisively with the men in whom those forces now precariously survive.

What these men stand for we will patiently and temperately disclose. We will give you undeniable proofs of incredible events. The catalogue of crimes will omit nothing that could be conceived by a pathological pride, cruelty, and lust for power. These men created in Germany, under the *Führerprinzip,* a National Socialist despotism equaled only by the dynasties of the ancient East. They took from the German people all those dignities and freedoms that we hold natural and inalienable rights in every human being. The people were compensated by inflaming and gratifying hatreds toward those who were marked as "scapegoats." Against their opponents, including Jews, Catholics, and free labor, the Nazis directed such a campaign of arrogance, brutality, and annihilation as the world has not witnessed since the pre-Christian ages. They excited the German ambition to be a "master race," which of course implies serfdom for others. They led their people on a mad gamble for domination. They diverted social energies and resources to the creation of what they thought to be an invincible war machine. They overran their neighbors. To sustain the "master race" in its war-making, they enslaved millions of human beings and brought them into Germany, where these hapless creatures now wander as "displaced persons." At length bestiality and bad faith reached such excess that they aroused the sleeping strength of imperiled Civilization. Its united efforts have ground the German war machine to fragments. But the struggle has left Europe a liberated yet prostrate land where a demoralized society struggles to survive. These are the fruits of the sinister forces that sit with these defendants in the prisoners' dock.

In justice to the nations and the men associated in this prosecution, I must remind you of certain difficulties which may leave their mark on this case. Never before in legal history has an effort been made to bring within the scope of a single litigation the developments of a decade, covering a whole Continent, and involving a score of nations, countless individuals, and innumerable events. Despite the magnitude of the task, the world has demanded immediate action. This demand has had to be met, though perhaps at the cost of finished craftsmanship. In my country, established courts, following familiar procedures, applying well-thumbed precedents, and dealing with the legal consequences of local and limited events seldom commence a trial within a year of the event in litigation. Yet less than eight months ago today the courtroom in which you sit was an enemy fortress in the hands of German SS troops. Less than eight months ago nearly all our witnesses and documents were in enemy hands. The law had not been codified, no procedures had been established, no Tribunal was in existence, no usable courthouse stood here, none of the hundreds of tons of official German documents had been examined, no prosecuting staff had been assembled, nearly all the present defendants were at large, and the four prosecuting powers had not yet joined in common cause to try them. I should be the last to deny that the case may well suffer from incomplete researches and quite likely will not be the example of professional work which any of the prosecuting nations would normally wish to sponsor. It is, however, a completely adequate case to the judgment we shall ask you to render, and its full development we shall be obliged to leave to historians.

Before I discuss particulars of evidence, some general considerations which may affect the credit of this trial in the eyes of the world should be candidly faced. There is a dramatic disparity between the circumstances of the accusers and of the accused that might discredit our work if we should falter, in even minor matters, in being fair and temperate.

Unfortunately, the nature of these crimes is such that both prosecution and judgment must be by victor nations over vanquished foes. The world-wide scope of the aggressions carried out by these men has left but few real neutrals. Either the victors must judge the vanquished or we must leave the defeated to judge themselves. After the first World War, we learned the futility of the latter course. The former high station of these defendants, the notoriety of their acts, and the adaptability of their conduct to provoke retaliation make it hard to distinguish between the demand for a just and measured retribution, and the unthinking cry for vengeance which arises from the anguish of war. It is our task, so far as humanly possible, to draw the line between the two. We must never forget that the record on which we judge these defendants today is the record on which history will judge us tomorrow. To pass these defendants a poisoned chalice is to put it to our own lips as well. We must summon such detachment and intellectual integrity to our task that this trial will commend itself to posterity as fulfilling humanity's aspirations to do justice.

At the very outset, let us dispose of the contention that to put these men to trial is to do them an injustice entitling them to some special consideration. These defendants may be hard pressed but they are not ill-used. Let us see what alternative they would have to being tried.

More than a majority of these prisoners surrendered to or were tracked down by forces of the United States. Could they expect us to make American custody a shelter for our enemies against the just wrath of our Allies? Did we spend American lives to capture them only to save them from punishment? Under the principles of the Moscow Declaration, those suspected war criminals who are not to be tried internationally must be turned over to individual governments for trial at the scene of their outrages. Many less responsible and less culpable American-held prisoners have been and will be turned over to other United Nations for local trial. If these defendants should succeed, for any reason, in escaping the condemnation of this Tribunal, or if they obstruct or abort this trial, those who are American-held prisoners will be delivered up to our continental Allies. For these defendants, however, we have set up an International Tribunal and have undertaken the burden of participating in a complicated effort to give them fair and dispassionate hearings. That is the best-known protection to any man with a defense worthy of being heard.

If these men are the first war leaders of a defeated nation to be prosecuted in the name of the law, they are also the first to be given a chance to plead for their lives in the name of the law. Realistically, the Charter of this Tribunal, which gives them a hearing, is also the source of their only hope. It may be that these men of troubled conscience, whose only wish is that the world forget them, do not regard a trial as a favor. But they do have a fair opportunity to defend themselves—a favor which these men, when in power, rarely extended to their fellow countrymen. Despite the fact that public opinion already condemns their acts, we agree that here they must be given a presumption of innocence, and we accept the burden of proving criminal acts and the responsibility of these defendants for their commission.

When I say that we do not ask for convictions unless we prove crime, I do not mean mere technical or incidental transgression of international conventions. We charge guilt on planned and intended conduct that involves moral as well as legal wrong. And we do not mean conduct that is a natural and human, even if illegal, cutting of corners, such as many of us might well have committed had we been in the defendants' positions. It is not because they yielded to the normal frailties of human beings that we accuse them. It is their abnormal and inhuman conduct which brings them to this bar.

We will not ask you to convict these men on the testimony of their foes. There is no count of the Indictment that cannot be proved by books and records. The Germans were always meticulous record keepers, and these defendants had their share of the Teutonic passion for thoroughness in putting things on paper. Nor were they without vanity. They arranged frequently to be photographed in action. We will show you their own films. You will see their own conduct and hear their own voices as these defendants re-enact for you, from the screen, some of the events in the course of the conspiracy.

We would also make clear that we have no purpose to incriminate the whole German people. We know that the Nazi Party was not put in power by a majority of the German vote. We know it came to power by an evil alliance between the most extreme of the Nazi revolutionists, the most unrestrained of the German reactionaries, and the most aggressive of the German militarists. If the German populace had willingly accepted the Nazi program, no Stormtroopers would have been needed in the early days of the Party and there would have been no need for concentration camps or the Gestapo, both of which institutions were inaugurated as soon as the Nazis gained control of the German state. Only after these lawless innovations proved successful at home were they taken abroad.

The German people should know by now that the people of the United States hold them in no fear, and in no hate. It is true that the Germans have taught us the horrors of modern warfare, but the ruin that lies from the Rhine to the Danube shows that we, like our Allies, have not been dull pupils. If we are not awed by German fortitude and proficiency in war, and if we are not persuaded of their political maturity, we do respect their skill in the arts of peace, their technical competence, and the sober, industrious and self-disciplined character of the masses of the German people. In 1933, we saw the German people recovering prestige in the commercial, industrial and artistic world after the setback of the last war. We beheld their progress neither with envy nor malice. The Nazi regime interrupted this advance. The recoil of the Nazi aggression has left Germany in ruins. The Nazi readiness to pledge the German word without hesitation and to break it without shame has fastened upon German diplomacy a reputation for duplicity that will handicap it for years. Nazi arrogance has made the boast of the "master race" a taunt that will be thrown at Germans the world over for generations. The Nazi nightmare has given the German name a new and sinister significance throughout the world which will retard Germany a century. The German, no less than the non-German world, has accounts to settle with these defendants.

The fact of the war and the course of the war, which is the central theme of our case, is history. From September 1, 1939, when the German armies crossed the Polish frontiers, until September 1942, when they met epic resistance at Stalingrad, German arms seemed invincible. Denmark and Norway, The Netherlands and France, Belgium and Luxembourg, the Balkans and Africa, Poland and the Baltic States, and parts of Russia, all had been overrun and conquered by swift, powerful, well-aimed blows. That attack upon the peace of the world is the crime against international society which brings into international cognizance crimes in its aid and preparation which otherwise might be only internal concerns. It was aggressive war, which the nations of the world had renounced. It was war in violation of treaties, by which the peace of the world was sought to be safeguarded.

This war did not just happen—it was planned and prepared for over a long period of time and with no small skill and cunning. The world has perhaps never seen such a concentration and stimulation of the energies of any people as that which enabled Germany twenty years after it was defeated, disarmed, and dismembered to come so near carrying out its plan to dominate Europe. Whatever else we may say of those who were the authors of this war, they did achieve a stupendous work in organization, and our first task is to examine the means by which these defendants and their fellow conspirators prepared and incited Germany to go to war.

In general, our case will disclose these defendants all uniting at some time with the Nazi Party in a plan which they well knew could be accomplished only by an outbreak of war in Europe. Their seizure of the German state, their subjugation of the German people, their terrorism and extermination of dissident elements, their planning and waging of war, their calculated and planned ruthlessness in the conduct of warfare, their deliberate and planned criminality toward conquered peoples—all these are ends for which they acted in concert; and all these are phases of the conspiracy, a conspiracy which reached one goal only to set out for another and more ambitious one. We shall also trace for you the intricate web of organizations which these men formed and utilized to accomplish these ends. We will show how the entire structure of offices and officials was dedicated to the criminal purposes and committed to use of the criminal methods planned by these defendants and their co-conspirators, many of whom war and suicide have put beyond reach.

It is my purpose to open the case, particularly under Count One of the Indictment, and to deal with the common plan or conspiracy to achieve ends possible only by resort to crimes against peace, war crimes, and crimes against humanity. My emphasis will not be on individual barbarities and perversions which may have occurred independently of any central plan. One of the dangers ever present is that this trial may be protracted by details of particular wrongs and that we will become lost in a "wilderness of single instances." Nor will I now dwell on the activity of individual defendants except as it may contribute to exposition of the common plan.

The case as presented by the United States will be concerned with the brains and authority back of all the crimes. These defendants were men of a station and rank which does not soil its own hands with blood. They were men who knew how to use lesser folk as tools. We want to reach the planners and designers, the inciters and leaders without whose evil architecture the world would not have been for so long scourged with the violence and lawlessness, and wracked with the agonies and convulsions of this terrible war.

THE LAWLESS ROAD TO POWER

The chief instrumentality of cohesion in plan and action was the National Socialist German Workers Party, known as the Nazi Party. Some of the defendants were with it from the beginning. Others joined only after success seemed to have validated its lawlessness or power had invested it with immunity from the processes of the law. Adolf Hitler became its supreme leader as "Führer" in 1921.

On the 24th of February, 1920, at Munich, it publicly had proclaimed its program. (1708–PS.) Some of its purposes would commend themselves to many good citizens, such as the demands for "profit-sharing in the great industries," "generous development of provision for old age," "creation and maintenance of a healthy middle class," "a land reform suitable to our national requirements," and "raising the standard of health." It also made a strong appeal to that sort of nationalism which in ourselves we call patriotism and in our rivals chauvinism. It demanded "equality of rights for the German people in its dealing with other nations and the evolution of the peace treaties of Versailles and St. Germaine." It demanded the "union of all Germans on the basis of the right of self-determination of peoples to form a Great Germany." It demanded "land and territory (colonies) for the enrichment of our people and the settlement of our surplus population." All these, of course, were legitimate objectives if they were to be attained without resort to aggressive warfare.

The Nazi Party from its inception, however, contemplated war. It demanded "the abolition of mercenary troops and the formation of a national army." It proclaimed that, "In view of the enormous sacrifice of life and property demanded of a nation by every war, personal enrichment through war must be regarded as a crime against the nation. We demand, therefore, the ruthless confiscation of all war profits." I do not criticize this policy. Indeed, I wish it were universal. I merely point out that in a time of peace, war was a preoccupation of the Party, and it started the work of making war less offensive to the masses of the people. With this it combined a program of physical training and sports for youth that became, as we shall see, the cloak for a secret program of military training.

The Nazi Party declaration also committed its members to an anti-Semitic program. It declared that no Jew or any person of non-German blood could be a member of the nation. Such persons were to be disfranchised, disqualified for office, subject to the alien laws, and entitled to nourishment only after the German population had first been provided for. All who had entered Germany after August 2, 1914 were to be required forthwith to depart, and all non-German immigration was to be prohibited.

The Party also avowed, even in those early days, an authoritarian and totalitarian program for Germany. It demanded creation of a strong central power with unconditional authority, nationalization of all businesses which had been "amalgamated," and a "reconstruction" of the national system of education which "must aim at teaching the pupil to understand the idea of the State (state sociology)." Its hostility to civil liberties and freedom of the press was distinctly announced in these words: "It must be forbidden to publish newspapers which do not conduce to the national welfare. We demand the legal prosecution of all tendencies in art or literature of a kind likely to disintegrate our life as a nation and the suppression of institutions which might militate against the above requirements."

The forecast of religious persecution was clothed in the language of religious liberty, for the Nazi program stated, "We demand liberty for all religious denominations in the State." But, it continues with the limitation, "so far as they are not a danger to it and do not militate against the morality and moral sense of the German race."

The Party program foreshadowed the campaign of terrorism. It announced, "We demand ruthless war upon those whose activities are injurious to the common interests," and it demanded that such offenses be published with death.

It is significant that the leaders of this Party interpreted this program as a belligerent one certain to precipitate conflict. The Party platform concluded, "The leaders of the Party swear to proceed regardless of consequences—if necessary, at the sacrifice of their lives—toward the fulfillment of the foregoing points." It is this Leadership Corps of the Party, not its entire membership, that stands accused as a criminal organization.

Let us now see how the leaders of the Party fulfilled their pledge to proceed regardless of consequences. Obviously, their foreign objectives, which were nothing less than to undo international treaties and to wrest territory from foreign control, as well as most of their internal program, could be accomplished only by possession of the machinery of the German state. The first effort, accordingly, was to subvert the Weimar Republic by violent revolution. An abortive *Putsch* at Munich in 1923 landed many of them in jail. The period of meditation which followed produced *Mein Kampf,* henceforth the source of law for the Party workers and a source of considerable revenue to its supreme leader. The Nazi plans for the violent overthrow of the feeble Republic then turned to plans for its capture.

No greater mistake could be made than to think of the Nazi Party in terms of the loose organizations which we of the Western World call "political parties." In discipline, structure, and method the Nazi Party was not adapted to the democratic process of persuasion. It was an instrument of conspiracy and of coercion. The Party was not organized to take over power in the German state by winning support of a majority of the German people. It was organized to seize power in defiance of the will of the people.

The Nazi Party, under the *Führerprinzip,* was bound by an iron discipline into a pyramid, with the Führer, Adolf Hitler, at the top and broadening into a numerous Leadership Corps, composed of overlords of a very extensive Party membership at the base. By no means all of those who may have supported the movement in one way or another were actual Party members. The membership took the Party oath which in effect, amounted to an abdication of personal intelligence and moral responsibility. This was the oath: "I vow inviolable fidelity to Adolf Hitler; I vow absolute obedience to him and to the leaders he designates for me." The membership in daily practice followed its leaders with an idolatry and self-surrender more Oriental than Western.

We will not be obliged to guess as to the motives or goal of the Nazi Party. The immediate aim was to undermine the Weimar

Republic. The order to all Party members to work to that end was given in a letter from Hitler of August 24, 1931 to Rosenberg, of which we will produce the original. Hitler wrote:

> I am just reading in the *Völkischer Beobachter*, edition 235/236, page 1, an article entitled "Does Wirth intend to come over?" The tendency of the article is to prevent on our part a crumbling away from the present form of government. I myself am traveling all over Germany to achieve exactly the opposite. May I therefore ask that my own paper will not stab me in the back with tactically unwise articles. . . . (047–PS.)

Captured film enables us to present the defendant, Alfred Rosenberg, who from the screen will himself tell you the story. The SA practiced violent interference with elections. We have the reports of the SD describing in detail how its members later violated the secrecy of elections in order to identify those who opposed them. One of these reports makes this explanation:

> . . . The control was effected in the following way: some members of the election-committee marked all the ballot papers with numbers. During the ballot itself, a voters' list was made up. The ballot-papers were handed out in numerical order, therefore it was possible afterwards with the aid of this list to find out the persons who cast No-votes or invalid votes. One sample of these marked ballot-papers is enclosed. The marking was done on the back of the ballot-papers with skimmed milk. . . . (R–142.)

The Party activity, in addition to all the familiar forms of political contest, took on the aspect of a rehearsal for warfare. It utilized a Party formation, *Die Sturmabteilungen*, commonly known as the SA. This was a voluntary organization of youthful and fanatical Nazis trained for the use of violence under semi-military discipline. Its members began by acting as bodyguards for the Nazi leaders and rapidly expanded from defensive to offensive tactics. They became disciplined ruffians for the breaking up of opposition meetings and the terrorization of adversaries. They boasted that their task was to make the Nazi Party "master of the streets." The SA was the parent organization of a number of others. Its offspring include *Die Schutzstaffeln*, commonly known as the SS, formed in 1925 and distinguished for the fanaticism and cruelty of its members; *Der Sicherheitsdienst*, known as the SD; and *Die Geheime Staatspolizei,* the Secret State Police, the infamous Gestapo formed in 1934 after Nazi accession to power.

A glance at a chart of the Party organization is enough to show how completely it differed from the political parties we know. It had its own source of law in the Führer and sub-Führers. It had its own courts and its own police. The conspirators set up a government within the Party to exercise outside the law every sanction that any legitimate state could exercise and many that it could not. Its chain of command was military, and its formations were martial in name as well as in function. They were composed of battalions set up to bear arms under military discipline, motorized corps, flying corps, and the infamous "Death Head Corps," which was not misnamed. The Party had its own secret police, its security units, its intelligence and espionage division, its raiding forces, and its youth forces. It established elaborate administrative mechanisms to identify and liquidate spies and informers, to manage concentration camps, to operate death vans, and to finance the whole movement. Through concentric circles of authority, the Nazi Party, as its leadership later boasted, eventually organized and dominated every phase of German life—but not until they had waged a bitter internal struggle characterized by brutal criminality. In preparation for this phase of their struggle, they created a Party police system. This became the pattern and the instrument of the police state, which was the first goal in their plan.

The Party formations, including the Leadership Corps of the Party, the SD, the SS, the SA, and the infamous Secret State Police, or Gestapo,—all these stand accused before you as criminal organizations; organizations which, as we will prove from their own documents, were recruited only from recklessly devoted Nazis, ready in conviction and temperament to do the most violent of deeds to advance the common program. They terrorized and silenced democratic opposition and were able at length to combine with political opportunists, militarists, industrialists, monarchists, and political reactionaries.

On January 30, 1933 Adolf Hitler became Chancellor of the German Republic. An evil combination, represented in the prisoners' dock by its most eminent survivors, had succeeded in possessing itself of the machinery of the German Government, a façade behind which they thenceforth would operate to make a reality of the war of conquest they so long had plotted. The conspiracy had passed into its second phase.

THE CONSOLIDATION OF NAZI POWER

We shall now consider the steps, which embraced the most hideous of crimes against humanity, to which the conspirators resorted in perfecting control of the German state and in preparing Germany for the aggressive war indispensable to their ends.

The Germans of the 1920's were a frustrated and baffled people as a result of defeat and the disintegration of their traditional government. The democratic elements, which were trying to govern Germany through the new and feeble machinery of the Weimar Republic, got inadequate support from the democratic forces of the rest of the world. It is not to be denied that Germany, when world-wide depression was added to her other problems, was faced with urgent and intricate pressures in her economic and political life which necessitated bold measures.

The internal measures by which a nation attempts to solve its problems are ordinarily of no concern to other nations. But the Nazi program from the first was recognized as a desperate program for a people still suffering the effects of an unsuccessful war. The Nazi policy embraced ends always recognized as attainable only by a renewal and a more successful outcome of war. The conspirators' answer to Germany's problems was nothing less than to plot the regaining of territories lost in the first World War and the acquisition of other fertile lands of Central Europe by dispossessing or exterminating those who inhabited them. They also contemplated destroying or permanently weakening all other neighboring peoples so as to win virtual domination of Europe and probably of the world. The precise limits of their ambition we need not define for it was and is as illegal to wage aggressive war for small stakes as for large ones.

We find at this period two governments in Germany—the real and the ostensible. The forms of the German Republic were maintained for a time, and it was the outward and visible government. But the real authority in the State was outside of and above the law and rested in the Leadership Corps of the Nazi Party.

THE NÜRNBERG CASE

On February 27, 1933, less than a month after Hitler became Chancellor, the Reichstag building was set on fire. The burning of this symbol of free parliamentary government was so providential for the Nazis that it was believed they staged the fire themselves. Certainly when we contemplate their known crimes, we cannot believe they would shrink from mere arson. It is not necessary, however, to resolve the controversy as to who set the fire. The significant point is in the use that was made of the fire and of the state of public mind it produced. The Nazis immediately accused the Communist Party of instigating and committing the crime, and turned every effort to portray the single act of arson as the beginning of a Communist revolution. Then, taking advantage of the hysteria, the Nazis met this phantom revolution with a real one. In the following December, the German Supreme Court with commendable courage and independence acquitted the accused Communists, but it was too late to influence the tragic course of events which the Nazi conspirators had set rushing forward.

Hitler, on the morning after the fire, obtained from the aged and ailing President von Hindenburg a Presidential decree suspending the extensive guarantees of individual liberty contained in the Constitution of the Weimar Republic. The decree provided that,

> Sections 114, 115, 117, 118, 123, 124, and 153 of the Constitution of the German Reich are suspended until further notice. Thus, restrictions on personal liberty, on the right of free expression of opinion, including freedom of the press, on the right of assembly and the right of association, and violations of the privacy of postal, telegraphic, and telephonic communications, and warrants for house-searches, orders for confiscations as well as restrictions on property, are also permissible beyond the legal limits otherwise prescribed. (1390–PS.)

The extent of the restrictions on personal liberty under the decree of February 28, 1933, may be understood by reference to the rights under the Weimar Constitution which were suspended:

> *Article 114.* The freedom of the person is inviolable. Curtailment or deprivation of personal freedom by a public authority is only permissible on a legal basis.

Persons who have been deprived of their freedom must be informed at the latest on the following day by whose authority and for what reasons the deprivation of freedom was ordered; opportunity shall be afforded them without delay of submitting objections to their deprivation of freedom.

Article 115. Every German's home is his sanctuary and is inviolable. Exceptions may only be made as provided by law.

Article 117. The secrecy of letters and all postal, telegraphic and telephonic communications is inviolable. Exceptions are inadmissible except by Reich law.

Article 118. Every German has the right, within the limits of the general laws, to express his opinions freely in speech, in writing, in print, in picture form or in any other way. No conditions of work or employment may detract from this right and no disadvantage may accrue to him from any person for making use of this right. . . .

Article 123. All Germans have the right to assemble peacefully and unarmed without giving notice and without special permission.

A Reich law may make previous notification obligatory for assemblies in the open air, and may prohibit them in the case of immediate danger to the public safety.

Article 124. All the Germans have the right to form associations or societies for purposes not contrary to criminal law. This right may not be curtailed by preventive measures. The same provisions apply to religious associations and societies.

Every association may become incorporated (*Erwerb der Rechtsfähigkeit*) according to the provisions of the civil law. The right may not be refused to any association on the grounds that its aims are political, social-political or religious.

Article 153. Property is guaranteed by the Constitution. Its content and limits are defined by the laws.

Expropriation can only take place for the public benefit and on a legal basis. Adequate compensation shall be granted, unless a Reich law orders otherwise. In the case of dispute concerning the amount of compensation, it shall be possible to submit the matter to the ordinary civil courts, unless Reich laws determine otherwise. Compensation must be paid if the Reich expropriates property belonging to the Lands, Communes, or public utility associations.

Property carries obligations. Its use shall also serve the common good. (2050–PS.)

It must be said in fairness to von Hindenburg that the Constitution itself authorized him temporarily to suspend these fundamental rights "if the public safety and order in the German Reich are considerably disturbed or endangered." It must also be acknowledged that President Ebert previously had invoked this power.

But the National Socialist coup was made possible because the terms of the Hitler-Hindenburg decree departed from all previous ones in which the power of suspension had been invoked. Whenever Ebert had suspended constitutional guarantees of individual rights, his decree had expressly revived the Protective Custody Act adopted by the Reichstag in 1916 during the previous war. This Act guaranteed a judicial hearing within twenty-four hours of arrest, gave a right to have counsel and to inspect all relevant records, provided for appeal, and authorized compensation from Treasury funds for erroneous arrests.

The Hitler-Hindenburg decree of February 28, 1933 contained no such safeguards. The omission may not have been noted by von Hindenburg. Certainly he did not appreciate its effect. It left the Nazi police and Party formations, already existing and functioning under Hitler, completely unrestrained and irresponsible. Secret arrest and indefinite detention, without charges, without evidence, without hearing, without counsel, became the method of inflicting inhuman punishment on any whom the Nazi police suspected or disliked. No court could issue an injunction, or writ of *habeas corpus,* or *certiorari.* The German people were in the hands of the police, the police were in the hands of the Nazi Party, and the Party was in the hands of a ring of evil men, of whom the defendants here before you are surviving and representative leaders.

The Nazi conspiracy, as we shall show, always contemplated not merely overcoming current opposition but exterminating elements which could not be reconciled with its philosophy of the state. It not only sought to establish the Nazi "new order" but to secure its sway, as Hitler predicted, "for a thousand years." Nazis were never in doubt or disagreement as to what these dissident elements were. They were concisely described by one of them, Colonel General von Fritsch, on December 11, 1938, in these words:

> Shortly after the first war I came to the conclusion that we should have to be victorious in three battles if Germany were to become

powerful again: 1. The battle against the working class—Hitler has won this. 2. Against the Catholic Church, perhaps better expressed against ultramontanism. 3. Against the Jews. (1947–PS.)

The warfare against these elements was continuous. The battle in Germany was but a practice skirmish for the world-wide drive against them. We have in point of geography and of time two groups of crimes against humanity—one within Germany before and during the war, the other in occupied territory during the war. But the two are not separated in Nazi planning. They are a continuous unfolding of the Nazi plan to exterminate peoples and institutions which might serve as a focus or instrument for overturning their "new world order" at any time. We consider those Crimes against Humanity in this address as manifestations of the one Nazi plan and discuss them according to Colonel General von Fritsch's classification.

I. THE BATTLE AGAINST THE WORKING CLASS

When Hitler came to power, there were in Germany three groups of trade unions. The General German Trade Union Confederation (ADGB) with twenty-eight affiliated unions, and the General Independent Employees Confederation (AFA) with thirteen federated unions together numbered more than 4,500,000 members. The Christian Trade Union had over 1,250,000 members.

The working people of Germany, like the working people of other nations, had little to gain personally by war. While labor is usually brought around to the support of the nation at war, labor by and large is a pacific, though by no means a pacifist force in the world. The working people of Germany had not forgotten in 1933 how heavy the yoke of the war lord can be. It was the workingmen who had joined the sailors and soldiers in the revolt of 1918 to end the first World War. The Nazis had neither forgiven nor forgotten. The Nazis program required that this part of the German population not only be stripped of power to resist diversion of its scanty comforts to armament, but also be wheedled or whipped into new and unheard-of sacrifices as part of the Nazi war preparation. Labor must be cowed, and that meant its organizations and means of cohesion and defense must be destroyed.

The purpose to regiment labor for the Nazi Party was avowed by Ley in a speech to workers on May 2, 1933, as follows:

> You may say what else do you want, you have the absolute power. True we have the power, but we do not have the whole people, we do not have you workers 100%, and it is you whom we want; we will not let you be until you stand with us in complete, genuine acknowledgment. (614–PS.)

The first Nazi attack was upon the two larger unions. On April 21, 1933 an order not even in the name of the Government, but of the Nazi Party was issued by the conspirator Robert Ley as "Chief of Staff of the political organization of the NSDAP," applicable to the Trade Union Confederation and the Independent Employees Confederation. It directed seizure of their properties and arrest of their principal leaders. The Party order directed Party organs which we here denounce as criminal associations, the SA and SS "to be employed for the occupation of the trade union properties, and for the taking into custody of personalities who come into question." And it directed the taking into "protective custody" of all chairmen and district secretaries of such unions and branch directors of the labor bank. (392–PS.)

These orders were carried out on May 2, 1933. All funds of the labor unions, including pension and benefit funds, were seized. Union leaders were sent to concentration camps. A few days later, on May 10, 1933, Hitler appointed Ley leader of the German Labor Front (*Deutsche Arbeitsfront*), which succeeded to the confiscated union funds. The German Labor Front, a Nazi controlled labor bureau, was set up under Ley to teach the Nazi philosophy to German workers and to weed out from industrial employment all who were backward in their lessons. (1940–PS.) "Factory Troops" were organized as an "ideological shock squad within the factory." (1817–PS.) The Party order provided that "outside of the German Labor Front, no other organization (whether of workers or of employees) is to exist." On June 24, 1933 the remaining Christian Trade Unions were seized pursuant to an order of the Nazi Party signed by Ley.

On May 19, 1933, this time by government decree, it was provided that "trustees" of labor, appointed by Hitler, should regulate the conditions of all labor contracts, replacing the former process of collective bargaining. (405–PS.) On November 30, 1934 a decree "regulating national labor" introduced the Führer principle into industrial relations. It provided that the owners of enterprises should be the "Führers" and the workers should be the followers. The enterpriser-Führers should "make decisions for employees and laborers in all matters concerning the enterprise." (1861–PS.) It was by such bait that the great German industrialists were induced to support the Nazi cause, to their own ultimate ruin.

Not only did the Nazis dominate and regiment German labor, but they forced the youth into the ranks of the laboring people they had thus led into chains. Under a compulsory labor service decree on June 26, 1935, young men and women between the ages of 18 and 25 were conscripted for labor. (1654–PS.) Thus was the purpose to subjugate German labor accomplished. In the words of Ley, this accomplishment consisted "in eliminating the association character of the trade union and employees' associations, and in its place we have substituted the conception 'soldiers of work'." The productive manpower of the German nation was in Nazi control. By these steps the defendants won the battle to liquidate labor unions as potential opposition and were enabled to impose upon the working class the burdens of preparing for aggressive warfare.

Robert Ley, the field marshal of the battle against labor, answered our indictment with suicide. Apparently he knew no better answer.

II. THE BATTLE AGAINST THE CHURCHES

The Nazi Party always was predominantly anti-Christian in its ideology. But we who believe in freedom of conscience and of religion base no charge of criminality on anybody's ideology. It is not because the Nazis themselves were irreligious or pagan, but because they persecuted others of the Christian faith that they become guilty of crime, and it is because the persecution was a step in the preparation for aggressive warfare that the offense becomes one of international consequence. To remove every moderating influence among the German people and to put its population on a total war footing, the conspirators devised and carried out a systematic and relentless repression of all Christian sects and churches.

We will ask you to convict the Nazis on their own evidence. Martin Bormann in June, 1941, issued a secret decree on the relation of Christianity and National Socialism. The decree provided:

> For the first time in German history the Führer consciously and completely has the leadership of the people in his own hand. With the party, its components and attached units the Führer has created for himself and thereby the German Reich leadership an instrument which makes him independent of the Church. All influences which might impair or damage the leadership of the people exercised by the Führer with help of the NSDAP, must be eliminated. More and more the people must be separated from the churches and their organs, the pastors. Of course, the churches must and will, seen from their viewpoint, defend themselves against this loss of power. But never again must an influence on leadership of the people be yielded to the churches. This (influence) must be broken completely and finally.
>
> Only the Reich government and by its direction the Party, its components and attached units have a right to leadership of the people. Just as the deleterious influences of astrologers, seers and other fakers are eliminated and suppressed by the State, so must the possibility of Church influence also be totally removed. Not until this has happened, does the State leadership have influence on the individual citizens. Not until then are people and Reich secure in their existence for all the future. (D–75.)

And how the Party had been securing the Reich from Christian influence, will be proved by such items as this teletype from the Gestapo, Berlin, to the Gestapo, Nürnberg on July 24, 1938. Let us hear their own account of events in Rottenburg:

> The Party on 23 July 1939 from 2100 on carried out the third demonstration against Bishop Sproll. Participants, about 2,500– 3,000, were brought in from outside by bus, etc. The Rottenburg populace again did not participate in the demonstration. This town took rather a hostile attitude to the demonstrations. The action got completely out of hand of the Party Member responsible for it. The demonstrators stormed the palace, beat in the gates and doors. About 150 to 200 people forced their way into the palace, searched the rooms, threw files out of the windows and rummaged through

the beds in the rooms of the palace. One bed was ignited. Before the fire got to the other objects of equipment in the rooms and the palace, the flaming bed could be thrown from the window and the fire extinguished. The Bishop was with Archbishop Groeber of Freiburg and the ladies and gentlemen of his menage in the chapel at prayer. About 25 to 30 people pressed into this chapel and molested those present. Bishop Groeber was taken for Bishop Sproll. He was grabbed by the robe and dragged back and forth. Finally the intruders realized that Bishop Groeber is not the one they are seeking. They could then be persuaded to leave the building. After the evacuation of the palace by the demonstrators I had an interview with Archbishop Groeber, who left Rottenburg in the night. Groeber wants to turn to the Führer and Reich Minister of the Interior, Dr. Frick, anew. On the course of the action, the damage done as well as the homage of the Rottenburg populace beginning today for the Bishop I shall immediately hand in a full report, after I am in the act of suppressing counter mass meetings. . . .

In case the Führer has instructions to give in this matter, I request that these be transmitted most quickly. . . . (848–PS.)

Later, defendant Rosenberg wrote to Bormann reviewing the proposal of Kerrl as Church Minister to place the Protestant Church under state tutelage and proclaim Hitler its Supreme head. Rosenberg was opposed, hinting that Nazism was to suppress the Christian Church completely after the war. (See also 098–PS.)

The persecution of all pacifist and dissenting sects, such as Jehovah's Witnesses and the Pentecostal Association, was peculiarly relentless and cruel. The policy toward the Evangelical Churches, however, was to use their influence for the Nazis' own purposes. In September 1933, Mueller was appointed the Führer's representative with power to deal with the "affairs of the Evangelical Church" in its relations to the State. Eventually, steps were taken to create a Reich Bishop vested with power to control this church. A long conflict followed, Pastor Niemöller was sent to a concentration camp, and extended interference with the internal discipline and administration of the churches occurred.

A most intense drive was directed against the Roman Catholic Church. After a strategic concordat with the Holy See, signed in July 1933 in Rome, which never was observed by the Nazi Party, a long and persistent persecution of the Catholic Church, its priesthood, and its members, was carried out. Church schools and educational institutions were suppressed or subjected to requirements of Nazi teaching inconsistent with the Christian faith. The property of the Church was confiscated and inspired vandalism directed against Church property was left unpunished. Religious instruction was impeded and the exercise of religion made difficult. Priests and bishops were laid upon, riots were stimulated to harass them, and many were sent to concentration camps.

After occupation of foreign soil, these persecutions went on with greater vigor than ever. We will present to you from the files of the Vatican the earnest protests made by the Vatican to Ribbentrop summarizing the persecutions to which the priesthood and the Church had been subjected in this twentieth century under the Nazi regime. Ribbentrop never answered them. He could not deny. He dared not justify.

III. CRIMES AGAINST THE JEWS

The most savage and numerous crimes planned and committed by the Nazis were those against the Jews. These in Germany, in 1933, numbered about 500,000. In the aggregate, they had made for themselves positions which excited envy, and had accumulated properties which excited the avarice of the Nazis. They were few enough to be helpless and numerous enough to be held up as a menace.

Let there be no misunderstanding about the charge of persecuting Jews. What we charge against these defendants is not those arrogances and pretensions which frequently accompany the intermingling of different peoples and which are likely, despite the honest efforts of government, to produce regrettable crimes and convulsions. It is my purpose to show a plan and design, to which all Nazis were fanatically committed, to annihilate all Jewish people. These crimes were organized and promoted by the Party Leadership, executed and protected by the Nazi officials, as we shall convince you by written orders of the Secret State Police itself.

The persecution of the Jews was a continuous and deliberate policy. It was a policy directed against other nations as well as

GERMAN PHOTOGRAPHS *contained in the report of SS General Stroop on the destruction of the Warsaw Ghetto and the elimination of a "proved total of 56,065. To that we have to add the number of those killed through blasting, fire, etc., which cannot be counted."*

against the Jews themselves. Anti-Semitism was promoted to divide and embitter the democratic peoples and to soften their resistance to the Nazi aggression. As Robert Ley declared in *Der Angriff*, on May 14, 1944, "The second German secret weapon is anti-Semitism because if it is constantly pursued by Germany, it will become a universal problem which all nations will be forced to consider."

Anti-Semitism also has been aptly credited with being a "spearhead of terror." The ghetto was the laboratory for testing repressive measures. Jewish property was the first to be expropriated, but the custom grew and included similar measures against anti-Nazi Germans, Poles, Czechs, Frenchmen, and Belgians. Extermination of the Jews enabled the Nazis to bring a practiced hand to similar measures against Poles, Serbs, and Greeks. The plight of the Jew was a constant threat to opposition or discontent among other elements of Europe's population—pacifists, conservatives, communists, Catholics, Protestants, socialists. It was, in fact, a threat to every dissenting opinion and to every non-Nazi's life.

The persecution policy against the Jews commenced with nonviolent measures, such as disfranchisement and discriminations against their religion, and the placing of impediments in the way of success in economic life. It moved rapidly to organized mass violence against them, physical isolation in ghettos, deportation, forced labor, mass starvation, and extermination. The Government, the Party formations indicted before you as criminal organizations, the Secret State Police, the Army, private and semipublic associations, and "spontaneous" mobs that were carefully inspired from official sources, were all agencies concerned in this persecution. Nor was it directed against individual Jews for personal bad citizenship or unpopularity. The avowed purpose was the destruction of the Jewish people as a whole, as an end in itself, as a measure of preparation for war, and as a discipline of conquered peoples.

The conspiracy or common plan to exterminate the Jew was so methodically and thoroughly pursued that despite the German defeat and Nazi prostration, this Nazi aim largely has succeeded. Only remnants of the European Jewish population remain in Germany, in the countries which Germany occupied, and in those which were her satellites or collaborators. Of the 9,600,000 Jews who lived in Nazi dominated Europe, sixty percent are authoritatively estimated to have perished. 5,700,000 Jews are missing from the countries in which they formerly lived, and over 4,500,000 cannot be accounted for by the normal death rate nor by immigration; nor are they included among displaced persons. History does not record a crime ever perpetrated against so many victims or one ever carried out with such calculated cruelty.

You will have difficulty, as I have, to look into the faces of these defendants and believe that in this twentieth century human beings could inflict such sufferings as will be proved here on their own countrymen as well as upon their so-called "inferior" enemies. Particular crimes, and the responsibility of defendants for them, are to be dealt with by the Soviet Government's Counsel, when committed in the East, and by Counsel for the Republic of France when committed in the West. I advert to them only to show their magnitude as evidence of a purpose and a knowledge common to all defendants, of an official plan rather than of a capricious policy of some individual commander, and to show such a continuity of Jewish persecution from the rise of the Nazi conspiracy to its collapse as forbids us to believe that any person could be identified with any part of Nazi action without approving this most conspicuous item of its program.

The Indictment itself recites many evidences of the anti-Semitic persecutions. The defendant Streicher led the Nazis in anti-Semitic bitterness and extremism. In an article appearing in *Der Stürmer* on March 19, 1942 he complained that Christian teachings have stood in the way of "radical solution of the Jewish question in Europe," and quoted enthusiastically as the twentieth century solution the Führer's proclamation of February 24, 1942 that "the Jew will be exterminated." And on November 4, 1943, Streicher declared in *Der Stürmer* that the Jews "have disappeared from Europe and that the Jewish 'Reservoir of the East' from which the Jewish plague has for centuries beset the people of Europe, has ceased to exist." Streicher now has the effrontery to tell us he is "only a Zionist"—he says he wants only to return the Jews to Palestine. But on May 7, 1942, his newspaper had this to say:

It is also not only an European problem! *The Jewish question is a world question!* Not only is Germany not safe in the face of the Jews as long as one Jew lives in Europe, but also the Jewish question is hardly solved in Europe so long as Jews live in the rest of the world.

And the defendant Hans Frank, a lawyer by profession I say with shame, summarized in his diary in 1944 the Nazi policy thus: "The Jews are a race which has to be eliminated; whenever we catch one, it is his end." (2233–PS p. 26, March 4, 1944.) And earlier, speaking of his function as Governor General of Poland, he confided to his diary this sentiment: "Of course I cannot eliminate all lice and Jews in only a year's time." (2233–PS, Vol. IV, 1940 p. 1158.) I could multiply endlessly this kind of Nazi ranting but I will leave it to the evidence and turn to the fruit of this perverted thinking.

The most serious of the actions against Jews were outside of any law, but the law itself was employed to some extent. There were the infamous Nürnberg decrees of September 15, 1935 (*Reichsgesetzblatt*, 1935, Part I, p. 1146.) The Jews were segregated into ghettos and put into forced labor; they were expelled from their professions; their property was expropriated; all cultural life, the press, the theater, and schools were prohibited them; and the SD was made responsible for them. (212–PS, 069–PS.) This was an ominous guardianship, as the following order for "The Handling of the Jewish Question" shows:

> The competency of the Chief of the Security Police and Security Service, who is charged with the mission of solving the European Jewish question, extends even to the occupied eastern provinces. . . .
>
> An eventual act by the civilian population against the Jews is not to be prevented as long as this is compatible with the maintenance of order and security in the rear of the fighting troops. . . .
>
> The first main goal of the German measures must be strict segregation of Jewry from the rest of the population. In the execution of this, first of all is the seizing of the Jewish populace by the introduction of a registration order and similar appropriate measures. . . .
>
> Then immediately, the wearing of the recognition sign consisting of a yellow Jewish star is to be brought about and all rights of freedom for Jews are to be withdrawn. They are to be placed in ghettos

and at the same time are to be separated according to sexes. The presence of many more or less closed Jewish settlements in White Ruthenia and in the Ukraine makes this mission easier. Moreover, places are to be chosen which make possible the full use of the Jewish manpower in case labor needs are present. . . .

The entire Jewish property is to be seized and confiscated with exception of that which is necessary for a bare existence. As far as the economic situation permits, the power of disposal of their property is to be taken from the Jews as soon as possible through orders and other measures given by the commissariat, so that the moving of property will quickly cease.

Any cultural activity will be completely forbidden to the Jew. This includes the outlawing of the Jewish press, the Jewish theaters and schools.

The slaughtering of animals according to Jewish rites is also to be prohibited. . . . (212–PS.)

The anti-Jewish campaign became furious in Germany following the assassination in Paris of the German Legation Councillor von Rath. Heydrich, Gestapo head, sent a teletype to all Gestapo and SD offices with directions for handling "spontaneous" uprising anticipated for the nights of November 9 and 10, 1938, so as to aid in destruction of Jewish-owned property and protect only that of Germans. No more cynical document ever came into evidence. Then there is a report by an SS Brigade Leader, Dr. Stahlecker, to Himmler, which recites that:

. . . Similarly, native anti-Semitic forces were induced to start pogroms against Jews during the first hours after capture, though this inducement proved to be very difficult. Following out orders, the Security Police was determined to solve the Jewish question with all possible means and most decisively. But it was desirable that the Security Police should not put in an immediate appearance, at least in the beginning, since the extraordinarily harsh measures were apt to stir even German circles. It had to be shown to the world that the native population itself took the first action by way of natural reaction against the suppression by Jews during several decades and against the terror exercised by the Communists during the preceding period. . . .

. . . In view of the extension of the area of operations and the great number of duties which had to be performed by the Security Police, it was intended from the very beginning to obtain the co-

operation of the reliable population for the fight against vermin—
that is mainly the Jews and Communists. Beyond our directing of
the first spontaneous actions of self-cleansing, which will be reported elsewhere, care had to be taken that reliable people should
be put to the cleansing job and that they were appointed auxiliary
members of the Security Police. . . .

. . . Kowno . . . To our surprise it was not easy at first to set
in motion an extensive pogrom against Jews. Klimatis, the leader
of the partisan unit, mentioned above, who was used for this purpose primarily, succeeded in starting a pogrom on the basis of
advice given to him by a small advanced detachment acting in
Kowno, and in such a way that no German order or German instigation was noticed from the outside. During the first pogrom in the
night from 25. to 26.6 the Lithuanian partisans did away with more
than 1,500 Jews, set fire to several synagogues or destroyed them
by other means and burned down a Jewish dwelling district consisting of about 60 houses. During the following nights about 2,300
Jews were made harmless in a similar way. In other parts of Lithuania similar actions followed the example of Kowno, though smaller
and extending to the Communists who had been left behind.

These self-cleansing actions went smoothly because the Army
authorities who had been informed showed understanding for this
procedure. From the beginning it was obvious that only the first
days after the occupation would offer the opportunity for carrying
out pogroms. After the disarmament of the partisans the self-cleansing actions ceased necessarily.

It proved much more difficult to set in motion similar cleansing
actions in Latvia. . . .

. . . From the beginning it was to be expected that the Jewish
problem in the East could not be solved by pogroms alone. In accordance with the basic orders received, however, the cleansing
activities of the Security Police had to aim at a complete annihilation
of the Jews. . . .

The sum total of the Jews liquidated in Lithuania amounts to
71,105. . . . (L–180.)

Of course, it is self-evident that these "uprisings" were managed by the government and the Nazi Party. If we were in doubt,
we could resort to Streicher's memorandum of April 14, 1939,
which says, "The anti-Jewish action of November 1938 did not
arise spontaneously from the people. . . . Part of the party formation have been charged with the execution of the anti-Jewish

action." (406–PS.) Jews as a whole were fined a billion Reichsmarks. They were excluded from all businesses, and claims against insurance companies for their burned properties were confiscated, all by decree of the defendant Göring. (*Reichsgesetzblatt*, 1938, Part I, pp. 1579–1582.)

Synagogues were the objects of a special vengeance. On November 10, 1938, the following order was given: "By order of the Group Commander, all Jewish synagogues in the area of Brigade 50 have to be blown up or set afire. . . . The operation will be carried out in civilian clothing. . . . Execution of the order will be reported. . . ." (1721–PS.) Some forty teletype messages from various police headquarters will tell the fury with which all Jews were pursued in Germany on those awful November nights. The SS troops were turned loose and the Gestapo supervised. Jewish-owned property was authorized to be destroyed. The Gestapo ordered twenty to thirty thousand "well-to-do Jews" to be arrested. Concentration camps were to receive them. Healthy Jews, fit for labor, were to be taken. (3051–PS.) As the German frontiers were expanded by war, so the campaign against the Jews expanded. The Nazi plan never was limited to extermination in Germany; always it contemplated extinguishing the Jew in Europe and often in the world. In the West, the Jews were killed and their property taken over. But the campaign achieved its zenith of savagery in the East. The Eastern Jew has suffered as no people ever suffered. Their sufferings were carefully reported to the Nazi authorities to show faithful adherence to the Nazi design. I shall refer only to enough of the evidence of these to show the extent of the Nazi design for killing Jews.

If I should recite these horrors in words of my own, you would think me intemperate and unreliable. Fortunately, we need not take the word of any witness but the Germans themselves. I invite you now to look at a few of the vast number of captured German orders and reports that will be offered in evidence, to see what a Nazi invasion meant. We will present such evidence as the report of "*Einsatzgruppe* (Action Group) A" of October 15, 1941, which boasts that in overrunning the Baltic States, "Native anti-Semitic forces were induced to start pogroms against the Jews during the first hours after occupation . . ." The report continues:

From the beginning it was to be expected that the Jewish problem in the East could not be solved by pogroms alone. In accordance with the basic orders received, however, the cleansing activities of the Security Police had to aim at a complete annihilation of the Jews. Special detachments reinforced by selected units—in Lithuania partisan detachments, in Latvia units of the Latvian auxiliary police —therefore performed extensive executions both in the towns and in rural areas. The actions of the execution detachments were performed smoothly.

The sum total of the Jews liquidated in Lithuania amounts to 71,105. During the pogroms in Kowno 3,800 Jews were eliminated, in the smaller towns about 1,200 Jews.

In Latvia, up to now a total of 30,000 Jews were executed. 500 were eliminated by pogroms in Riga. (L-180.)

This is a captured report from the Commissioner of Sluzk on October 30, 1941, which describes the scene in more detail. It says:

. . . The first lieutenant explained that the police battalion had received the assignment to effect the liquidation of all Jews here in the town of Sluzk, within two days. . . . Then I requested him to postpone the action one day. However, he rejected this with the remark that he had to carry out this action everywhere and in all towns and that only two days were allotted for Sluzk. Within those two days, the town of Sluzk had to be cleared of Jews by all means. . . . All Jews without exception were taken out of the factories and shops and deported in spite of our agreement. It is true that part of the Jews was moved by way of the ghetto where many of them were processed and still segregated by me, but a large part was loaded directly on trucks and liquidated without further delay outside of the town. . . . For the rest, as regards the execution of the action. I must point out to my deepest regret that the latter bordered already on sadism. The town itself offered a picture of horror during the action. With indescribable brutality on the part of both the German police officers and particularly the Lithuanian partisans, the Jewish people, but also among them White Ruthenians, were taken out of their dwellings and herded together. Everywhere in the town shots were to be heard and in different streets the corpses of shot Jews accumulated. The White Ruthenians were in greatest distress to free themselves from the encirclement. Regardless of the fact that the Jewish people, among whom were also tradesmen, were mistreated in a terribly barbarous way in the face

59

of the White Ruthenian people, the White Ruthenians themselves were also worked over with rubber clubs and rifle butts. There was no question of an action against the Jews any more. It rather looked like a revolution. . . . (1104–PS.)

There are reports which merely tabulate the numbers slaughtered. An example is an account of the work of *Einsatzgruppen* of Sipo and SD in the East, which relates that—

In Estonia, all Jews were arrested immediately upon the arrival of the Wehrmacht. Jewish men and women above the age of 16 and capable of work were drafted for forced labor. Jews were subjected to all sorts of restrictions and all Jewish property was confiscated.

All Jewish males above the age of 16 were executed, with the exception of doctors and elders. Only 500 of an original 4,500 Jews remained.

37,180 persons have been liquidated by the Sipo and SD in White Ruthenia during October.

In one town, 337 Jewish women were executed for demonstrating a "provocative attitude." In another, 380 Jews were shot for spreading vicious propaganda.

And so the report continues, listing town after town, where hundreds upon hundreds of Jews were murdered.

In Witebsk 3,000 Jews were liquidated because of the danger of epidemics.

In Kiew, 33,771 Jews were executed on September 29 and 30 in retaliation for some fires which were set off there.

In Shitomir, 3,145 Jews "had to be shot" because, judging from experience they had to be considered as the carriers of Bolshevik propaganda.

In Cherson, 410 Jews were executed in reprisal against acts of sabotage.

In the territory east of the Dnepr, the Jewish problem was "solved" by the liquidation of 4,891 Jews and by putting the remainder into labor battalions of up to 1,000 persons. (R–102.)

Other accounts tell not of the slaughter so much as of the depths of degradation to which the tormentors stooped. For example, we will show the report made to defendant Rosenberg about the army and the SS in the area under Rosenberg's jurisdiction, which recited the following:

Details: In presence of SS man, a Jewish dentist has to break all gold teeth and fillings out of mouth of German and Russian Jews *before* they are executed.

Men, women and children are locked into barns and burned alive.

Peasants, women and children are shot on pretext that they are suspected of belonging to bands. (R–135.)

We of the Western World heard of gas wagons in which Jews and political opponents were asphyxiated. We could not believe it. But here we have the report of May 16, 1942 from the German SS officer, Becker, to his supervisor in Berlin which tells this story:

Gas vans in C group can be driven to execution spot, which is generally stationed 10 to 15 kms. from main road only in dry weather. Since those to be executed become frantic if conducted to this place, such vans become immobilized in wet weather.

Gas vans in D group camouflaged as cabin trailers, but vehicles well known to authorities and civilian population which calls them "Death Vans."

Writer of letter (Becker) ordered all men to keep as far away as possible during gassing. Unloading van has "atrocious spiritual and physical effect" on men and they should be ordered not to participate in such work. (501–PS.)

I shall not dwell on this subject longer than to quote one more sickening document which evidences the planned and systematic character of the Jewish persecutions. I hold a report written with Teutonic devotion to detail, illustrated with photographs to authenticate its almost incredible text, and beautifully bound in leather with the loving care bestowed on a proud work. It is the original report of the SS Brigadier General Stroop in charge of the destruction of the Warsaw Ghetto, and its title page carries the inscription, "The Jewish Ghetto in Warsaw no longer exists." It is characteristic that one of the captions explains that the photograph concerned shows the driving out of Jewish "bandits"; those whom the photograph shows being driven out are almost entirely women and little children. It contains a day-by-day account of the killings mainly carried out by the SS organization, too long to relate, but let me quote General Stroop's summary:

The resistance put up by the Jews and bandits could only be suppressed by energetic actions of our troops day and night. *The*

Reichsführer SS ordered, therefore on 23 April 1943 the cleaning out of the ghetto with utter ruthlessness and merciless tenacity. I, therefore, decided to destroy and burn down the entire ghetto without regard to the armament factories. These factories were systematically dismantled and then burned. Jews usually left their hideouts, but frequently remained in the burning buildings and jumped out of the windows only when the heat became unbearable. They then tried to crawl with broken bones across the street into buildings which were not afire. Sometimes they changed their hideouts during the night into the ruins of burned buildings. Life in the sewers was not pleasant after the first week. Many times we could hear loud voices in the sewers. SS men or policemen climbed bravely through the manholes to capture these Jews. Sometimes they stumbled over Jewish corpses; sometimes they were shot at. Tear gas bombs were thrown into the manholes and the Jews driven out of the sewers and captured. Countless numbers of Jews were liquidated in sewers and bunkers through blasting. The longer the resistance continued the tougher became the members of the Waffen SS police and Wehrmacht who always discharged their duties in an exemplary manner. Frequently Jews who tried to replenish their food supplies during the night or to communicate with neighboring groups were exterminated. (1061–PS.)

This action eliminated, says the SS commander, "a proved total of 56,065. To that we have to add the number of those killed through blasting, fire, etc., which cannot be counted."

We charge that all atrocities against Jews were the manifestation and culmination of the Nazi plan to which every defendant here was a party. I know very well that some of these men did take steps to spare some particular Jew for some personal reason from the horrors that awaited the unrescued Jew. Some protested that particular atrocities were excessive, and discredited the general policy. While a few defendants may show efforts to make specific exceptions to the policy of Jewish extermination, I have found no instance in which any defendant opposed the policy itself or sought to revoke or even modify it.

Determination to destroy the Jews was a binding force which at all times cemented the elements of this conspiracy. On many internal policies there were differences among the defendants. But there is not one of them who has not echoed the rallying cry of Nazism—*Deutschland erwache, Juda verrecke!* (*Germany awake, Jewry perish!*)

TERRORISM AND PREPARATION FOR WAR

How a government treats its own inhabitants generally is thought to be no concern of other governments or of international society. Certainly few oppressions or cruelties would warrant the intervention of foreign powers. But the German mistreatment of Germans is now known to pass in magnitude and savagery any limits of what is tolerable by modern civilization. Other nations, by silence, would take a consenting part in such crimes. These Nazi persecutions, moreover, take character as international crimes because of the purpose for which they were undertaken.

The purpose, as we have seen, of getting rid of the influence of free labor, the churches, and the Jews was to clear their obstruction to the precipitation of aggressive war. If aggressive warfare in violation of treaty obligation is a matter of international cognizance, the preparations for it must also be of concern to the international community. Terrorism was the chief instrument for securing the cohesion of the German people in war purposes. Moreover, these cruelties in Germany served as atrocity practice to discipline the membership of the criminal organization to follow the pattern later in occupied countries.

Through the police formations that before you are accused as criminal organizations, the Nazi Party leaders, aided at some point in their basic and notorious purpose by each of the individual defendants instituted a reign of terror. These espionage and police organizations were utilized to hunt down every form of opposition and to penalize every nonconformity. These organizations early founded and administered concentration camps— Buchenwald in 1933, Dachau in 1934. But these notorious names were not alone. Concentration camps came to dot the German map and to number scores. At first they met with resistance from some Germans. We have a captured letter from Minister of Justice Gürtner to Hitler which is revealing. A Gestapo official had been prosecuted for crimes committed in the camp at Hohnstein, and the Nazi Governor of Saxony had promptly asked that

63

the proceeding be quashed. The Minister of Justice in June 1935 protested because, as he said:

> In this camp unusually grave mistreatments of prisoners have occurred at least since Summer 1933. The prisoners not only were beaten with whips without cause, similarly as in the Concentration Camp Bredow near Stettin till they lost consciousness, but they were also tortured in other manners, e.g. with the help of a dripping apparatus constructed exclusively for this purpose, under which prisoners had to stand until they were suffering from serious purulent wounds of the scalp. . . . (787–PS.)

I shall not take time to detail the ghastly proceedings in these concentration camps. Beatings, starvings, tortures, and killings were routine—so routine that the tormentors became blasé and careless. We will show you a report of discovery that in Plötzens one night, one hundred and eighty-six persons were executed while there were orders for only one hundred and eighty. Another report describes how the family of one victim received two urns of ashes by mistake. Inmates were compelled to execute each other. In 1942, they were paid five Reichsmarks per execution, but on June 27, 1942, SS General Gluecks ordered commandants of all concentration camps to reduce this honorarium to three cigarettes. In 1943, the Reichsleader of the SS and Chief of German Police ordered the corporal punishments on Russian women to be applied by Polish women and vice versa, but the price was not frozen. "As reward, a few cigarettes" was authorized. Under the Nazis, human life had been progressively devalued until it finally became worth less than a handful of tobacco —ersatz tobacco. There were, however, some traces of the milk of human kindness. On August 11, 1942, an order went from Himmler to the commanders of fourteen concentration camps that "only German prisoners are allowed to beat other German prisoners." 2189–PS.

Mystery and suspense were added to cruelty in order to spread torture from the inmate to his family and friends. Men and women disappeared from their homes or business or from the streets, and no word came of them. The omission of notice was not due to overworked staff; it was due to policy. The Chief of the SD and Sipo reported that in accordance with orders from the Führer anxiety should be created in the minds of the family of the arrested person. (668–PS.) Deportations and secret arrests were labeled, with a Nazi wit which seems a little ghoulish, "*Nacht und Nebel*" (Night and Fog). (L–90, 833–PS.) The decree ordering these actions makes this explanation:

> The decree carries a basic innovation. The Führer and Commander-in-Chief of the Armed Forces commands that crimes of the specified sort committed by civilians of the occupied territories are to be punished by the pertinent courts-martial in the occupied territories *only* when
>
> (a) the sentence calls for the death penalty, and
> (b) the sentence is pronounced within 8 days after the arrest.
>
> Only when both conditions are met does the Führer and Commander-in-Chief of the Armed Forces hope for the desired deterrent effect from the conduct of punitive proceedings in the occupied territories.
>
> In other cases in the future the accused are to be secretly brought to Germany and the further conduct of the trial carried on here. The deterrent effect of those measures lies
>
> (a) in allowing the disappearance of the accused without a trace,
> (b) therein, that no information whatsoever may be given about their whereabouts and their fate. (833–PS.)

To clumsy cruelty, scientific skill was added. "Undesirables" were exterminated by injection of drugs into the bloodstream, by asphyxiation in gas chambers. They were shot with poison bullets, to study the effects. (L–103.)

Then, to cruel experiments the Nazi added obscene ones. These were not the work of underling degenerates but of masterminds high in the Nazi conspiracy. On May 20, 1942, General Field Marshal Milch authorized SS General Wolff to go ahead at Dachau Camp with so-called "cold experiments"; and four female gypsies were supplied for the purpose. Himmler gave permission to carry on these "experiments" also in other camps. (1617–PS.) At Dachau, the reports of the "doctor" in charge show that victims were immersed in cold water until their body temperature was reduced to 28 degrees centigrade (82.4 degrees Fahrenheit), when they all died immediately. (1618–PS.) This was in August 1942. But the "doctor's" technique improved. By February, 1943, he was able to report that thirty persons were chilled to 27 to 29 degrees, their hands and feet frozen white, and their bodies "rewarmed" by a hot bath. But the Nazi scientific triumph was "rewarming with animal heat." The victim, all but frozen to death, was surrounded with bodies of living women until he revived and responded to his environment by having sexual intercourse. (1616–PS.) Here Nazi degeneracy reached its nadir.

I dislike to encumber the record with such morbid tales, but we are in the grim business of trying men as criminals, and these are the things their own agents say happened. We will show you these concentration camps in motion pictures, just as the Allied armies found them when they arrived, and the measures General Eisenhower had to take to clean them up. Our proof will be disgusting and you will say I have robbed you of your sleep. But these are the things which have turned the stomach of the world and set every civilized hand against Nazi Germany.

Germany became one vast torture chamber. Cries of its victims were heard round the world and brought shudders to civilized people everywhere. I am one who received during this war most atrocity tales with suspicion and skepticism. But the proof here will be so overwhelming that I venture to predict not one word I have spoken will be denied. These defendants will only deny personal responsibility or knowledge.

Under the clutch of the most intricate web of espionage and intrigue that any modern state has endured, and persecution and torture of a kind that has not been visited upon the world in many centuries, the elements of the German population which were both decent and courageous were annihilated. Those which were decent but weak were intimidated. Open resistance, which had never been more than feeble and irresolute, disappeared. But resistance, I am happy to say, always remained, although it was manifest in only such events as the abortive effort to assassinate Hitler on July 20, 1944. With resistance driven underground, the Nazi had the German state in his own hands.

But the Nazis not only silenced discordant voices. They created positive controls as effective as their negative ones. Propaganda organs, on a scale never before known, stimulated the Party and Party formations with a permanent enthusiasm and abandon such as we democratic people can work up only for a few days before a general election. They inculcated and practiced the *Führer-prinzip* which centralized control of the Party and of the Party-controlled state over the lives and thought of the German people, who are accustomed to look upon the German state by whomever controlled with a mysticism that is incomprehensible to my people.

All these controls from their inception were exerted with unparalleled energy and single-mindedness to put Germany on a war footing. We will show from the Nazis' own documents their secret training of military personnel, their secret creation of a military air force. Finally, a conscript army was brought into being. Financiers, economists, industrialists, joined in the plan and promoted elaborate alterations in industry and finance to support an unprecedented concentration of resources and energies upon preparations for war. Germany's rearmament so outstripped the strength of her neighbors that in about a year she was able to crush the whole military force of Continental Europe, exclusive of that of Soviet Russia, and then to push the Russian armies back to the Volga. These preparations were of a magnitude which surpassed all need of defense and every defendant, and every intelligent German, well understood them to be for aggressive purposes.

EXPERIMENTS IN AGGRESSION

Before resorting to open aggressive warfare, the Nazis undertook some rather cautious experiments to test the spirit and resistance of those who lay across their path. They advanced, but only as others yielded, and kept in a position to draw back if they found a temper that made persistence dangerous.

On March 7, 1936, the Nazis reoccupied the Rhineland and then proceeded to fortify it in violation of the Treaty of Versailles and the Pact of Locarno. They encountered no substantial resistance and were emboldened to take the next step, which was the acquisition of Austria. Despite repeated assurances that Germany had no designs on Austria, invasion was perfected. Threat of attack forced Schuschnigg to resign as Chancellor of Austria and put the Nazi defendant Seyss-Inquart in his place. The latter immediately opened the frontier and invited Hitler to invade Austria "to preserve order." On March 12 the invasion began.

The next day, Hitler proclaimed himself Chief of the Austrian State, took command of its armed forces, and a law was enacted annexing Austria to Germany.

Threats of aggression had succeeded without arousing resistance. Fears nevertheless had been stirred. They were lulled by an assurance to the Czechoslovak government that there would be no attack on that country. We will show that the Nazi government already had detailed plans for the attack. We will lay before you the documents in which these conspirators planned to create an incident to justify their attack. They even gave consideration to assassinating their own Ambassador at Prague in order to create a sufficiently dramatic incident. They did precipitate a diplomatic crisis which endured through the summer. Hitler set September 30 as the day when troops should be ready for action. Under the threat of immediate war, the United Kingdom and France concluded a pact with Germany and Italy at Munich on September 29, 1938 which required Czechoslovakia to acquiesce in the cession of the Sudetenland to Germany. It was consummated by German occupation on October 1, 1938.

The Munich Pact pledged no further aggression against Czechoslovakia, but the Nazi pledge was lightly given and quickly broken. On March 15, 1939, in defiance of the treaty of Munich itself, the Nazis seized and occupied Bohemia and Moravia, which constituted the major part of Czechoslovakia not already ceded to Germany. Once again the West stood aghast, but it dreaded war, it saw no remedy except war, and it hoped against hope that the Nazi fever for expansion had run its course. But the Nazi world was intoxicated by these unresisted successes in open alliance with Mussolini and covert alliance with Franco. Then, having made a deceitful, delaying peace with Russia, the conspirators entered upon the final phase of the plan to renew war.

WAR OF AGGRESSION

I will not prolong this address by detailing the steps leading to the war of aggression which began with the invasion of Poland on September 1, 1939. The further story will be unfolded to you from documents including those of the German High Command itself. The plans had been laid long in advance. As early as 1935

OPENING STATEMENT

Hitler appointed the defendant Schacht to the position of "General Deputy for the War Economy." (2261–PS.) We have the diary of General Jodl (1784–PS.), the "Plan Otto," Hitler's own order for attack on Austria in case trickery failed (C–102.); the "Plan Green" (388–PS.) which was the blueprint for attack on Czechoslovakia; the plans for the War in the West (376–PS, 375–PS.); Funk's letter to Hitler dated August 25, 1939, detailing the long course of economic preparation (699–PS.); Keitel's top secret mobilization order for 1939–40 prescribing secret steps to be taken during a "period of tension" during which no "'state of war' will be publicly declared even if open war measures against the foreign enemy will be taken." This later order (1639–A–PS.) is in our possession despite a secret order issued on March 16, 1945, when Allied troops were advancing into the heart of Germany, to burn these plans. We have also Hitler's directive, dated December 18, 1940, for the "Barbarossa Contingency" outlining the strategy of the attack upon Russia. (446–PS.) We have detailed information concerning "Case White," the plan for attack on Poland. (C–120.) That attack began the war. The plan was issued by Keitel on April 3, 1939. The attack did not come until September. Steps in preparation for the attack were taken by subordinate commanders, one of whom issued an order on June 14 providing that:

The Commander-in-Chief of the Army has ordered the working out of a *plan of deployment against Poland* which takes in account the demands of the political leadership *for the opening of war by surprise and for quick success* . . .

I declare it the duty of the Commanding Generals, the divisional commanders and the commandants to limit as much as possible the number of persons who will be informed, and to limit the extent of the information, and ask that all suitable measures be taken to prevent persons not concerned from getting information . . .

The operation, in order to forestall an orderly Polish mobilization and concentration, is to be opened by surprise with forces which are for the most part armored and motorized, placed on alert in the neighborhood of the border. The initial superiority over the Polish frontier-guards and surprise that can be expected with certainty are to be maintained by quickly bringing up other parts of the army as well to counteract the marching up of the Polish Army. . . .

If the development of the political situation should show that a surprise at the beginning of the war is out of question, because of well advanced defense preparations on the part of the Polish Army, the Commander-in-Chief of the Army will order the opening of the hostilities only after the assembling of sufficient additional forces. The basis of all preparations will be to surprise the enemy. . . . (2327–PS.)

We have also the order for the invasion of England, signed by Hitler and initialed by Keitel and Jodl. It is interesting that it commences with a recognition that although the British military position is "hopeless," they show not the slightest sign of giving in. (442–PS.)

Not the least incriminating are the minutes of Hitler's meeting with his high advisers. As early as November 5, 1937, Hitler told defendants Göring, Raeder, and Neurath, among others, that German rearmament was practically accomplished and that he had decided to secure by force, starting with a lightning attack on Czechoslovakia and Austria, greater living space for Germans in Europe no later than 1943–45 and perhaps as early as 1938. (386–PS.) On May 23, 1939, the Führer advised his staff that—

It is a question of expanding our living space in the East and of securing our food supplies . . . over and above the natural fertility, thoroughgoing German exploitation will enormously increase the surplus.

There is therefore no question of sparing Poland, and we are left with the decision:

To attack Poland at the first suitable opportunity.

We cannot expect a repetition of the Czech affair. There will be war. (L–79.)

On August 22, 1939 Hitler again addressed members of the High Command, telling them when the start of military operations would be ordered. He disclosed that for propaganda purposes, he would provoke a good reason. "It will make no difference," he announced, "whether this reason will sound convincing or not. After all, the victor will not be asked whether he talked the truth or not. We have to proceed brutally. The stronger is always right." (1014–PS.) On November 23, 1939, after the Germans had invaded Poland, Hitler made this explanation:

OPENING STATEMENT

. . . For the first time in history we have to fight on only one front, the other front is at present free. But no one can know how long that will remain so. I have doubted for a long time whether I should strike in the east and then in the west. Basically I did not organize the armed forces in order not to strike. The decision to strike was always in me. Earlier or later I wanted to solve the problem. Under pressure it was decided that the east was to be attacked first. . . . (789–PS.)

We know the bloody sequel. Frontier incidents were staged. Demands were made for cession of territory. When Poland refused, the German forces invaded on September 1, 1939. Warsaw was destroyed; Poland fell. The Nazis, in accordance with plan, moved swiftly to extend their aggression throughout Europe and to gain the advantage of surprise over their unprepared neighbors. Despite repeated and solemn assurances of peaceful intentions, they invaded Denmark and Norway on April 9, 1940; Belgium, The Netherlands and Luxembourg on May 10, 1940; Yugoslavia and Greece on April 6, 1941.

As part of the Nazi preparation for aggression against Poland and her allies, Germany, on August 23, 1939 had entered into a non-aggression pact with Soviet Russia. It was only a delaying treaty intended to be kept no longer than necessary to prepare for its violation. On June 22, 1941, pursuant to long matured plans, the Nazis hurled troops into Soviet territory without any declaration of war. The entire European world was aflame.

CONSPIRACY WITH JAPAN

The Nazi plans of aggression called for use of Asiatic allies and they found among the Japanese men of kindred mind and purpose. They were brothers, under the skin.

Himmler records a conversation he had on January 31, 1939, with General Oshima, Japanese Ambassador at Berlin. He wrote:

Furthermore, he (Oshima) had succeeded up to now to send 10 Russians with bombs across the Caucasian frontier. These Russians had the mission to kill Stalin. A number of additional Russians, whom he had also sent across, had been shot at the frontier (2195–PS.)

THE NÜRNBERG CASE

On September 27, 1940, the Nazis concluded a German-Italian-Japanese ten-year military and economic alliance by which those powers agreed "to stand by and co-operate with one another in regard to their efforts in Greater East Asia and regions of Europe respectively wherein it is their prime purpose to establish and maintain a new order of things. . . ."

On March 5, 1941, a top secret directive was issued by defendant Keitel. It stated that "The Führer has ordered instigation of Japan's active participation in the war" and directed that "Japan's military power has to be strengthened by the disclosure of German war experiences and support of a military, economic and technical nature has to be given." The aim was stated to be to crush England quickly, "thereby keeping the United States out of the war." (C–75.)

On March 29, 1941, Ribbentrop told Matsuoka, the Japanese Foreign Minister, that the German Army was ready to strike against Russia. Matsuoka reassured Ribbentrop about the Far East. Japan, he reported, was acting at the moment as though she had no interest whatever in Singapore, but "intends to strike when the right moment comes." (1877–PS.) On April 5, 1941, Ribbentrop urged Matsuoka that entry of Japan into the war would "hasten the victory" and would be more in the interest of Japan than of Germany since it would give Japan a unique chance to fulfill her national aims and to play a leading part in Eastern Asia. (1882–PS.)

The proofs in this case will also show that the leaders of Germany were planning war against the United States from its Atlantic as well as instigating it from its Pacific approaches. A captured memorandum from the Führer's headquarters, dated October 29, 1940, asks certain information as to air bases and supply and reports further that

> The Führer is at present occupied with the question of the occupation of the Atlantic islands with a view to the prosecution of war against America at a later date. Deliberations on this subject are being embarked upon here. (376–PS.)

On December 7, 1941, a day which the late President Roosevelt declared "will live in infamy," victory for German aggression seemed certain. The Wehrmacht was at the gates of Moscow.

OPENING STATEMENT

Taking advantage of the situation, and while her plenipotentiaries were creating a diplomatic diversion in Washington, Japan without declaration of war treacherously attacked the United States at Pearl Harbor and the Philippines. Attacks followed swiftly on the British Commonwealth, and The Netherlands in the Southwest Pacific. These aggressions were met in the only way they could be met, with instant declarations of war and with armed resistance which mounted slowly through many long months of reverse until finally the Axis was crushed to earth and deliverance for its victims was won.

CRIMES IN THE CONDUCT OF WAR

Even the most warlike of peoples have recognized in the name of humanity some limitations on the savagery of warfare. Rules to that end have been embodied in international conventions to which Germany became a party. This code had prescribed certain restraints as to the treatment of belligerents. The enemy was entitled to surrender and to receive quarter and good treatment as a prisoner of war. We will show by German documents that these rights were denied, that prisoners of war were given brutal treatment and often murdered. This was particularly true in the case of captured airmen, often my countrymen.

It was ordered that captured English and American airmen should no longer be granted the status of prisoners of war. They were to be treated as criminals and the Army was ordered to refrain from protecting them against lynching by the populace. (R–118.) The Nazi government, through its police and propaganda agencies, took pains to incite the civilian population to attack and kill airmen who crash-landed. The order, given by the SS Reichsführer, Himmler, on August 10, 1943, directed that,

> It is not the task of the police to interfere in clashes between German and English and American flyers who have bailed out.

This order was transmitted on the same day by SS *Obersturmbannführer* Brand of Himmler's Personal Staff to all Senior Executive SS and Police officers, with these directions:

> I am sending you the inclosed order with the request that the Chief of the Regular Police and of the Security Police be informed. They

are to make this instruction known to their subordinate officers verbally. (R–110.)

Similarly, we will show Hitler's top secret order, dated October 18, 1942, that commandos, regardless of condition, were "to be slaughtered to the last man" after capture. (498–PS.) We will show the circulation of secret orders, one of which was signed by Hess, to be passed orally to civilians, that enemy fliers or parachutists were to be arrested or liquidated. (062–PS.) By such means were murders incited and directed.

This Nazi campaign of ruthless treatment of enemy forces assumed its greatest proportions in the fight against Russia. Eventually all prisoners of war were taken out of control of the Army and put in the hands of Himmler and the SS. (058–PS.) In the East, the German fury spent itself. Russian prisoners were ordered to be branded. They were starved. I shall quote passages from a letter written February 28, 1942 by defendant Rosenberg to defendant Keitel:

> The fate of the Soviet prisoners of war in Germany is on the contrary a tragedy of the greatest extent. Of 3.6 millions of prisoners of war, only several hundred thousand are still able to work fully. A large part of them has starved, or died, because of the hazards of the weather. Thousands also died from spotted fever.
>
> The camp commanders have forbidden the civilian population to put food at the disposal of the prisoners, and they have rather let them starve to death.
>
> In many cases, when prisoners of war could no longer keep up on the march because of hunger and exhaustion, they were shot before the eyes of the horrified civilian population, and the corpses were left.
>
> In numerous camps, no shelter for the prisoners of war was provided at all. They lay under the open sky during rain or snow. Even tools were not made available to dig holes or caves.
>
> Finally, the shooting of prisoners of war must be mentioned: For instance, in various camps, all the "Asiatics" were shot. (081–PS.)

Civilized usage and conventions to which Germany was a party had prescribed certain immunities for civilian populations unfortunate enough to dwell in lands overrun by hostile armies. The German occupation forces, controlled or commanded by men on trial before you, committed a long series of outrages against the inhabitants of occupied territory that would be incredible except for captured orders and the captured reports showing the fidelity with which these orders were executed.

We deal here with a phase of common criminality designed by the conspirators as part of the common plan. We can appreciate why these crimes against their European enemies were not of a casual character but were planned and disciplined crimes when we get at the reason for them. Hitler told his officers on August 22, 1939, that "The main objective in Poland is the destruction of the enemy and not the reaching of a certain geographical line." (1014–PS.) The project of deporting promising youth from occupied territories was approved by Rosenberg on the theory that "a desired weakening of the biological force of the conquered people is being achieved." (031–PS.) To Germanize or to destroy was the program. Himmler announced, "Either we win over any good blood that we can use for ourselves and give it a place in our people or, gentlemen—you may call this cruel, but nature is cruel—we destroy this blood." As to "racially good types" Himmler further advised, "Therefore, I think that it is our duty to take their children with us, to remove them from their environment if necessary by robbing or stealing them." (L–70.) He urged deportation of Slavic children to deprive potential enemies of future soldiers.

The Nazi purpose was to leave Germany's neighbors so weakened that even if she should eventually lose the war, she would still be the most powerful nation in Europe. Against this background, we must view the plan for ruthless warfare, which means a plan for the commission of war crimes and crimes against humanity.

Hostages in large numbers were demanded and killed. Mass punishments were inflicted, so savage that whole communities were extinguished. Rosenberg was advised of the annihilation of three unidentified villages in Slovakia. In May 1943, another village of about forty farms and two hundred and twenty inhabitants was ordered wiped out. The entire population was ordered shot, the cattle and property impounded, and the order required that "the village will be destroyed totally by fire." A secret report from Rosenberg's Reich Ministry of Eastern Territory reveals that:

Food rations allowed the Russian population are so low that they fail to secure their existence and provide only for minimum subsistence of limited duration. The population does not know if they will still live tomorrow. They are faced with death by starvation. The roads are clogged by hundreds of thousands of people, sometimes as many as one million according to the estimate of experts, who wander around in search of nourishment.

Sauckel's action has caused great unrest among the civilians. Russian girls were deloused by men, nude photos in forced positions were taken, women doctors were locked into freight cars for the pleasure of the transport commanders, women in night shirts were fettered and forced through the Russian towns to the railroad station, etc. All this material has been sent to the OKH.

Perhaps the deportation to slave labor was the most horrible and extensive slaving operation in history. On few other subjects is our evidence so abundant or so damaging. In a speech made on January 25, 1944, the defendant Frank, Governor General of Poland boasted, "I have sent 1,300,000 Polish workers into the Reich." The defendant Sauckel reported that "out of the five million foreign workers who arrived in Germany not even 200,000 came voluntarily." This fact was reported to the Führer and defendants Speer, Göring, and Keitel (R–124.) Children of ten to fourteen years were impressed into service by telegraphic order from Rosenberg's Ministry for Occupied Eastern Territories:

> The Command is further charged with the transferring of worth-while Russian youth between 10–14 years of age, to the Reich. The authority is not affected by the changes connected with the evacuation and transportation to the reception camps of Pialystok, Krajewo, and Olitei. The Führer wishes that this activity be increased even more. (200–PS.)

When enough labor was not forthcoming, prisoners of war were forced in war work in flagrant violation of international conventions. (016–PS.) Slave labor came from France, Belgium, Holland, Italy, and the East. Methods of recruitment were violent. (R–124, 018–PS, 204–PS.) The treatment of these slave laborers was stated in general terms, not difficult to translate into concrete deprivations, in a letter to the defendant Rosenberg from the defendant Sauckel, which stated:

OPENING STATEMENT

All *prisoners of war,* from the *territories* of the West as well of the East, actually in Germany, must be completely incorporated into the German armament and munition industries. Their production must be brought to the highest possible level. . . .

The complete employment of all prisoners of war as well as the use of a gigantic number of new foreign civilian workers, men and women, has become an undisputable necessity for the solution of the mobilization of labor program in this war.

All the men must be fed, sheltered and treated in such a way as to exploit them to the highest possible extent at the lowest conceivable degree of expenditure. . . . (016–PS.)

In pursuance of the Nazi plan permanently to reduce the living standards of their neighbors and to weaken them physically and economically, a long series of crimes were committed. There was extensive destruction, serving no military purpose, of the property of civilians. Dikes were thrown open in Holland almost at the close of the war not to achieve military ends but to destroy the resources and retard the economy of the thrifty Netherlanders.

There was carefully planned economic syphoning off of the assets of occupied countries. An example of the planning is shown by a report on France dated December 7, 1942 made by the Economic Research Department of the Reichsbank. The question arose whether French occupation costs should be increased from 15 million Reichsmarks per day to 25 million Reichsmarks per day. The Reichsbank analyzed French economy to determine whether it could bear the burden. It pointed out that the armistice had burdened France to that date to the extent of 18½ billion Reichsmarks, equaling 370 billion francs. It pointed out that the burden of these payments within two and a half years equaled the aggregate French national income in the year 1940, and that the amount of payments handed over to Germany in the first six months of 1942 corresponded to the estimate for the total French revenue for that whole year. The report concluded, "In any case, the conclusion is inescapable that relatively heavier tributes have been imposed on France since the armistice in June 1940 than upon Germany after the World War. In this connection, it must be noted that the economic powers of France never equaled those of the German Reich and that vanquished France could not draw on foreign economic and financial resources in the same degree as Germany after the last World War."

The defendant Funk was the Reich Minister of Economics and President of the Reichsbank; the defendant Ribbentrop was Foreign Minister; the defendant Göring was Plenipotentiary for the Four-Year Plan, and all of them participated in the exchange of views of which this captured document is a part. (2149–PS.) Notwithstanding this analysis by the Reichsbank, they proceeded to increase the imposition on France from 15 million Reichsmarks daily to 25 million daily.

It is small wonder that the bottom has been knocked out of French economy. The plan and purpose of the thing appears in a letter from General Stülpnagel, head of the German Armistice Commission, to the defendant Jodl as early as September 14, 1940, when he wrote, "The slogan 'Systematic weakening of France' has already been surpassed by far in reality."

Not only was there a purpose to debilitate and demoralize the economy of Germany's neighbors for the purpose of destroying their competitive position, but there was looting and pilfering on an unprecedented scale. We need not be hypocritical about this business of looting. I recognize that no army moves through occupied territory without some pilfering as it goes. Usually the amount of pilfering increases as discipline wanes. If the evidence in this case showed no looting except of that sort, I certainly would ask no conviction of these defendants for it.

But we will show you that looting was not due to the lack of discipline or to the ordinary weaknesses of human nature. The German organized plundering, planned it, disciplined it, and made it official just as he organized everything else, and then he compiled the most meticulous records to show that he had done the best job of looting that was possible under the circumstances. And we have those records.

The defendant Rosenberg was put in charge of a systematic plundering of the art objects of Europe by direct order of Hitler dated January 29, 1940. (136–PS.) On April 16, 1943 Rosenberg reported that up to April 7, 92 railway cars with 2,775 cases containing art objects had been sent to Germany; and that 53 pieces of art had been shipped to Hitler direct, and 594 to the defendant Göring. The report mentioned something like 20,000 pieces of seized art and the main locations where they were stored. (015–PS.)

Moreover, this looting was glorified by Rosenberg. Here we have 39 leather bound tabulated volumes of his inventory, which in due time we will offer in evidence. One cannot but admire the artistry of this Rosenberg report. The Nazi taste was cosmopolitan. Of the 9,455 articles inventoried, there were included 5,255 paintings, 297 sculptures, 1,372 pieces of antique furniture, 307 textiles, and 2,224 small objects of art. Rosenberg observed that there were approximately 10,000 more objects still to be inventoried. (015–PS.) Rosenberg himself estimated that the values involved would come close to a billion dollars. (090–PS.)

I shall not go into further details of the war crimes and crimes against humanity committed by the Nazi gangster ring whose leaders are before you. It is not the purpose in my part of this case to deal with the individual crimes. I am dealing with the common plan or design for crime and will not dwell upon individual offenses. My task is only to show the scale on which these crimes occurred, and to show that these are the men who were in the responsible positions and who conceived the plan and design which renders them answerable, regardless of the fact that the plan was actually executed by others.

At length, this reckless and lawless course outraged the world. It recovered from the demoralization of surprise attack, assembled its forces, and stopped these men in their tracks. Once success deserted their banners, one by one the Nazi satellites fell away. Sawdust Cæsar collapsed. Resistance forces in every occupied country arose to harry the invader. Even at home, Germans saw that Germany was being led to ruin by these mad men, and the attempt on July 20, 1944 to assassinate Hitler, an attempt fostered by men of highest station, was a desperate effort by internal forces to stop short of ruin. Quarrels broke out among the failing conspirators, and the decline of the Nazi power was more swift than its ascendancy. German armed forces surrendered, its government disintegrated, its leaders committed suicide by the dozen, and by the fortunes of war these defendants fell into our hands. Although they are not by any means all the guilty ones, they are survivors among the most responsible. Their names appear over and over in the documents and their faces grace the photographic evidence. We have here the surviving top politicians, militarists, financiers, diplomats, administrators, and propagandists of the Nazi movement. Who was responsible for these crimes if they were not?

THE LAW OF THE CASE

The end of the war and capture of these prisoners presented the victorious Allies with the question whether there is any legal responsibility on high-ranking men for acts which I have described. Must such wrongs either be ignored or redressed in hot blood? Is there no standard in the law for a deliberate and reasoned judgment on such conduct?

The Charter of this Tribunal evidences a faith that the law is not only to govern the conduct of little men, but that even rulers are, as Lord Chief Justice Coke put it to King James, "under God and the law." The United States believed that the law long has afforded standards by which a juridical hearing could be conducted to make sure that we punish only the right men and for the right reasons. Following the instructions of the late President Roosevelt and the decision of the Yalta Conference, President Truman directed representatives of the United States to formulate a proposed International Agreement, which was submitted during the San Francisco Conference to Foreign Ministers of the United Kingdom, the Soviet Union, and the Provisional Government of France. With many modifications, that proposal has become the Charter of this Tribunal.

But the Agreement which sets up the standards by which these prisoners are to be judged does not express the views of the signatory nations alone. Other nations with diverse but highly respected systems of jurisprudence also have signified adherence to it. These are Belgium, The Netherlands, Denmark, Norway, Czechoslovakia, Luxembourg, Poland, Greece, Yugoslavia, Ethiopia, Australia, Haiti, Honduras, Panama, New Zealand, Venezuela, and India. You judge, therefore, under an organic act which represents the wisdom, the sense of justice, and the will of twenty-one governments, representing an overwhelming majority of all civilized people.

The Charter by which this Tribunal has its being embodies certain legal concepts which are inseparable from its jurisdiction and which must govern its decision. These, as I have said, also are conditions attached to the grant of any hearing to defendants. The validity of the provisions of the Charter is conclusive upon us all whether we have accepted the duty of judging or of prosecuting under it, as well as upon the defendants, who can point to no other law which gives them a right to be heard at all. My able and experienced colleagues believe, as do I, that it will contribute to the expedition and clarity of this trial if I expound briefly the application of the legal philosophy of the Charter to the facts I have recited.

While this declaration of the law by the Charter is final, it may be contended that the prisoners on trial are entitled to have it applied to their conduct only most charitably if at all. It may be said that this is new law, not authoritatively declared at the time they did the acts it condemns, and that this declaration of the law has taken them by surprise.

I cannot, of course, deny that these men are surprised that this is the law; they really are surprised that there is any such thing as law. These defendants did not rely on any law at all. Their program ignored and defied all law. That this is so will appear from many acts and statements, of which I cite but a few. In the Führer's speech to all military commanders on November 23, 1939, he reminded them that at the moment Germany had a pact with Russia, but declared, "Agreements are to be kept only as long as they serve a certain purpose." Later on in the same speech he announced, "A violation of the neutrality of Holland and Belgium will be of no importance." (789–PS.) A top secret document, entitled "Warfare as a Problem of Organization," dispatched by the Chief of the High Command to all Commanders on April 19, 1938, declared that "the normal rules of war toward neutrals may be considered to apply on the basis whether operation of rules will create greater advantages or disadvantages for belligerents." (L–211.) And from the files of the German Navy Staff, we have a "Memorandum on Intensified Naval War," dated October 15, 1939, which begins by stating a desire to comply with International Law. "However," it continues, "if decisive successes are expected from any measure considered as a war necessity, it must be carried through even if it is not in agreement with International Law." (L–184.) International Law, natural law,

German law, any law at all was to these men simply a propaganda device to be invoked when it helped and to be ignored when it would condemn what they wanted to do. That men may be protected in relying upon the law at the time they act is the reason we find laws of retrospective operation unjust. But these men cannot bring themselves within the reason of the rule which in some systems of jurisprudence prohibits *ex post facto* laws. They cannot show that they ever relied upon International Law in any state or paid it the slightest regard.

The Third Count of the Indictment is based on the definition of war crimes contained in the Charter. I have outlined to you the systematic course of conduct toward civilian populations and combat forces which violates international conventions to which Germany was a party. Of the criminal nature of these acts at least, the defendants had, as we shall show, clear knowledge. Accordingly, they took pains to conceal their violations. It will appear that the defendants Keitel and Jodl were informed by official legal advisors that the orders to brand Russian prisoners of war, to shackle British prisoners of war, and to execute commando prisoners were clear violations of International Law. Nevertheless, these orders were put into effect. The same is true of orders issued for the assassination of General Giraud and General Weygand, which failed to be executed only because of a ruse on the part of Admiral Canaris, who was himself later executed for his part in the plot to take Hitler's life on July 20, 1944.

The Fourth Count of the Indictment is based on crimes against humanity. Chief among these are mass killings of countless human beings in cold blood. Does it take these men by surprise that murder is treated as a crime?

The First and Second Counts of the Indictment add to these crimes the crime of plotting and waging wars of aggression and wars in violation of nine treaties to which Germany was a party. There was a time, in fact I think the time of the first World War, when it could not have been said that war inciting or war making was a crime in law, however reprehensible in morals.

Of course, it was under the law of all civilized peoples a crime for one man with his bare knuckles to assault another. How did it come that multiplying this crime by a million, and adding firearms to bare knuckles, made a legally innocent act? The doctrine was that one could not be regarded as criminal for committing the usual violent acts in the conduct of legitimate warfare. The age of imperialistic expansion during the eighteenth and nineteenth centuries added the foul doctrine, contrary to the teachings of early Christian and International Law scholars such as Grotius, that all wars are to be regarded as legitimate wars. The sum of these two doctrines was to give war making a complete immunity from accountability to law.

This was intolerable for an age that called itself civilized. Plain people, with their earthy common sense, revolted at such fictions and legalisms so contrary to ethical principles and demanded checks on war immunity. Statesmen and international lawyers at first cautiously responded by adopting rules of warfare designed to make the conduct of war more civilized. The effort was to set legal limits to the violence that could be done to civilian populations and to combatants as well.

The common sense of men after the first World War demanded, however, that the law's condemnation of war reach deeper, and that the law condemn not merely uncivilized ways of waging war, but also the waging in any way of uncivilized wars—wars of aggression. The world's statesmen again went only as far as they were forced to go. Their efforts were timid and cautious and often less explicit than we might have hoped. But the 1920s did outlaw aggressive war.

The re-establishment of the principle that there are unjust wars and that unjust wars are illegal is traceable in many steps. One of the most significant is the Briand-Kellogg Pact of 1928, by which Germany, Italy, and Japan, in common with practically all the nations of the world, renounced war as an instrument of national policy, bound themselves to seek the settlement of disputes only by pacific means, and condemned recourse to war for the solution of international controversies. This pact altered the legal status of a war of aggression. As Mr. Stimson, the United States Secretary of State, put it in 1932, such a war "is no longer to be the source and subject of rights. It is no longer to be the principle around which the duties, the conduct, and the rights of nations revolve. It is an illegal thing. . . . By that very act, we have made obsolete many legal precedents and have given the legal profession the task of re-examining many of its codes and treaties."

The Geneva Protocol of 1924 for the Pacific Settlement of International Disputes, signed by the representatives of forty-eight governments, declared that "a war of aggression constitutes . . . an international crime." The Eighth Assembly by the League of Nations in 1927, on unanimous resolution of the representatives of forty-eight member nations, including Germany, declared that a war of aggression constitutes an international crime. At the Sixth Pan-American Conference of 1928, the twenty-one American Republics unanimously adopted a resolution stating that "war of aggression constitutes an international crime against the human species."

A failure of these Nazis to heed, or to understand the force and meaning of this evolution in the legal thought of the world is not a defense or a mitigation. If anything, it aggravates their offense and makes it the more mandatory that the law they have flouted be vindicated by juridical application to their lawless conduct. Indeed, by their own law—had they heeded any law—these principles were binding on these defendants. Article 4 of the Weimar Constitution provided that "the generally accepted rules of International Law are to be considered as binding integral parts of the law of the German Reich." (2050–PS.) Can there be any doubt that the outlawry of aggressive war was one of the "generally accepted rules of International Law" in 1939?

Any resort to war—to any kind of a war—is a resort to means that are inherently criminal. War inevitably is a course of killings, assaults, deprivations of liberty, and destruction of property. An honestly defensive war is, of course, legal and saves those lawfully conducting it from criminality. But inherently criminal acts cannot be defended by showing that those who committed them were engaged in a war, when war itself is illegal. The very minimum legal consequence of the treaties making aggressive wars illegal is to strip those who incite or wage them of every defense the law ever gave, and to leave war-makers subject to judgment by the usually accepted principles of the law of crimes.

But if it be thought that the Charter, whose declarations concededly bind us all, does contain new law I still do not shrink from demanding its strict application by this Tribunal. The rule of law in the world, flouted by the lawlessness incited by these defendants, had to be restored at the cost to my country of over a million casualties, not to mention those of other nations. I cannot subscribe to the perverted reasoning that society may advance and strengthen the rule of law by the expenditure of morally innocent lives but that progress in the law may never be made at the price of morally guilty lives.

It is true, of course, that we have no judicial precedent for the Charter. But International Law is more than a scholarly collection of abstract and immutable principles. It is an outgrowth of treaties and agreements between nations and of accepted customs. Yet every custom has its origin in some single act, and every agreement has to be initiated by the action of some state. Unless we are prepared to abandon every principle of growth for International Law, we cannot deny that our own day has the right to institute customs and to conclude agreements that will themselves become sources of a newer and strengthened International Law. International Law is not capable of development by the normal processes of legislation for there is no continuing international legislative authority. Innovations and revisions in International Law are brought about by the action of governments designed to meet a change in circumstances. It grows, as did the Common Law, through decisions reached from time to time in adapting settled principles to new situations. The fact is that when the law evolves by the case method, as did the Common Law and as International Law must do if it is to advance at all, it advances at the expense of those who wrongly guessed the law and learned too late their error. The law, so far as International Law can be decreed, had been clearly pronounced when these acts took place. Hence, I am not disturbed by the lack of judicial precedent for the inquiry we propose to conduct.

The events I have earlier recited clearly fall within the standards of crimes, set out in the Charter, whose perpetrators this Tribunal is convened to judge and punish fittingly. The standards for war crimes and crimes against humanity are too familiar to need comment. There are, however, certain novel problems in applying other precepts of the Charter which I should call to your attention.

THE CRIME AGAINST PEACE

A basic provision of the Charter is that to plan, prepare, initiate, or wage a war of aggression, or a war in violation of international treaties, agreements, and assurances, or to conspire or participate in a common plan to do so is a crime.

It is perhaps a weakness in this Charter that it fails itself to define a war of aggression. Abstractly, the subject is full of difficulty and all kinds of troublesome hypothetical cases can be conjured up. It is a subject which, if the defense should be permitted to go afield beyond the very narrow charge in the Indictment, would prolong the trial and involve the Tribunal in insoluble political issues. But so far as the question can properly be involved in this case, the issue is one of no novelty and is one on which legal opinion has well crystallized.

One of the most authoritative sources of International Law on this subject is the Convention for the Definition of Aggression signed at London on July 3, 1933, by Rumania, Estonia, Latvia, Poland, Turkey, The Soviet Union, Persia, and Afghanistan. The subject has also been considered by international committees and by commentators whose views are entitled to the greatest respect. It had been little discussed prior to the first World War but has received much attention as International Law has evolved its outlawry of aggressive war. In the light of these materials of International Law, and so far as relevant to the evidence in this case, I suggest that an "aggressor" is generally held to be that state which is the first to commit any of the following actions:

(1) Declaration of war upon another State;

(2) Invasion by its armed forces, with or without a declaration of war, of the territory of another State;

(3) Attack by its land, naval, or air forces, with or without a declaration of war, on the territory, vessels, or aircraft of another State;

(4) Provision of support to armed bands formed in the territory of another State, or refusal, notwithstanding the request of the invaded State, to take in its own territory, all the measures in its power to deprive those bands of all assistance or protection.

And I further suggest that it is the general view that no political, military, economic, or other considerations shall serve as an excuse or justification for such actions; but exercise of the right of legitimate self-defense, that is to say, resistance to an act of aggression, or action to assist a state which has been subjected to aggression, shall not constitute a war of aggression.

It is upon such an understanding of the law that our evidence of a conspiracy to provoke and wage an aggressive war is prepared and presented. By this test each of the series of wars begun by these Nazi leaders was unambiguously aggressive.

It is important to the duration and scope of this trial that we bear in mind the difference between our charge that this war was one of aggression and a position that Germany had no grievances. We are not inquiring into the conditions which contributed to causing this war. They are for history to unravel. It is no part of our task to vindicate the European *status quo* as of 1933, or as of any other date. The United States does not desire to enter into discussion of the complicated pre-war currents of European politics, and it hopes this trial will not be protracted by their consideration. The remote causations avowed are too insincere and inconsistent, too complicated and doctrinaire to be the subject of profitable inquiry in this trial. A familiar example is to be found in the *Lebensraum* slogan, which summarized the contention that Germany needed more living space as a justification for expansion. At the same time that the Nazis were demanding more space for the German people, they were demanding more German people to occupy space. Every known means to increase the birth rate, legitimate and illegitimate, was utilized. *Lebensraum* represented a vicious circle of demand—from neighbors more space, and from Germans more progeny. We do not need to investigate the verity of doctrines which led to constantly expanding circles of aggression. It is the plot and the act of aggression which we charge to be crimes.

Our position is that whatever grievances a nation may have, however objectionable it finds the *status quo,* aggressive warfare is an illegal means for settling those grievances or for altering those conditions. It may be that the Germany of the 1920s and 1930s faced desperate problems, problems that would have warranted the boldest measures short of war. All other methods—

persuasion, propaganda, economic competition, diplomacy—were open to an aggrieved country, but aggressive warfare was outlawed. These defendants did make aggressive war, a war in violation of treaties. They did attack and invade their neighbors in order to effectuate a foreign policy which they knew could not be accomplished by measures short of war. And that is as far as we accuse or propose to inquire.

THE LAW OF INDIVIDUAL RESPONSIBILITY

The Charter also recognizes individual responsibility on the part of those who commit acts defined as crimes, or who incite others to do so, or who join a common plan with other persons, groups or organizations to bring about their commission. The principle of individual responsibility for piracy and brigandage, which have long been recognized as crimes punishable under International Law, is old and well established. That is what illegal warfare is. This principle of personal liability is a necessary as well as logical one if International Law is to render real help to the maintenance of peace. An International Law which operates only on states can be enforced only by war because the most practicable method of coercing a state is warfare. Those familiar with American history know that one of the compelling reasons for adoption of our Constitution was that the laws of the Confederation, which operated only on constituent states, were found ineffective to maintain order among them. The only answer to recalcitrance was impotence or war. Only sanctions which reach individuals can peacefully and effectively be enforced. Hence, the principle of the criminality of aggressive war is implemented by the Charter with the principle of personal responsibility.

Of course, the idea that a state, any more than a corporation, commits crimes is a fiction. Crimes always are committed only by persons. While it is quite proper to employ the fiction of responsibility of a state or corporation for the purpose of imposing a collective liability, it is quite intolerable to let such a legalism become the basis of personal immunity.

The Charter recognizes that one who has committed criminal acts may not take refuge in superior orders nor in the doctrine that his crimes were acts of states. These twin principles working together have heretofore resulted in immunity for practically everyone concerned in the really great crimes against peace and mankind. Those in lower ranks were protected against liability by the orders of their superiors. The superiors were protected because their orders were called acts of state. Under the Charter, no defense based on either of these doctrines can be entertained. Modern civilization puts unlimited weapons of destruction in the hands of men. It cannot tolerate so vast an area of legal irresponsibility.

Even the German Military Code provides that:

> If the execution of a military order in the course of duty violates the criminal law, then the superior officer giving the order will bear the sole responsibility therefor. However, the obeying subordinate will share the punishment of the participant: (1) if he has exceeded the order given to him, or (2) if it was within his knowledge that the order of his superior officer concerned an act by which it was intended to commit a civil or military crime or trangression. (*Reichsgesetzblatt*, 1926, No. 37, p. 278, Art. 47.)

Of course, we do not argue that the circumstances under which one commits an act should be disregarded in judging its legal effect. A conscripted private on a firing squad cannot expect to hold an inquest on the validity of the execution. The Charter implies common sense limits to liability just as it places common sense limits upon immunity. But none of these men before you acted in minor parts. Each of them was entrusted with broad discretion and exercised great power. Their responsibility is correspondingly great and may not be shifted to that fictional being, "the State," which cannot be produced for trial, cannot testify, and cannot be sentenced.

The Charter also recognizes a vicarious liability, which responsibility is recognized by most modern systems of law, for acts committed by others in carrying out a common plan or conspiracy to which a defendant has become a party. I need not discuss the familiar principles of such liability. Every day in the courts of countries associated in this prosecution, men are convicted for acts that they did not personally commit but for which they were held responsible because of membership in illegal combinations or plans or conspiracies.

THE POLITICAL, POLICE, AND MILITARY
ORGANIZATIONS

Accused before this Tribunal as criminal organizations are certain political and police organizations which the evidence will show to have been instruments of cohesion in planning and executing the crimes I have detailed. Perhaps the worst of the movement were the Leadership Corps of the NSDAP, the *Schutzstaffeln* or "SS," and the *Sturmabteilungen* or "SA," and the subsidiary formations which these include. These were the Nazi Party leadership, espionage, and policing groups. They were the real government, above and outside of any law. Also accused as organizations are the Reich Cabinet and the Secret State Police, or Gestapo, which were fixtures of the government but animated solely by the Nazi Party.

Except for a late period when some compulsory recruiting was done in the SS, membership in all these militarized formations was voluntary. The police organizations were recruited from ardent partisans who enlisted blindly to do the dirty work the leaders planned. The Reich Cabinet was the governmental façade for Nazi Party Government and in its members legal as well as actual responsibility was vested for the entire program. Collectively they were responsible for the program in general, individually they were especially responsible for segments of it. The finding which we ask you to make, that these are criminal organizations, will subject members to punishment to be hereafter determined by appropriate tribunals, unless some personal defense—such as becoming a member under threat to person, to family, or inducement by false representation, or the like—be established. Every member will have a chance to be heard in the subsequent forum on his personal relation to the organization, but your finding in this trial will conclusively establish the criminal character of the organization as a whole.

We have also accused as criminal organizations the High Command and the General Staff of the German Armed Forces. We recognize that to plan warfare is the business of professional soldiers in every country. But it is one thing to plan strategic moves in the event war comes, and it is another thing to plot and intrigue to bring on that war. We will prove the leaders of the

German General Staff and of the High Command to have been guilty of just that. Military men are not before you because they served their country. They are here because they mastered it, along with these others, and drove it to war. They are not here because they lost the war but because they started it. Politicians may have thought of them as soldiers, but soldiers know they were politicians. We ask that the General Staff and the High Command, as defined in the Indictment, be condemned as a criminal group whose existence and tradition constitute a standing menace to the peace of the world.

These individual defendants did not stand alone in crime and will not stand alone in punishment. Your verdict of "guilty" against these organizations will render *prima-facie* guilty, as nearly as we can learn, thousands upon thousands of members now in custody of United States forces and other armies.

THE RESPONSIBILITY OF THIS TRIBUNAL

To apply the sanctions of the law to those whose conduct is found criminal by the standards I have outlined, is the responsibility committed to this Tribunal. It is the first court ever to undertake the difficult task of overcoming the confusion of many tongues and the conflicting concepts of just procedure among divers systems of law, so as to reach a common judgment. The tasks of all of us are such as to make heavy demands on patience and good will. Although the need for prompt action has admittedly resulted in imperfect work on the part of the prosecution, four great nations bring you their hurriedly assembled contributions of evidence. What remains undiscovered we can only guess. We could, with witnesses' testimony, prolong the recitals of crime for years—but to what avail? We shall rest the case when we have offered what seems convincing and adequate proof of the crimes charged without unnecessary cumulation of evidence. We doubt very much whether it will be seriously denied that the crimes I have outlined took place. The effort will undoubtedly be to mitigate or escape personal responsibility.

Among the nations which unite in accusing these defendants the United States is perhaps in a position to be the most dispassionate, for, having sustained the least injury, it is perhaps the least animated by vengeance. Our American cities have not been

bombed by day and by night, by humans and by robots. It is not
our temples that have been laid in ruins. Our countrymen have
not had their homes destroyed over their heads. The menace of
Nazi aggression, except to those in actual service, has seemed
less personal and immediate to us than to European peoples. But
while the United States is not first in rancor, it is not second in
determination that the forces of law and order be made equal to
the task of dealing with such international lawlessness as I have
recited here.

Twice in my lifetime, the United States has sent its young manhood across the Atlantic, drained its resources, and burdened
itself with debt to help defeat Germany. But the real hope and
faith that has sustained the American people in these great efforts
was that victory for ourselves and our Allies would lay the basis
for an ordered international relationship in Europe and would
end the centuries of strife on this embattled continent.

Twice we have held back in the early stages of European conflict in the belief that it might be confined to a purely European
affair. In the United States, we have tried to build an economy
without armament, a system of government without militarism,
and a society where men are not regimented for war. This purpose, we know now, can never be realized if the world periodi-
cally is to be embroiled in war. The United States cannot, generation after generation, throw its youth or its resources onto the
battlefields of Europe to redress the lack of balance between
Germany's strength and that of her enemies, and to keep the
battles from our shores.

The American dream of a peace and plenty economy, as well
as the hopes of other nations, can never be fulfilled if those nations
are involved in a war every generation so vast and devastating
as to crush the generation that fights and burden the generation
that follows. But experience has shown that wars are no longer
local. All modern wars become world wars eventually. And none
of the big nations at least can stay out. If we cannot stay out of
wars, our only hope is to prevent wars.

I am too well aware of the weaknesses of juridical action alone
to contend that in itself your decision under this Charter can
prevent future wars. Judicial action always comes after the event.
Wars are started only on the theory and in the confidence that

they can be won. Personal punishment, to be suffered only in the event the war is lost, will probably not be a sufficient deterrent to prevent a war where the war-makers feel the chances of defeat to be negligible.

But the ultimate step in avoiding periodic wars, which are inevitable in a system of international lawlessness, is to make statesmen responsible to law. And let me make clear that while this law is first applied against German aggressors, the law includes, and if it is to serve a useful purpose it must condemn aggression by any other nations, including those which sit here now in judgment. We are able to do away with domestic tyranny and violence and aggression by those in power against the rights of their own people only when we make all men answerable to the law. This trial represents mankind's desperate effort to apply the discipline of the law to statesmen who have used their powers of state to attack the foundations of the world's peace and to commit aggressions against the rights of their neighbors.

The usefulness of this effort to do justice is not to be measured by considering the law or your judgment in isolation. This trial is part of the great effort to make the peace more secure. One step in this direction is the United Nations organization, which may take joint political action to prevent war if possible, and joint military action to insure that any nation which starts a war will lose it. This Charter and this trial, implementing the Kellogg-Briand Pact, constitute another step in the same direction—juridical action of a kind to ensure that those who start a war will pay for it personally.

While the defendants and the prosecutors stand before you as individuals, it is not the triumph of either group alone that is committed to your judgment. Above all personalities there are anonymous and impersonal forces whose conflict makes up much of human history. It is yours to throw the strength of the law back of either the one or the other of these forces for at least another generation. What are the real forces that are contending before you?

No charity can disguise the fact that the forces which these defendants represent, the forces that would advantage and delight in their acquittal, are the darkest and most sinister forces in society—dictatorship and oppression, malevolence and passion, militarism and lawlessness. By their fruits we best know them. Their acts have bathed the world in blood and set civilization back a century. They have subjected their European neighbors to every outrage and torture, every spoliation and deprivation that insolence, cruelty, and greed could inflict. They have brought the German people to the lowest pitch of wretchedness, from which they can entertain no hope of early deliverance. They have stirred hatreds and incited domestic violence on every continent. These are the things that stand in the dock shoulder to shoulder with these prisoners.

The real complaining party at your bar is Civilization. In all our countries it is still a struggling and imperfect thing. It does not plead that the United States, or any other country, has been blameless of the conditions which made the German people easy victims to the blandishments and intimidations of the Nazi conspirators.

But it points to the dreadful sequence of aggressions and crimes I have recited, it points to the weariness of flesh, the exhaustion of resources, and the destruction of all that was beautiful or useful in so much of the world, and to greater potentialities for destruction in the days to come. It is not necessary among the ruins of this ancient and beautiful city, with untold members of its civilian inhabitants still buried in its rubble, to argue the proposition that to start or wage an aggressive war has the moral qualities of the worst of crimes. The refuge of the defendants can be only their hope that International Law will lag so far behind the moral sense of mankind that conduct which is crime in the moral sense must be regarded as innocent in law.

Civilization asks whether law is so laggard as to be utterly helpless to deal with crimes of this magnitude by criminals of this order of importance. It does not expect that you can make war impossible. It does expect that your juridical action will put the forces of International Law, its precepts, its prohibitions and, most of all, its sanctions, on the side of peace, so that men and women of good will in all countries may have "leave to live by no man's leave, underneath the law."

IV

THE LAW UNDER WHICH NAZI ORGANIZATIONS ARE ACCUSED OF BEING CRIMINAL. ARGUMENT BY ROBERT H. JACKSON, CHIEF OF COUNSEL FOR THE UNITED STATES. NÜRNBERG, GERMANY, FEBRUARY 28, 1946.

MAY IT PLEASE THE TRIBUNAL:

The unconditional surrender of Germany created, for the victors, novel and difficult problems of law and administration. Since it is the first such surrender of an entire and modernly organized society, precedents and past experiences are of little help in guiding our policy toward the vanquished. The responsibility implicit in demanding and accepting capitulation of a whole people must of necessity include a duty to discriminate justly and intelligently between opposing elements of the population which bore dissimilar relations to the policies and conduct which led to the catastrophe. This differentiation is the objective of those provisions of the Charter which authorize this Tribunal to declare organizations or groups to be criminal. Understanding of the problem which the instrument attempts to solve is essential to its interpretation and application.

I. THE PROBLEM OF THE NAZI ORGANIZATIONS

One of the sinister peculiarities of German society at the time of the surrender was that the state itself played only a subordinate role in the exercise of political power, while the really drastic controls over German society were organized outside its nominal government. This was accomplished through an elaborate network of closely knit and exclusive organizations of selected volunteers, oath-bound to execute without delay and without question the commands of the Nazi leaders.

These organizations penetrated the whole German life. The country was subdivided into little Nazi principalities of about fifty households each, and every such community had its recognized party leaders, its party police, and its undercover party spies. These were combined into larger units with higher ranking leaders, executioners, and spies. The whole formed a pyramid of power outside of the law, with the Führer at its apex, and with the local Party officials as its broad base resting heavily on the German population. The Nazi despotism, therefore, did not consist of these individual defendants alone. A thousand little Führers dictated, a thousand imitation Görings strutted, a thousand Schirachs incited the youth, a thousand Sauckels worked slaves, a thousand Streichers and Rosenbergs stirred hate, a thousand Kaltenbrunners and Franks tortured and killed, a thousand Schachts and Speers and Funks administered, financed, and supported the movement. The Nazi movement was an integrated force in city and county and hamlet. The Party power resulting from this system of organizations first rivaled, and then dominated, the power of the state itself.

The primary vice of this web of organizations was that they were used to transfer the power of coercing men from the government and the law to the Nazi leaders. Liberty, self-government, and security of person and property do not exist except where the power of coercion is possessed only by the state and is exercised only in obedience to law. The Nazis, however, set up a private system of coercion, outside of and immune from law, with Party-controlled concentration camps and firing squads to administer privately decreed sanctions. Without responsibility to law and without warrant from any court, they were enabled to seize property, take away liberty, and even take life itself.

These organizations had a calculated and decisive part in the barbaric extremes of the Nazi movement. They served cleverly to exploit mob psychology and to manipulate the mob. Multiplying the numbers of persons in a common enterprise tends to diminish each individual's sense of moral responsibility and to increase his sense of security. The Nazi leaders were masters of this technique. They manipulated these organizations to make before the German populace impressive exhibitions of numbers and of power. These were used to incite a mob spirit and then riotously to gratify the popular hates they had inflamed and the Germanic ambition they had inflated.

These organizations indoctrinated and practiced violence and terrorism. They provided the systematized, aggressive, and dis-

*HE UNITED STATES ASKS THAT LEADING NAZI ORGANIZATIONS
BE DECLARED CRIMINAL*

"*The Nazis set up a private system of coercion, outside of and
immune from law, with Party-controlled concentration camps
and firing squads to administer privately decreed sanctions.
Without responsibility to law, and without warrant from any
court, they were enabled to seize property, take away liberty,
and even to take life itself.*"

JUSTICE JACKSON, ARGUMENT ON ORGANIZATIONS

ciplined execution throughout Germany and the occupied countries of the whole catalogue of crimes we have proven. The flowering of the system is represented in the fanatical SS General Ohlendorf, who told this Tribunal without shame or trace of pity how he personally directed the putting to death of ninety thousand men, women, and children. No tribunal ever listened to a recital of such wholesale murder as this Tribunal heard from him and from Wisliceny, a fellow officer of the SS. Their own testimony shows the responsibility of the SS for the extermination program which took the lives of five million Jews, a responsibility the organization welcomed and discharged methodically, remorselessly, and thoroughly. These crimes are unprecedented ones because of the shocking numbers of victims. They are even more shocking and unprecedented because of the large number of persons who united to perpetrate them. All scruple or conscience of a very large segment of the German people was committed to Nazi keeping, and its devotees felt no personal sense of guilt as they went from one extreme measure to another. On the other hand, they developed a contest in cruelty and a competition in crime. Ohlendorf from the witness stand accused other SS commanders, whose killings exceeded his, of "exaggerating" their figures.

There could be no justice and no wisdom in an occupation policy which imposed upon passive and unorganized and inarticulate Germans the same burdens as it placed upon those who voluntarily banded themselves together in these powerful and notorious gangs. One of the basic requirements, both of justice and of successful administration of the occupation responsibility of the victors, is a segregation of these organized elements from the masses of Germans for separate treatment.

It seems beyond controversy that to punish a few top leaders but to leave this web of organized bodies unscotched in the midst of German post-war society, would be to foster the nucleus of a new Nazidom. The members are accustomed to an established chain of centralized command, they have formed a habit and developed a technique of both secret and open co-operation. They still nourish a blind devotion to the suspended, but not abandoned, Nazi program. They will keep alive the hates and ambitions which generated the orgy of crime we have proved.

They are carriers, from this generation to the next, of the infection of aggressive and ruthless war. The Tribunal has seen on the screen how easily an assemblage that ostensibly is only a common labor force can be in fact a military training unit drilling with shovels. The next war and the next pogroms will be hatched in the nests of these organizations as surely as we leave their membership with its prestige and influence undiminished by condemnation and punishment.

The menace of these organizations is the more impressive when we consider the demoralized state of German society. It will be years before there can be established in the German state any political authority that is not inexperienced and provisional. It cannot quickly acquire the stability of a government aided by long habit of obedience and traditional respect. The intrigue, obstruction, and possible overthrow, which older and established governments fear from conspiratorial groups, is a real and present danger to any stable social order in the Germany of today and of tomorrow.

In so far as the Charter of this Tribunal contemplates a justice of retribution, it is obvious that it could not overlook these organized instruments and instigators of past crimes. In opening this case, I said that the United States does not seek to convict the whole German people of crime. But it is equally important that this trial shall not serve to absolve the whole German people except twenty-two men in the dock. The wrongs that have been done to the world by these defendants and their top confederates was not done by their will or by their strength alone. The success of their designs was made possible because great numbers of Germans organized themselves to become the fulcrum and the lever by which the power of these leaders was extended and magnified. If this trial fails to condemn these organized confederates for their share of responsibility for this catastrophe, it will be construed as their exoneration.

But the Charter was not concerned with retributive justice alone. It manifests a constructive policy influenced by exemplary and preventive considerations. The primary objective of requiring that the surrender be unconditional was to clear the way for reconstruction of German society on such a basis that it will not again threaten the peace of Europe and of the world.

Temporary measures of the occupation authorities may, by necessity, have been more arbitrary and applied with less discrimination than befits a permanent policy. Under existing denazification policy, no member of the Nazi Party or its formations may be employed in any position, other than ordinary labor, or in any business enterprise unless he is found to have been only a nominal Nazi. Persons in certain categories whose standing in the community is one of prominence or influence, are required to meet this standard, and those who do not may be denied further participation in their businesses or professions. It is mandatory to remove or exclude from public office and from positions of importance in quasi-public and private enterprise persons falling within approximately ninety specified categories deemed to consist of either active Nazis, Nazi supporters, or militarists. The property of such persons is blocked.

It is recognized by the Control Council, as it was by the framers of the Charter, that a permanent long-term program should be based on a more careful and more individual discrimination than was possible with sweeping temporary measures. There is a movement now within the Control Council for reconsideration of its whole denazification policy and procedure. The action of this Tribunal in declaring, or in failing to declare, the accused organizations criminal has a vital bearing on future occupation policy.

It was the intent of the Charter to utilize the hearing processes of this Tribunal to identify and condemn those Nazi and militaristic forces that were so organized as to constitute a continuing menace to the long-term objectives for which our respective countries have spent the lives of their men. It is in the light of this great purpose that we must examine the provisions of the Charter.

II. THE PROCEDURE FOR CONDEMNING ORGANIZATIONS

It was obvious that the conventional litigation procedures could not, without some modification, be adapted to this task. No system of jurisprudence has yet evolved any satisfactory technique for handling a great multiplicity of common charges against a multitude of accused persons. The number of individual defendants that fairly can be tried in a single proceeding probably does not greatly exceed the number now in your dock. Moreover, the number of separate trials in which the same voluminous evidence as to common plan must be repeated is very limited as a practical matter. Yet adversary hearing procedures are the best assurance the law has evolved that decisions will be well considered and just. The task of the framers of the Charter was to find a way to overcome these obstacles to practicable and early decision without sacrificing the fairness implicit in hearings. The solution prescribed by the Charter is certainly not faultless, but not one of its critics has ever proposed an alternative that would not either deprive the individual of any hearing or contemplate such a multitude of long trials as to be impracticable. In any case, it is the plan adopted by our respective governments and our duty here is to make it work.

The plan which was adopted in the Charter essentially is a severance of the general issues which would be common to all individual trials from the particular issues which would differ in each trial. The plan is comparable to that employed in certain war-time legislation of the United States (*Yakus* v. *United States*, 321 U.S. 414, 64 Sup. Ct. 660). The general issues are to be determined with finality in one trial before the International Tribunal. In this trial, every accused organization must be defended by counsel and must be represented by at least one leading member, and other individual members may apply to be heard. Their applications may be granted if the Tribunal thinks justice requires it. The only issue in this trial concerns the collective criminality of the organization or group. It is to be adjudicated by what amounts to a declaratory judgment. It does not decree any punishment either against the organization or against the individual members.

The only specification as to the effect of this Tribunal's declaration that an organization is criminal is contained in Article 10 of the Charter which provides:

> In cases where a group or organization is declared criminal by the Tribunal, the competent national authority of any Signatory shall have the right to bring individuals to trial for membership therein before national, military or occupation courts. In any such case the

criminal nature of the group or organization is considered proved and shall not be questioned.

Unquestionably, it would be competent for the Charter to have declared flatly that membership in any of these named organizations is criminal and should be punished accordingly. If there had been such an enactment, it would not have been open to an individual who was being tried for membership in the organization to contend that the organization was not in fact criminal. The framers of the Charter, at a time before the evidence adduced here was available, did not care to find organizations criminal by fiat. They left that issue to determination after relevant facts were developed by adversary proceedings. Plainly, the individual member is better off because of the procedure of the Charter, which leaves that finding of criminality to this body after hearings at which the organization must, and the individual may, be represented.

The groups and organizations named in the Indictment are not "on trial" in the conventional sense of that term. They are more nearly under investigation as they might be before a grand jury in Anglo-American practice. Article 9 recognizes a distinction between *the declaration* of a group or organization as criminal and "*the trial* of any individual member thereof." The power of the Tribunal to try is confined to "persons," and the Charter does not expand that term by definition, as statutes sometimes do, to include other than natural persons. The groups or organizations named in the Indictment were not as entities served with process. The Tribunal is not empowered to impose any sentence upon them as entities, nor to convict any person because of membership.

It is to be observed that the Charter does not *require* subsequent proceedings against anyone. It provides only that the competent national authorities "*shall have the right* to bring individuals to trial for membership therein."

The Charter is silent as to the form these trials should take. It was not deemed wise, on the information available when the Charter was drawn up, that the Charter should regulate subsequent proceedings. Nor was it necessary to do so. There is a continuing legislative authority, representing all four signatory nations, competent to take over where the Charter leaves off. Legislative supplementation of the Charter is necessary to confer jurisdiction on local courts, to define procedures, and to prescribe different penalties for different forms of activity.

Fear has been expressed, however, that the Charter's silence as to future proceedings means that great numbers of members will be rounded up and automatically punished as a result of a declaration of an organization to be criminal. It also has been suggested that this is, or may be, the consequence of Article II, 1 (d) of Control Council Act No. 10, which defines as a crime "membership in categories of a criminal group or organization declared criminal by the International Military Tribunal." A purpose to inflict punishments without a right of hearing cannot be spelled out of the Charter, and would be offensive to both its letter and its spirit. And I do not find in Control Council Act. No. 10 any inconsistency with the Charter. Of course, to reach all individual members will require numerous hearings. But they will involve only narrow issues; many accused will have no answers to charges if they are clearly stated, and the proceedings should be expeditious and nontechnical.

But I think it is clear that before any person is punishable for membership in a criminal organization, he is entitled to a hearing on the facts of his case. The Charter does not authorize the national authorities to punish membership without a hearing—it gives them only the right to "bring individuals to trial." That means what it says. A trial means there is something to try.

As to trials of the individual members, the Charter denies only one of the possible defenses of an accused: he may not relitigate the question whether the organization itself was a criminal one. Nothing precludes him from denying that his participation was voluntary and proving he acted under duress; he may prove that he was deceived or tricked into membership; he may show that he had withdrawn; or he may prove that his name on the rolls is a case of mistaken identity.

The membership which the Charter and the Control Council Act make criminal, of course, implies a genuine membership involving the volition of the member. The act of affiliation with the organization must have been intentional and voluntary. Legal compulsion or illegal duress, actual fraud or trick of which one is a victim has never been thought to be the victim's crime and such an unjust result is not to be implied now. The extent of the member's knowledge of the criminal character of the organization is, however, another matter. He may not have known on the day he joined but may have remained a member after learning the fact. And he is chargeable not only with what he knew but with all of which he reasonably was put on notice.

There are safeguards to assure that this program will be carried out in good faith. Prosecution under the declaration is discretionary, and if there were purpose to punish without trial, it would have been already done without waiting for the declaration. We think the Tribunal will presume that Signatory powers which have voluntarily submitted to this process will carry it out faithfully.

The Control Council Act applies only to "categories of membership declared criminal." This language recognizes a power in this Tribunal to limit the effect of its declaration. I do not think, for reasons I will later state, that this should be construed or availed of so as to try here any issues as to sub-groups or sections or individuals which can be tried later. It should, I think, be construed to mean, not those limitations which must be defined by detailed evidence, but limitations of principle such as those I have outlined as already implied. It does not require this Tribunal to delve into evidence to condition its judgment, if it sees fit, to apply only to intentional, voluntary, and knowing membership. It does not supplant later trials but guides them.

It cannot be said that a plan, such as we have here, for the severance of general issues common to many cases from particular issues applicable only to individual defendants and for the litigation of each type of issue in separate Tribunals specially adapted to their different tasks is lacking in reasonableness or fair play. And while it presents unusual procedural difficulties, I do not think it presents any insurmountable ones.

III. CRITERIA, PRINCIPLES, AND PRECEDENTS FOR DECLARING COLLECTIVE CRIMINALITY

The substantive law which governs the inquiry into criminality of organizations is, in its large outline, old and well settled and fairly uniform in all systems of law. It is true that we are dealing with a procedure easy to abuse, and one often feared as an interference with liberty of assembly or as an imposition of "guilt by association." It also is true that proceedings against organizations are closely akin to the conspiracy charge, which is the great dragnet of the law, rightly watched by courts lest it be abused.

The fact is, however, that every form of government has considered it necessary to treat some organizations as criminal. Not even the most tolerant of governments can permit the accumulation of power in private organizations to a point where it rivals, obstructs, or dominates the government itself. To do so would be to grant designing men a liberty to destroy liberty. It was the very complacency and tolerance as well as the impotence of the Weimar Republic towards the growing organization of Nazi power which spelled the death of German freedom.

Protection of the citizen's liberty has required even free governments to enact laws making criminal those aggregations of power which threaten to impose their will on unwilling citizens. Every one of the nations signatory to this Charter has laws making certain types of organizations criminal. The Ku Klux Klan in the United States flourished at about the same time as the Nazi movement in Germany. It appealed to the same hates, practiced the same extra-legal coercions, and likewise terrorized by weird nighttime ceremonials. Like the Nazi Party it was composed of a core of fanatics, but enlisted support of some respectable persons who knew it was wrong, but thought it was winning. It eventually provoked a variety of legislative acts directed against such organizations.

The Congress of the United States also has enacted legislation outlawing certain organizations. A recent example is the Act of June 28, 1940 (c. 439, Title I, Section 2, 54 Stat. 671, 18 USCA 10), which provides in part as follows:

(a) It shall be unlawful for any person . . .
(3) to organize or help to organize any society, group, or assembly of persons who teach, advocate, or encourage the overthrow or destruction of any government in the United States by force or violence; or to be or become a member of, or affiliate with, any such society, group, or assembly of persons, knowing the purposes thereof.

LAW ACCUSING NAZI ORGANIZATIONS

There is much legislation by states of the American union creating analogous offenses. An example is to be found in the Act of California (Statutes 1919, Chapter 188, p. 281), which after defining "criminal syndicalism" provides:

> Section 2. Any person who . . . (4) organizes or assists in organizing, or is or knowingly becomes a member of, any organization, society, group or assemblage of persons organized or assembled to teach or aid and abet criminal syndicalism . . . is guilty of a felony and punishable by imprisonment.

Precedents in English law for outlawing organizations and punishing membership therein are old and consistent with the Charter. One of the first is the British India Act No. 30, enacted November 14, 1836. Section 1 provides:

> It is hereby enacted that whoever shall be proved to have belonged either before or after the passing of this Act to any gang of thugs either within or without the territories of the East India Company shall be punished with imprisonment for life with hard labour.

Other precedents in English legislation are the Unlawful Societies Act of 1799 (3 George III, Chapter 79); the Seditious Meetings Act of 1817 (57 George III, Chapter 19); the Seditious Meetings Act of 1846 (9 and 10 Victoria, Chapter 33); the Public Order Act of 1936 and Defense Regulation 18 (b). This latter, not without opposition, was intended to protect the integrity of the British Government against the fifth-column activities of this same Nazi conspiracy.

Soviet Russia punishes as a crime the formation of and membership in a criminal gang. Criminologists of the U.S.S.R. call this crime the "crime of banditry," a term appropriate to the German organizations.

French criminal law makes membership in subversive organizations a crime. Membership in the criminal gang is a crime in itself. (Articles 265–268, French Penal Code, "*Association de Malfaiteurs*," Garaud, *Précis de Droit Criminel*, 1934 Edition Sirey, p. 1518 et seq. See also Act of December 18, 1893.)

For German precedents, it is neither seemly nor necessary to go to the Nazi regime. Under the Empire and the Weimar Republic, however, German jurisprudence deserved respect and it presents both statutory and juridical examples of declarations of the criminality of organizations. Among statutory examples are:

1. The German Criminal Code enacted in 1871. Section 128 was aimed against secret associations, and 129 was directed against organizations inimical to the state.
2. The law of March 22, 1921 against paramilitary organizations.
3. The law of July 21, 1922 against organizations aimed at overthrowing the constitution of the Reich.

Section 128 of the Criminal Code of 1871, is especially pertinent. It reads:

The participation in an organization the existence, constitution, or purposes of which are to be kept secret from the government, or in which obedience to unknown superiors or unconditional obedience to known superiors is pledged, is punishable by imprisonment up to six months for the members and from one month to one year for the founders and officers. Public officials may be deprived of the right to hold public office for a period of from one to five years.

Under the Empire, various Polish national unions were the subject of criminal prosecution. Under the Republic judicial judgments, in 1927–8, held criminal the entire Communist Party of Germany. In 1922 and 1928, judgments were entered against the political Leadership Corps of the Communist Party which included all of its so-called "body of functionaries," corresponding to the Leadership Corps of the Nazi Party which we have accused. The judgment included every cashier, every employee, every delivery boy and messenger, and every district leader. In 1930 a judgment of criminality against the "Union of Red Front Fighters" of the Communist Party made no discrimination between leaders and ordinary members.

Most significant of all is the fact that on May 30, 1924, German courts rendered judgment that the whole Nazi Party was a criminal organization. This decision referred not only to the Leadership Corps, which we are indicting here, but to all other members as well. The whole subsequent rise to power of the Nazi Party was in the shadow of this judgment of illegality.

The German courts in dealing with criminal organizations proceeded on the theory that all members were held together by a common plan in which each one participated even though at various levels. Moreover, the fundamental principles of responsibility of members, as stated by the German Supreme Court, are strikingly like the principles that govern the Anglo-American law of conspiracy. Among them were these:

1. It is a matter of indifference whether all the members pursued the forbidden aims. It is enough if a part exercised the forbidden activity. (R.G. VIa 97/22 of the 8.5.22.)

2. It is a matter of indifference whether the members of the group or association agrees with the aims, tasks, means of working and means of fighting. (R.G. 58, 401 of the 24.10.24.)

3. The real attitude of mind of the participants is a matter of indifference. Even if they had the intention of not participating in criminal efforts, or hindering them, this can not eliminate their responsibility. (R.G. 58, 401 of the 24.10.24.)

Organizations with criminal ends are everywhere regarded as in the nature of criminal conspiracies and their criminality is judged by the application of conspiracy principles. The reason why they are offensive to law-governed people has been succinctly stated as follows:

The reason for finding criminal liability in case of a combination to effect an unlawful end or to use unlawful means, where none would exist, even though the act contemplated were actually committed by an individual, is that a combination of persons to commit a wrong, either as an end or as a means to an end, is so much more dangerous, because of its increased power to do wrong, because it is more difficult to guard against and prevent the evil designs of a group of persons than of a single person, and because of the terror which fear of such a combination tends to create in the minds of people. (*Miller on Criminal Law*, 1932, p. 110.)

The Charter, in Article 6, provides that:

Leaders, organizers, instigators and accomplices participating in the formulation or execution of a common plan or conspiracy to commit any of the foregoing crimes are responsible for all acts performed by any persons in execution of such plan.

The individual defendants are arraigned at your bar on this charge which, if proved, makes them responsible for the acts of others in execution of the common plan.

The Charter did not define responsibility for the acts of others in terms of "conspiracy" alone. The crimes were defined in nontechnical but inclusive terms, and embraced formulating and executing a "common plan" as well as participating in a "conspiracy." It was feared that to do otherwise might import into the proceedings technical requirements and limitations which have grown up around the term "conspiracy." There are some divergences between the Anglo-American concept of conspiracy and that of either Soviet, French, or German jurisprudence. It was desired that concrete cases be guided by the broader considerations inherent in the nature of the social problem, rather than controlled by refinements of any local law.

Now, except for procedural difficulties arising from their multitude, there is no reason why every member of any Nazi organization accused here could not have been indicted and convicted as a part of the conspiracy under Article 6 even if the Charter had never mentioned organizations at all. Voluntary affiliation constituted a definite act of adherence to some common plan and purpose. These did not pretend to be merely social or cultural groups; admittedly they were united for action. In the case of several of the Nazi organizations, the fact of confederation was evidenced by formal induction into membership, the taking of an oath, the wearing of a distinctive uniform, the submission to a discipline. That all members of each Nazi organization did combine under a common plan to achieve some end by combined efforts is abundantly established.

The criteria for determining the collective guilt of those who thus adhered to a common plan obviously are those which would test the legality of any combination or conspiracy. Did it contemplate illegal methods or aim at illegal ends? If so, the liability of each member of one of these Nazi organizations for the acts of every other member is not essentially different from the liability for conspiracy enforced in courts of the United States against businessmen who combine in violation of the anti-trust laws, or of other defendants accused under narcotic drugs laws, sedition acts, or other federal penal enactments.

Among the principles every day enforced in courts of Great Britain and the United States in dealing with conspiracy are these:

1. No meeting or formal agreement is necessary. It is sufficient, although one performs one part and other persons other parts, if there be concert of action and working together understandingly with a common design to accomplish a common purpose.

2. One may be liable even though he may not have known who his fellow conspirators were, or just what part they were to take, or what acts they committed, and though he did not take personal part in them or was absent when criminal acts occurred.

3. There may be liability for acts of fellow conspirators although the particular acts were not intended or anticipated, if they were done in execution of the common plan.

4. It is not necessary to liability that one be a member of a conspiracy at the same time as other actors, or at the time of criminal acts. When one becomes a party to it, he adopts and ratifies what has gone before and remains responsible until he abandons the conspiracy with notice to his fellow conspirators.

Of course, members of criminal organizations or conspiracies who personally commit crimes are individually punishable for those crimes exactly as are those who commit the same offenses without organizational backing. But the very gist of the crime of conspiracy or membership in a criminal association is liability for acts one did not personally commit but which his acts facilitated or abetted. The crime is to combine with others and to participate in the unlawful common effort, however innocent the personal acts of the participant when considered by themselves.

The very innocent act of mailing a letter is enough to implicate one in a conspiracy if the purpose of the letter is to advance a criminal plan. There are countless examples of this doctrine in Anglo-American jurisprudence.

The sweep of the law of conspiracy is an important consideration in determining the criteria of guilt for organizations. Certainly the vicarious liability imposed in consequence of voluntary membership, formalized by oath, dedicated to a common organizational purpose and submission to a discipline and chain of command, can not be less than that which follows from informal co-operation with a nebulous group to a common end as is sufficient in conspiracy. This meets the suggestion that the prosecution is required to prove every member, or every part, fraction, or division of the membership to be guilty of criminal acts. The suggestion ignores the conspiratorial nature of the charge. Such an interpretation also would reduce the Charter to an unworkable absurdity. To concentrate in one International Tribunal inquiries requiring such detailed evidence as to each member would set a task not possible of completion within the lives of living men.

It is easy to toss about such a plausible but superficial cliche as, "One should be convicted for his activities, not for his membership." But this ignores the fact that membership in Nazi bodies was itself an activity. It was not something passed out to a passive citizen like a handbill. Even a nominal membership may aid and abet a movement greatly. Does anyone believe that Hjalmar Schacht sitting in the front row of the Nazi Party Congress of 1935, wearing the insignia of the Party, was included in the Nazi propaganda films merely for artistic effect? This great banker's mere loan of his name to this shady enterprise gave it a lift and a respectability in the eyes of every hesitating German. There may be instances in which membership did not aid and abet the organizational ends and means, but individual situations of that kind are for appraisal in the later hearings and not by this Tribunal. By and large, the use of organization affiliation is a quick and simple, but at the same time fairly accurate, outline of the contours of a conspiracy to do what the organization actually did. It is the only one workable at this stage of the trial. It can work no injustice because before any individual can be punished, he can submit the facts of his own case to further and more detailed judicial scrutiny.

While the Charter does not so provide, we think that on ordinary legal principles the burden of proof to justify a declaration of criminality is upon the prosecution. It is discharged, we think, when we establish the following:

1. The organization or group in question must be some aggregation of persons associated in some identifiable relationship with a collective general purpose.

2. While the Charter does not so declare, we think it implied that membership in such an organization must be generally voluntary. That does not require proof that every member was a volunteer. Nor does it mean that an organization is not to be considered vol-

untary if the defense proves that some minor fraction or small percentage of its membership was compelled to join. The test is a common-sense one: Was the organization on the whole one which persons were free to join or to stay out of? Membership is not made involuntary by the fact that it was good business or good politics to identify one's self with the movement. Any compulsion must be of the kind which the law normally recognizes, and threats of political or economic retaliation would be of no consequence.

3. The aims of the organization must be criminal in that it was designing to perform acts denounced as crimes in Article 6 of the Charter. No other act would authorize conviction of an individual and therefore no other act would authorize conviction of an organization in connection with the conviction of the individual.

4. The criminal aims or methods of the organization must have been of such character that its membership in general may properly be charged with knowledge of them. This again is not specifically required by the Charter. Of course, it is not incumbent on the prosecution to establish the individual knowledge of every member of the organization or to rebut the possibility that some may have joined in ignorance of its true character.

5. Some individual defendant must have been a member of the organization and must be convicted of some act on the basis of which the organization is declared to be criminal.

IV. DEFINITION OF ISSUES FOR TRIAL

The progress of this trial will be expedited by clear definition of the issues to be tried. I have indicated what we consider to be the proper criteria of guilt. There are also subjects which we think are not relevant before this Tribunal, some of which are mentioned in the specific questions asked by the Tribunal.

Only a single ultimate issue is before this Tribunal for decision. That is, whether accused organizations properly may be characterized as criminal ones or as innocent ones. Nothing is relevant here that does not bear on a question that would be common to the case of every member. Any matter which would be exculpating for some members but not for all is irrelevant here.

We think it is not relevant to this proceeding at this stage that one or many members were conscripted if in general the membership was voluntary. It may be conceded that conscription is a good defense for an individual charged with membership in a criminal organization, but an organization can have criminal purposes and commit criminal acts even if a portion of its membership consists of persons who were compelled to join it. The issue of conscription is not pertinent to this proceeding but it is pertinent to the trials of individuals for membership in organizations declared criminal by this Tribunal.

We also think it is not relevant to this proceeding that one or more members of the named organizations were ignorant of its criminal purposes or methods if its purposes or methods were open and notorious. An organization may have criminal purposes and commit criminal acts although one or many of its members were without personal knowledge thereof. If a person joined what he thought was a social club but what in fact was a gang of cutthroats and murderers, his lack of knowledge would not exonerate the gang considered as a group, although it might possibly be a factor in extenuation of a charge of criminality brought against him for mere membership in the organization. Even then the test would be not what the man knew, but what, as a person of common understanding, he should have known.

It is not relevant to this proceeding that one or more members of the named organizations were themselves innocent of unlawful acts. This proposition is basic to the entire theory of the declaration of organizational criminality. The purpose of declaring the criminality of organizations, as in every conspiracy charge, is punishment for aiding crimes, although the precise perpetrators may never be found or identified. We know that the Gestapo and SS, as organizations, were given principal responsibility for the extermination of the Jewish people in Europe —but beyond a few isolated instances, we can never establish which members of the Gestapo or SS actually carried out the murders. Any member guilty of direct participation in such crimes can be tried on the charge of having committed specific crimes in addition to the general charge of membership in a criminal organization. Therefore, it is wholly immaterial that one or more members of the organizations were themselves allegedly innocent of specific wrongdoing. The purpose of this proceeding is not to reach instances of individual criminal conduct, even in subsequent trials, and, therefore, such considerations are irrelevant here.

Another question raised by the Tribunal is the period of time during which the groups or organizations named in the Indictment are claimed by the prosecution to have been criminal. The prosecution believes that each organization should be declared criminal during the period referred to in the Indictment. We do not contend that the Tribunal is without power to condition its declaration so as to cover a lesser period of time than that set forth in the Indictment. The prosecution feels, however, that there is in the record at this time adequate evidence to support the charge of criminality with respect to each of the named organizations during the full period of time set forth in the Indictment.

Another question raised by the Tribunal is whether any classes of persons included within the accused groups or organizations should be excluded from the declaration of criminality. It is, of course, necessary that the Tribunal relate its declaration to some identifiable group or organization. The Tribunal, however, is not expected or required to be bound by formalities of organization. In framing the Charter, the use was deliberately avoided of terms or concepts which would involve this trial in legal technicalities about "juristic persons" or "entities." Systems of jurisprudence are not uniform in the refinements of these fictions. The concept of the Charter, therefore, is a nontechnical one. "Group" or "organization" should be given no artificial or sophistical meaning. The word "group" was used in the Charter as a broader term, implying a looser and less formal structure or relationship than is implied in the term "organization." The terms mean in the context of the Charter what they mean in the ordinary speech of people. The test to identify a group or organization is, we submit, a natural and common-sense one.

It is important to bear in mind that while the Tribunal no doubt has power to make its own definition of the groups it will declare criminal, the precise composition and membership of groups and organizations is not an issue for trial here. There is no Charter requirement and no practical need for the Tribunal to define a group or organization with such particularity that its precise composition or membership is thereby determined. The creation of a mechanism for later trial of such issues was a recognition that the declaration of this Tribunal is not decisive of such questions and is likely to be so general as to comprehend persons who on more detailed inquiry will prove to be outside of it. An effort by this Tribunal to try questions of exculpation of individuals, few or many, would unduly protect the trial, transgress the limitation of the Charter, and quite likely do some mischief by attempting to adjudicate precise boundaries on evidence which is not directed to that purpose.

The prosecution stands upon the language of the Indictment and contends that each group or organization should be declared criminal as an entity and that no inquiry should be entered upon and no evidence entertained as to the exculpation of any class or classes of persons within such descriptions. Practical reasons of conserving the Tribunal's time combine with practical considerations for the defendants. A single trial held in one city to deal with questions of excluding thousands of defendants living all over Germany could not be expected to do justice to each member unless it was expected to endure indefinitely. Provision for later, local trial of individual relationships protects the rights of members better than can possibly be done in proceedings before this Tribunal.

With respect to the Gestapo, the United States consents to exclude persons employed in purely clerical, stenographic, janitorial, or similar unofficial routine tasks. As to the Nazi Leadership Corps we abide by the position taken at the time of submission of the evidence, that the following should be included: the Führer, the *Reichsleitung* (i.e., the Reichsleiters, main departments and office holders), the Gauleiters and their staff officers, the Kreisleiters and their staff officers, the Ortsgruppenleiters, the Zellenleiters and the Blockleiters, but not members of the staff of the last three officials. As regards the SA, it is considered advisable that the Declaration expressly exclude (1) wearers of the SA Sports Badge; (2) SA controlled Home Guard Units (*SA Wehrmannschaften*) which were not strictly part of the SA; (3) the *Marchabteilungen* of the NSKOV. (National Socialist League for Disabled Veterans), and (4) the SA Reserve so as to include only the active part of the organization, and that members who were never in any part of that organization other than the Reserve should be excluded.

The prosecution does not feel that there is evidence of the

severability of any class or classes of persons within the organizations accused which would justify any further concessions and feels that no other part of the named groups should be excluded. In this connection, we would again stress the principles of conspiracy. The fact that a section of an organization itself committed no criminal act, or may have been occupied in technical or administrative functions, does not relieve that section of criminal responsibility if its activities contributed to the accomplishment of the criminal enterprise.

V. FURTHER STEPS BEFORE THIS TRIBUNAL

Over 45,000 persons have joined in communications to this Tribunal asking to be heard in connection with the accusations against organizations. The volume of these applications has caused apprehension as to further proceedings. No doubt there are difficulties yet to be overcome, but my study indicates that the difficulties are greatly exaggerated.

The Tribunal is vested with wide discretion as to whether it will entertain an application to be heard. The prosecution would be anxious, of course, to have every application granted that is necessary, not only to do justice but to avoid the appearance of doing anything less than justice. And we do not consider that expediting this trial is so important as affording a fair opportunity to present all really pertinent facts.

Analysis of the conditions which have brought about this flood of applications indicates that their significance is not proportionate to their numbers. The Tribunal sent out 200,000 printed notices of the right to appear before it and defend. They were sent to allied prisoner of war and internment camps. The notice was published in all German-language papers and was repeatedly broadcast over the radio. The 45,000 persons who responded with applications to be heard came principally from about fifteen prisoner of war and internment camps in British or United States control. Those received included an approximate 12,000 from Dachau, 10,000 from Langwasser, 7,500 from Auerbach, 4,000 from Staumuehle, 2,500 from Garmisch, and several hundred from each of the others.

We undertook investigation of these applications from Auerbach camp as properly typical of all. This camp is for prisoners of war, predominantly SS members, and its prisoners number 16,964 enlisted men and 923 officers. The notice of the International Tribunal was posted in each barracks and was read to all inmates. The applications to the Tribunal were forewarded without censorship. Applications to defend were made by 7,509 SS members.

Investigation indicates that these were filed in direct response to the notice and that no action was directed or inspired from any other source within the camp. All who were interrogated professed no knowledge of any SS crimes or of SS criminal purpose, but expressed interest only in their individual fate. Our investigators report no indication that the SS members had additional evidence or information to submit on the general question of the criminality of the SS as an organization. They seemed to think it necessary to make the application to this Tribunal in order to protect themselves.

Examination of the applications made to the Tribunal indicates that most members do not profess to have evidence on the general issue triable here. They assent that the writer has neither committed, witnessed, nor known of the crimes charged against the organization. On a proper definition of the issues such an application is insufficient on its face.

A careful examination of the Tribunal's notice, to which these applications respond, will indicate that the notice contains no word which would inform a member, particularly a layman, of the narrowness of the issues here, or of the later opportunity of each member, if and when prosecuted, to present personal defenses. On the other hand, I think the notice creates the impression that every member may be convicted and punished by this Tribunal and that his only chance to be heard is here.

In view of these facts we suggest consideration of the following program for completion of this trial as to organizations:

1. That the Tribunal formulate and express in an order the scope of the issues and the limitations on the issues to be heard by it.

2. That a notice, adequately informing members as to the limitation on issues and the opportunity for later individual trial, be sent to all applicants and published as was the original notice.

3. That a panel of masters be appointed as authorized in Article 17 (e) of the Charter to examine applications and report those

insufficient on their own statements, and to go to the camps and supervise the taking of any relevant evidence. Defense counsel and prosecution representatives should of course attend and be heard before the masters. The masters should reduce any evidence to deposition form and report the whole to the Tribunal to be introduced as a part of its record.

4. The representative principle may also be employed to simplify this task. Members of particular organizations in particular camps might well be invited to choose one or more to represent them in presenting evidence.

It may not be untimely to remind the Tribunal and defense counsel that the prosecution has omitted from evidence many relevant documents which show repetition of crimes by these organizations in order to save time by avoiding cumulative evidence. It is not too much to expect that cumulative evidence of a negative character will likewise be limited.

Some concern has been expressed as to the number of persons who might be affected by the declarations of criminality we have asked. Some people seem more susceptible to the shock of a million punishments than to the shock of five million murders. At most the number of punishments will never catch up with the number of crimes. However, it is impossible to state even with approximate accuracy the number of persons who might be affected. Figures from German sources seriously exaggerate the number, because they do not take account of heavy casualties in the latter part of the war, and make no allowance for duplication of membership which was large. For example, the evidence is to the effect that seventy-five percent of the Gestapo men also were members of the SS. We know that the United States forces have in detention a roughly estimated 130,000 persons who appear to be members of accused organizations. I have no figures from other Allied forces. But how many of these actually would be prosecuted, instead of being dealt with under the denazification program, no one can foretell. Whatever the number, of one thing we may be sure: it is so large that a thorough inquiry by this Tribunal into each case would prolong its session beyond endurance. All questions as to whether individuals or sub-groups of accused organizations should be excepted from the Declaration of Criminality should be left for local courts, located near the home of the accused and near sources of evidence. These courts can work in one or at most in two languages, instead of four, and can hear evidence which both parties direct to the specific issues.

VI. CONCLUSION

This is not the time to review the evidence against particular organizations which, we take it, should be reserved for summation after all of the evidence is presented. But it is timely to say that the selection of the six organizations named in the Indictment was not a matter of chance. The chief reasons they were chosen are these: collectively they were the ultimate repositories of all power in the Nazi regime; they were not only the most powerful, but the most vicious organizations in the regime; and they were organizations in which membership was generally voluntary.

The Nazi Leadership Corps consisted of the directors and principal executors of the Nazi Party, which was the force lying behind and dominating the whole German state. The Reichs Cabinet was the façade through which the Nazi Party translated its will into legislative, administrative, and executive acts. The two pillars on which the security of the regime rested were the armed forces, directed and controlled by the General Staff and High Command, and the police forces—the Gestapo, the SA, the SD, and the SS. These organizations exemplify all the evil forces of the Nazi regime.

These organizations were also selected because, while representative, they were not so large or extensive as to make it probable that innocent, passive, or indifferent Germans might be caught up in the same net with the guilty. State officialdom is represented, but not all administrative officials or department heads or civil servants; only the *Reichsregierung*, the very heart of Nazidom within the government, is named. The armed forces are accused, but not the average soldier or officer, no matter how high-ranking. Only the top policy makers—the General Staff and High Command—are named. The police forces are accused—but not every policeman, not the ordinary police which performed only normal police functions. Only the most terroristic and repressive police elements—the Gestapo and SD—

are named. The Nazi Party is accused, but not every Nazi voter, not even every member; only the leaders, the *Politische Leiter*. And not even every Party official or worker is included; only "the bearers of sovereignty," in the metaphysical jargon of the Party, who were the actual commanding officers and their staff officers on the highest levels, are accused. The "formations" or strong arms of the Party are accused, but not every one of the seven formations, nor any of the twenty or more supervised or affiliated Party groups. Nazi organizations in which membership was compulsory, either legally or in practice (like the Hitler Youth and the *Deutsche Studentschaft*); Nazi professional organizations (like the Civil Servants Organization, the National Socialist Teachers Organization, and the National Socialist Lawyers Organization); Nazi organizations having some legitimate purpose (like the welfare organizations)—these have not been indicted. Only two formations are named, the SA and the SS, the oldest of the Nazi organizations, groups which had no purpose other than carrying out the Nazi schemes and which actively participated in every crime denounced in the Charter.

In administering preventive justice with a view to forestalling repetition of these crimes against peace, crimes against humanity, and war crimes, it would be a greater catastrophe to acquit these organizations than it would be to acquit the entire twenty-two individual defendants in the box. These defendants' power for harm is spent. That of these organizations goes on. If they are exonerated here the German people will infer that they did no wrong and will easily be regimented in reconstituted organizations under new names, behind the same program.

In administering retributive justice it would be possible to exonerate these organizations only by concluding that no crimes have been committed by the Nazi regime. Their sponsorship of every Nazi purpose and their confederation to execute every measure to attain those ends is beyond denial. A failure to condemn these organizations under the terms of the Charter can only mean that such Nazi ends and means cannot be considered criminal, and that the Charter of the Tribunal is considered a nullity.

119

V

CLOSING ADDRESS, DELIVERED BY ROBERT H. JACKSON, CHIEF OF COUNSEL FOR THE UNITED STATES, AT THE PALACE OF JUSTICE, NÜRNBERG, GERMANY, JULY 26, 1946.

MR. PRESIDENT AND MEMBERS OF THE TRIBUNAL:

An advocate can be confronted with few more formidable tasks than to select his closing arguments where there is great disparity between his appropriate time and his available material. In eight months—a short time as state trials go—we have introduced evidence which embraces as vast and varied a panorama of events as ever has been compressed within the frame work of a litigation. It is impossible in summation to do more than outline with bold strokes the vitals of this trial's mad and melancholy record, which will live as the historical text of the twentieth century's shame and depravity.

It is common to think of our own time as standing at the apex of civilization, from which the deficiencies of preceding ages may patronizingly be viewed in the light of what is assumed to be "progress." The reality is that in the long perspective of history the present century will not hold an admirable position, unless its second half is to redeem its first. These two-score years in this twentieth century will be recorded in the book of years as one of the most bloody in all annals. Two World Wars have left a legacy of dead which number more than all the armies engaged in any war that made ancient or medieval history. No half-century ever witnessed slaughter on such a scale, such cruelties and inhumanities, such wholesale deportations of peoples into slavery, such annihilations of minorities. The terror of Torquemada pales before the Nazi inquisition. These deeds are the overshadowing historical facts by which generations to come will remember this decade. If we cannot eliminate the causes and prevent the repetition of these barbaric events, it is not an irresponsible prophecy to say that this twentieth century may yet succeed in bringing the doom of civilization.

Goaded by these facts, we have moved to redress the blight on the record of our era. The defendants complain that our pace is too fast. In drawing the Charter of this Tribunal, we thought we were recording an accomplished advance in International Law. But they say that we have outrun our times, that we have anticipated an advance that should be, but has not yet been made. The Agreement of London, whether it originates or merely records, at all events marks a transition in International Law which roughly corresponds to that in the evolution of local law when men ceased to punish local crime by "hue and cry" and began to let reason and inquiry govern punishment. The society of nations has emerged from the primitive "hue and cry," the law of "catch and kill." It seeks to apply sanctions to enforce International Law, but to guide their application by evidence, law, and reason instead of outcry. The defendants denounce the law under which their accounting is asked. Their dislike for the law which condemns them is not original. It has been remarked before that

> No man e'er felt the halter draw
> With good opinion of the law.

I shall not labor the law of this case. The position of the United States was explained in my opening statement. My distinguished colleague, the Attorney General of Great Britain, will reply on behalf of all the Chief Prosecutors to the defendants' legal attack. At this stage of the proceedings, I shall rest upon the law of these crimes as laid down in the Charter. The defendants, who except for the Charter would have no right to be heard at all, now ask that the legal basis of this trial be nullified. This Tribunal, of course, is given no power to set aside or to modify the Agreement between the Four Powers, to which eighteen other nations have adhered. The terms of the Charter are conclusive upon every party to these proceedings.

In interpreting the Charter, however, we should not overlook the unique and emergent character of this body as an International Military Tribunal. It is no part of the constitutional mechanism of internal justice of any of the Signatory nations. Germany has unconditionally surrendered, but no peace treaty has been signed or agreed upon. The Allies are still technically in a state of war with Germany, although the enemy's political and military institutions have collapsed. As a Military Tribunal, it is a continuation of the war effort of the Allied nations. As an International Tribunal, it is not bound by the procedural and substantive refinements of our respective judicial or constitutional systems, nor will its rulings introduce precedents into any country's internal civil system of justice. As an International Military Tribunal, it rises above the provincial and transient and seeks guidance not only from International Law but also from the basic principles of jurisprudence which are assumptions of civilization and which long have found embodiment in the codes of all nations.

Of one thing we may be sure. The future will never have to ask, with misgiving: "What could the Nazis have said in their favor?" History will know that whatever could be said, they were allowed to say. They have been given the kind of a trial which they, in the days of their pomp and power, never gave to any man.

But fairness is not weakness. The extraordinary fairness of these hearings is an attribute of our strength. The prosecution's case, at its close, seemed inherently unassailable because it rested so heavily on German documents of unquestioned authenticity. But it was the weeks upon weeks of pecking at this case by one after another of the defendants that has demonstrated its true strength. The fact is that the testimony of the defendants has removed any doubts of guilt which, because of the extraordinary nature and magnitude of these crimes, may have existed before they spoke. They have helped write their own judgment of condemnation.

But justice in this case has nothing to do with some of the arguments put forth by the defendants or their counsel. We have not previously and we need not now discuss the merits of all their obscure and tortuous philosophy. We are not trying them for possession of obnoxious ideas. It is their right, if they choose, to renounce the Hebraic heritage in the civilization of which Germany was once a part. Nor is it our affair that they repudiated the Hellenic influence as well. The intellectual bankruptcy and moral perversion of the Nazi regime might have been no concern of International Law had it not been utilized to goose-step the

Herrenvolk across international frontiers. It is not their thoughts, it is their overt acts which we charge to be crimes. Their creed and teachings are important only as evidence of motive, purpose, knowledge, and intent.

We charge unlawful aggression but we are not trying the motives, hopes, or frustrations which may have led Germany to resort to aggressive war as an instrument of policy. The law, unlike politics, does not concern itself with the good or evil in the *status quo*, nor with the merits of grievances against it. It merely requires that the *status quo* be not attacked by violent means and that policies be not advanced by war. We may admit that overlapping ethnological and cultural groups, economic barriers, and conflicting national ambitions created in the 1930s, as they will continue to create, grave problems for Germany as well as for the other peoples of Europe. We may admit too that the world had failed to provide political or legal remedies which would be honorable and acceptable alternatives to war. We do not underwrite either the ethics or the wisdom of any country, including my own, in the face of these problems. But we do say that it is now, as it was for sometime prior to 1939, illegal and criminal for Germany or any other nation to redress grievances or seek expansion by resort to aggressive war.

Let me emphasize one cardinal point. The United States has no interest which would be advanced by the conviction of any defendant if we have not proved him guilty on at least one of the counts charged against him in the Indictment. Any result that the calm and critical judgment of posterity would pronounce unjust would not be a victory for any of the countries associated in this prosecution. But in summation we now have before us the tested evidences of criminality and have heard the flimsy excuses and paltry evasions of the defendants. The suspended judgment with which we opened this case is no longer appropriate. The time has come for final judgment and if the case I present seems hard and uncompromising, it is because the evidence makes it so.

I perhaps can do no better service than to try to lift this case out of the morass of detail with which the record is full and put before you only the bold outlines of a case that is impressive in its simplicity. True, its thousands of documents and more thousands of pages of testimony deal with an epoch, and cover a continent, and touch almost every branch of human endeavor. They illuminate specialties, such as diplomacy, naval development and warfare, land warfare, the genesis of air warfare, the politics of the Nazi rise to power, the finance and economics of totalitarian war, sociology, penology, mass psychology, and mass pathology. I must leave it to experts to comb the evidence and write volumes on their specialties, while I picture in broad strokes the offenses whose acceptance as lawful would threaten the continuity of civilization. I must, as Kipling put it, "splash at a ten-league canvas with brushes of comet's hair."

THE CRIMES OF THE NAZI REGIME

The strength of the case against these defendants under the conspiracy count, which it is the duty of the United States to argue, is in its simplicity. It involves but three ultimate inquiries: first, have the acts defined by the Charter as crimes been committed; second, were they committed pursuant to a common plan or conspiracy; third, are these defendants among those who are criminally responsible?

The charge requires examination of a criminal policy, not of a multitude of isolated, unplanned, or disputed crimes. The substantive crimes upon which we rely, either as goals of a common plan or as means for its accomplishment, are admitted. The pillars which uphold the conspiracy charge may be found in five groups of overt acts, whose character and magnitude are important considerations in appraising the proof of conspiracy.

I. THE SEIZURE OF POWER AND SUBJUGATION OF GERMANY TO A POLICE STATE

The Nazi Party seized control of the German state in 1933. "Seizure of power" is a characterization used by defendants and defense witnesses, and so apt that it has passed into both history and everyday speech.[1]

The Nazi junta in the early days lived in constant fear of overthrow. Göring, in 1934, pointed out that its enemies were legion and said:

---

[1] Notes for the Closing Address will be found on page 163 *et seq.*

Therefore the concentration camps have been created, where we have first confined thousands of Communists and Social Democrat functionaries.[2]

In 1933 Göring forecast the whole program of purposeful cruelty and oppression when he publicly announced:

Whoever in the future raises a hand against a representative of the National Socialist movement or of the state, must know that he will lose his life in a very short while.[3]

New political crimes were created to this end. It was made a treason, punishable with death, to organize or support a political party other than the Nazi Party.[1] Circulating a false or exaggerated statement, or one which would harm the state or even the Party, was made a crime.[5] Laws were enacted of such ambiguity that they could be used to punish almost any innocent act. It was, for example, made a crime to provoke "any act contrary to the public welfare."[6]

The doctrine of punishment by analogy was introduced to enable conviction for acts which no statute forbade.[7] Minister of Justice Gürtner explained that National Socialism considered every violation of the goals of life which the community set up for itself to be a wrong per se, and that the act could be punished even though it was not contrary to existing "formal" law.[8]

The Gestapo and the SD were instrumentalities of an espionage system which penetrated public and private life.[9] Göring controlled a personal wire-tapping unit.[10] All privacy of communication was abolished.[11] Party Blockleiters, appointed over every fifty households, continuously spied on all within their ken.[12] Upon the strength of this spying, individuals were dragged off to "protective custody" and to concentration camps, without legal proceedings of any kind,[13] and without statement of any reason therefor.[14] The partisan political police were exempted from effective legal responsibility for their acts.[15]

With all administrative offices in Nazi control and with the Reichstag reduced to impotence, the judiciary remained the last obstacle to this reign of terror.[16] But its independence was soon overcome and it was reorganized to dispense a venal justice.[17] Judges were ousted for political or racial reasons and were spied upon and put under pressure to join the Nazi Party.[18] After the Supreme Court had acquitted three of the four men whom the Nazis accused of setting the Reichstag fire, its jurisdiction over treason cases was transferred to a newly established "People's Court" consisting of two judges and five Party officials.[19] The German film of this "People's Court" in operation, which we showed in this chamber, revealed its presiding judge pouring partisan abuse upon speechless defendants.[20] Special courts were created to try political crimes, only Party members were appointed judges,[21] and "Judges Letters" instructed the puppet judges as to the "general lines" they must follow.[22]

The result was the removal of all peaceable means either to resist or to change the government. Having sneaked through the portals of power, the Nazis slammed the gate in the face of all others who might also aspire to enter. Since the law was what the Nazis said it was, every form of opposition was rooted out, and every dissenting voice throttled. Germany was in the clutch of a police state, which used the fear of the concentration camp as a means to enforce nonresistance. The Party was the state, the state was the Party, and terror by day and death by night were the policy of both.

II. THE PREPARATION AND WAGING OF WARS OF AGGRESSION

From the moment the Nazis seized power, they set about by feverish but stealthy efforts, in defiance of the Versailles Treaty, to arm for war. In 1933 they found no air force. By 1939 they had 21 squadrons, consisting of 240 echelons or about 2,400 first-line planes, together with trainers and transports. In 1933 they found an army of 3 infantry and 3 cavalry divisions. By 1939 they had raised and equipped an army of 51 divisions, 4 of which were fully motorized and 4 of which were panzer divisions. In 1933 they found a navy of 1 cruiser and 6 light cruisers. By 1939 they had built a navy of 4 battleships, 1 aircraft carrier, 6 cruisers, 22 destroyers, and 54 submarines. They had also built up in that period an armament industry as efficient as that of any country in the world.[23]

These new weapons were put to use, commencing in September 1939, in a series of undeclared wars against nations with which Germany had arbitration and nonaggression treaties, and in violation of repeated assurances.[24] On September 1, 1939 this rearmed Germany attacked Poland. The following April witnessed the invasion and occupation of Denmark and Norway, and May saw the overrunning of Belgium, the Netherlands, and Luxembourg. Another spring found Yugoslavia and Greece under attack, and in June 1941 came the invasion of Soviet Russia. Then Japan, which Germany had embraced as a partner, struck without warning at Pearl Harbor in December 1941 and four days later Germany declared war on the United States.

We need not trouble ourselves about the many abstract difficulties that can be conjured up about what constitutes aggression in doubtful cases. I shall show you, in discussing the conspiracy, that by any test ever put forward by any responsible authority, by all the canons of plain sense, these were unlawful wars of aggression in breach of treaties and in violation of assurances.

III. WARFARE IN DISREGARD OF INTERNATIONAL LAW

It is unnecessary to labor this point on the facts. Göring asserts that the Rules of Land Warfare were obsolete, that no nation could fight a total war within their limits.[25] He testified that the Nazis would have denounced the Conventions to which Germany was a party, but that General Jodl wanted captured German soldiers to continue to benefit from their observance by the Allies.[26]

It was, however, against the Soviet people and Soviet prisoners that Teutonic fury knew no bounds, in spite of a warning by Admiral Canaris that the treatment was in violation of International Law.[27]

We need not, therefore, for purposes of the conspiracy count, recite the revolting details of starving, beating, murdering, freezing, and mass extermination admittedly used against the eastern soldiery. Also, we may take as established or admitted that the lawless conduct such as shooting British and American airmen, mistreatment of western prisoners of war, forcing French prisoners of war into German war work, and other deliberate violations of the Hague and Geneva Conventions, did occur, and in obedience to highest levels of authority.[28]

IV. ENSLAVEMENT AND PLUNDER OF POPULATIONS
IN OCCUPIED COUNTRIES

The defendant Sauckel, Plenipotentiary General for the Utilization of Labor,[29] is authority for the statement that "out of five million foreign workers who arrived in Germany, not even 200,000 came voluntarily."[30] It was officially reported to defendant Rosenberg that in his territory "recruiting methods were used which probably have their origin in the blackest period of the slave trade." [31] Sauckel himself reported that male and female agents went hunting for men, got them drunk, and "shanghaied" them to Germany.[32] These captives were shipped in trains without heat, food, or sanitary facilities. The dead were thrown out at stations, and the newborn were thrown out the windows of moving trains.[33]

Sauckel ordered that "all the men must be fed, sheltered, and treated in such a way as to exploit them to the highest possible extent at the lowest conceivable degree of expenditure."[34] About two million of these were employed directly in the manufacture of armaments and munitions.[35] The director of the Krupp locomotive factory in Essen complained to the company that Russian forced laborers were so underfed that they were too weakened to do their work,[36] and the Krupp doctor confirmed their pitiable condition.[37] Soviet workers were put in camps under Gestapo guards, who were allowed to punish disobedience by confinement in a concentration camp or by hanging on the spot.[38]

Populations of occupied countries were otherwise exploited and oppressed unmercifully. Terrorism was the order of the day. Civilians were arrested without charges, committed without counsel, executed without hearing. Villages were destroyed, the male inhabitants shot or sent to concentration camps, the women sent to forced labor, and the children scattered abroad.[39] The extent of the slaughter in Poland alone was indicated by Frank, who reported:

If I wanted to have a poster put up for every seven Poles who were shot, the forests of Poland would not suffice for producing the paper for such posters.[40]

Those who will enslave men cannot be expected to refrain from plundering them. Boastful reports show how thoroughly and scientifically the resources of occupied lands were sucked into the German war economy, inflicting shortage, hunger, and inflation upon the inhabitants.[41] Besides this grand plan to aid the German war effort there were the sordid activities of the Rosenberg *Einsatzstab,* which pillaged art treasures for Göring and his fellow bandits.[42] It is hard to say whether the spectacle of Germany's number two leader urging his people to give up every comfort and strain every sinew on essential war work while he rushed around confiscating art by the trainload should be cast as tragedy or comedy. In either case it was a crime.

International Law at all times before and during this war spoke with precision and authority respecting the protection due civilians of an occupied country,[43] and the slave trade and plunder of occupied countries were at all times flagrantly unlawful.

V. PERSECUTION AND EXTERMINATION OF JEWS AND CHRISTIANS

The Nazi movement will be of evil memory in history because of its persecution of the Jews, the most far-flung and terrible racial persecution of all time. Although the Nazi Party neither invented nor monopolized anti-Semitism, its leaders from the very beginning embraced it, incited it, and exploited it. They used it as "the psychological spark that ignites the mob." After the seizure of power, it became an official state policy. The persecution began in a series of discriminatory laws eliminating the Jews from the civil service, the professions, and economic life. As it became more intense it included segregation of Jews in ghettos and exile. Riots were organized by Party leaders to loot Jewish business places and to burn synagogues. Jewish property was confiscated and a collective fine of a billion marks was imposed upon German Jewry. The program progressed in fury and irresponsibility to the "final solution." This consisted of sending all Jews who were fit to work to concentration camps as slave laborers, and all who were not fit, which included children under twelve and people over fifty, as well as any others judged unfit by an SS doctor, to concentration camps for extermination.[44]

Adolf Eichmann, the sinister figure who had charge of the extermination program, has estimated that the anti-Jewish activities resulted in the killing of six million Jews. Of these, four million were killed in extermination institutions, and two million were killed by *Einsatzgruppen*, mobile units of the Security Police and SD which pursued Jews in the ghettos and in their homes and slaughtered them by gas wagons, by mass shooting in anti-tank ditches, and by every device which Nazi ingenuity could conceive. So thorough and uncompromising was this program that the Jews of Europe as a race no longer exist, thus fulfilling the diabolic "prophecy" of Adolf Hitler at the beginning of the war.[45]

Of course, any such program must reckon with the opposition of the Christian church. This was recognized from the very beginning. Defendant Bormann wrote all Gauleiters in 1941 that "National Socialism and Christian concepts are irreconcilable," and that the people must be separated from the churches and the influence of the churches totally removed.[46] Defendant Rosenberg even wrote dreary treatises advocating a new and weird Nazi religion.[47]

The Gestapo appointed "church specialists" who were instructed that the ultimate aim was "destruction of the confessional churches."[48] The record is full of specific instances of the persecution of clergymen,[49] the confiscation of church property,[50] interference with religious publications,[51] disruption of religious education,[52] and suppression of religious organizations.[53]

The chief instrumentality for persecution and extermination was the concentration camp, sired by defendant Göring and nurtured under the overall authority of defendants Frick and Kaltenbrunner.

The horrors of these iniquitous places have been vividly disclosed by documents[54] and testified to by witnesses.[55] The Tribunal must be satiated with ghastly verbal and pictorial portrayals. From your records it is clear that the concentration camps were the first and worst weapon of oppression used by the National Socialist state, and that they were the primary means utilized for the persecution of the Christian church and the extermination of the Jewish race. This has been admitted to you by some of the defendants from the witness stand.[56] In the words of defendant Frank:

A thousand years will pass and this guilt of Germany will still not be erased.[57]

These, then, were the five great substantive crimes of the Nazi regime. Their commission, which cannot be denied, stands admitted. The defendant Keitel, who is in a position to know the facts, has given the Tribunal what seems to be a fair summation of the case on these facts:

The defendant has declared that he admits the contents of the general Indictment to be proved from the objective and factual point of view (that is to say, not every individual case) and this in consideration of the law of procedure governing this trial. It would be senseless, despite the possibility of refuting several documents or individual facts to attempt to shake the Indictment as a whole.[58]

I pass now to the inquiry whether these groups of criminal acts were integrated in a common plan or conspiracy.

THE COMMON PLAN OR CONSPIRACY

The prosecution submits that these five categories of premeditated crimes were not separate and independent phenomena but that all were committed pursuant to a common plan or conspiracy. The defense admits that these classes of crimes were committed but denies that they are connected one with another as parts of a single program.

The central crime in this pattern of crime, the kingpin which holds them all together, is the plot for aggressive war. The chief reason for international cognizance of these crimes lies in this fact. Have we established the plan or conspiracy to make aggressive war?

Certain admitted or clearly proven facts help answer that question. First is the fact that such war of aggression did take place. Second, it is admitted that from the moment the Nazis came to power, every one of them and every one of the defendants worked like beavers to prepare for *some* war. The question therefore comes to this: were they preparing for the war which did occur, or were they preparing for some war which never has happened? It is probably true that in the early days none of them had in mind what month of what year war would begin, the exact dispute which would precipitate it, or whether its first impact would be Austria, Czechoslovakia, or Poland. But I submit that the defendants either knew or are chargeable with knowledge that the war for which they were making ready would be a war of German aggression. This is partly because there was no real expectation that any power or combination of powers would attack Germany. But it is chiefly because the inherent nature of the German plans was such that they were certain sooner or later to meet resistance and that they could then be accomplished only by aggression.

The plans of Adolf Hitler for aggression were just as secret as *Mein Kampf,* of which over six million copies were published in Germany. He not only openly advocated overthrowing the Treaty of Versailles, but made demands which went far beyond a mere rectification of its alleged injustices.[59] He avowed an intention to attack neighboring states and seize their lands,[60] which he said would have to be won with "the power of a triumphant sword."[61] Here, for every German to hearken to, were the "ancestral voices prophesying war."

Göring has testified in this courtroom that at his first meeting with Hitler, long before the seizure of power:

> I noted that Hitler had a definite view of the impotency of protest and, as a second point, that he was of the opinion that Germany should be freed of the peace of Versailles. . . . We did not say we shall have to have a war and defeat our enemies; this was the aim and the methods had to be adapted to the political situation.[62]

When asked if this goal were to be accomplished by war if necessary, Göring did not deny that eventuality but evaded a direct answer by saying: "We did not even debate about those things at that time." He went on to say that the aim to overthrow the Treaty of Versailles was open and notorious and that "Every German in my opinion was for its modification, and there was no doubt that this was a strong inducement for joining the

Party."[63] Thus, there can be no possible excuse for any person who aided Hitler to get absolute power over the German people, or took a part in his regime, to fail to know the nature of the demands he would make on Germany's neighbors.

Immediately after the seizure of power the Nazis went to work to implement these aggressive intentions by preparing for war. They first enlisted German industrialists in a secret rearmament program. Twenty days after the seizure of power Schacht was host to Hitler, Göring, and some twenty leading industrialists. Among them were Krupp von Bohlen of the great Krupp armament works and representatives of I. G. Farben and other Ruhr heavy industries. Hitler and Göring explained their program to the industrialists, who became so enthusiastic that they set about to raise three million Reichsmarks to strengthen and confirm the Nazi Party in power.[64] Two months later Krupp was working to bring a reorganized association of German industry into agreement with the political aims of the Nazi government.[65] Krupp later boasted of the success in keeping the German war industries secretly alive and in readiness despite the disarmament clauses of the Versailles Treaty, and recalled the industrialists' enthusiastic acceptance of "the great intentions of the Führer in the rearmament period of 1933–39."[66]

Some two months after Schacht had sponsored this first meeting to gain the support of the industrialists, the Nazis moved to harness industrial labor to their aggressive plans. In April 1933 Hitler ordered Dr. Ley "to take over the trade unions," numbering some six million members. By Party directive Ley seized the unions, their property, and their funds. Union leaders, taken into "protective custody" by the SS and SA were put into concentration camps.[67] The free labor unions were then replaced by a Nazi organization known as the German Labor Front, with Dr. Ley as its head. It was expanded until it controlled over twenty-three million members.[68] Collective bargaining was eliminated, the voice of labor could no longer be heard as to working conditions, and the labor contract was prescribed by "trustees of labor" appointed by Hitler.[69] The war purpose of this labor program was clearly acknowledged by Robert Ley five days after war broke out, when he declared in a speech that:

133

We National Socialists have monopolized all resources and all our energies during the past seven years so as to be able to be equipped for the supreme effort of battle.[70]

The Nazis also proceeded at once to adapt the government to the needs of war. In April 1935 the Cabinet formed a Defense Council, the working committee of which met frequently thereafter. In the meeting of May 23, 1933, at which defendant Keitel presided, the members were instructed that

> No document must be lost since otherwise the enemy propaganda would make use of it. Matters communicated orally cannot be proven; they can be denied by us in Geneva.[71]

In January 1934, with defendant Jodl present, the Council planned a mobilization calendar and mobilization order for some 240,000 industrial plants. Again it was agreed that nothing should be in writing so that "the military purpose may not be traceable."[72]

On May 21, 1933 the top secret Reich Defense Law was enacted. Defendant Schacht was appointed Plenipotentiary General for War Economy with the task of secretly preparing all economic forces for war and, in the event of mobilization, of financing the war.[73] Schacht's secret efforts were supplemented in October 1936 by the appointment of defendant Göring as Commissioner of the Four Year Plan, with the duty of putting the entire economy in a state of readiness for war within four years.[74]

A secret program for the accumulation of the raw materials and foreign credits necessary for extensive rearmament was also set on foot immediately upon seizure of power. In September 1934 the Minister of Economics was already complaining that:

> The task of stockpiling is being hampered by the lack of foreign currency; the need for secrecy and camouflage also is a retarding influence.[75]

Foreign currency controls were at once established.[76] Financing was delegated to the wizard Schacht, who conjured up the MEFO bill to serve the dual objectives of tapping the short-term money market for rearmament purposes while concealing the amount of these expenditures.[77]

The spirit of the whole Nazi administration was summed up

by Göring at a meeting of the Council of Ministers, which included Schacht, on May 27, 1936, when he said,

All measures are to be considered from the standpoint of an assured waging of war.[78]

The General Staff, of course, also had to be enlisted in the war plans. Most of the Generals, attracted by the prospect of rebuilding their armies, became willing accomplices. The holdover Minister of War von Blomberg and the Chief of Staff General von Fritsch, however, were not cordial to the increasingly belligerent policy of the Hitler regime, and by vicious and obscene plotting they were discredited and removed in January 1938.[79] Thereupon, Hitler assumed for himself Supreme Command of the Armed Forces, and the positions of von Blomberg and von Fritsch were filled by others who became, as Blomberg said of Keitel, "a willing tool in Hitler's hands for every one of his decisions."[80] The Generals did not confine their participation to merely military matters. They participated in all major diplomatic and political maneuvers, such as the Obersalzburg meeting where Hitler, flanked by Keitel and other top Generals, issued his virtual ultimatum to Schuschnigg.[81]

As early as November 5, 1937, the plan to attack had begun to take definiteness as to time and victim. In a meeting which included defendants Raeder, Göring, and von Neurath, Hitler stated the cynical objective:

The question for Germany is where the greatest possible conquest could be made at the lowest possible cost.

He discussed various plans for the invasion of Austria and Czechoslovakia, indicating clearly that he was thinking of these territories not as ends in themselves, but as means for further conquest. He pointed out that considerable military and political assistance would be afforded by possession of these lands and discussed the possibility of constituting from them new armies up to a strength of about twelve divisions. The aim he stated boldly and baldly as the acquisition of additional living space in Europe, and recognized that "the German question can be solved only by way of force."[82]

Six months later, emboldened by the bloodless Austrian conquest, Hitler, in a secret directive to Keitel, stated his "unalterable decision to smash Czechoslovakia by military action in the near future."[83] On the same day, Jodl noted in his diary that the Führer had stated his final decision to destroy Czechoslovakia soon and had initiated military preparations all along the line.[84] By April the plan had been perfected to attack Czechoslovakia "with lightning-swift action as the result of an 'incident.' "[85] All along the line preparations became more definite for a war of expansion, on the assumption that it would result in world-wide conflict. In September 1938 Admiral Carls officially commented on a "Draft Study of Naval Warfare Against England":

> There is full agreement with the main theme of the study.
> 1. If according to the Führer's decision Germany is to acquire a position as a world power, she needs not only sufficient colonial possessions but also secure naval communications and secure access to the ocean.
> 2. Both requirements can only be fulfilled in opposition to Anglo-French interests and will limit their position as world powers. It is unlikely that they can be achieved by peaceful means. The decision to make Germany a world power therefore forces upon us the necessity of making the corresponding preparations for war.
> 3. War against England means at the same time war against the Empire, against France, probably against Russia as well, and a large number of countries overseas; in fact, against one-half to one-third of the whole world.
> It can only be justified and have a chance of success if it is prepared economically as well as politically and militarily and waged with the aim of conquering for Germany an outlet to the ocean.[86]

This Tribunal knows what categorical assurances were given to an alarmed world after the *Anschluss,* after Munich, and after the occupation of Bohemia and Moravia, that German ambitions were realized and that Hitler had "no further territorial demands to make in Europe."[87] The record of this trial shows that those promises were calculated deceptions and that those high in the bloody brotherhood of Nazidom knew it.

As early as April 15, 1938, Göring pointed out to Mussolini and Ciano that the possession of those territories would make possible an attack on Poland.[88] Ribbentrop's Ministry wrote on August 26, 1938 that:

After the liquidation of the Czechoslovakian question, it will be generally assumed that Poland will be next in turn.[89]

Hitler, after the Polish invasion, boasted that it was the Austrian and Czechoslovakian triumphs by which "the basis for the action against Poland was laid."[90] Göring suited the act to the purpose and gave immediate instructions to exploit for the further strengthening of Germany the war potential, first of the Sudetenland, and then of the whole Protectorate.[91]

By May 1939 the Nazi preparations had ripened to the point that Hitler confided to defendants Göring, Raeder, Keitel, and others, his readiness "to attack Poland at the first suitable opportunity," even though he recognized that "further successes cannot be attained without the shedding of blood." The larcenous motives behind this decision he made plain in words that echoed the covetous theme of *Mein Kampf*:

Circumstances must be adapted to aims. This is impossible without invasion of foreign states or attacks upon foreign property. Living space, in proportion to the magnitude of the state, is the basis of all power—further successes cannot be attained without expanding our living space in the east. . . .[92]

While a credulous world slumbered, snugly blanketed with perfidious assurances of peaceful intentions, the Nazis prepared not merely as before for *a* war, but now for *the* war. The defendants Göring, Keitel, Raeder, Frick, and Funk, with others, met as the Reich Defense Council in June 1939. The minutes, authenticated by Göring, are revealing evidence of the way in which each step of Nazi planning dovetailed with every other. These five key defendants, three months before the first Panzer unit had knifed into Poland, were laying plans for "employment of the *population* in wartime," and had gone so far as to classify industry for priority in labor supply "after five million servicemen had been called up." They decided upon measures to avoid "confusion when mobilization takes place," and declared a purpose "to gain and maintain the lead in the decisive initial weeks of a war." They then planned to use in production prisoners of war, criminal prisoners, and concentration camp inmates. They then decided on "compulsory work for women in wartime." They had already passed on applications from 1,172,000 specialist work-

137

men for classification as indispensable, and had approved 727,000 of them. They boasted that orders to workers to report for duty "are ready and tied up in bundles at the labor offices." And they resolved to increase the industrial manpower supply by bringing into Germany "hundreds of thousands of workers" from the Protectorate to be "housed together in hutments."[93]

It is the minutes of this significant conclave of many key defendants which disclose how the plan to start the war was coupled with the plan to wage the war through the use of illegal sources of labor to maintain production. Hitler, in announcing his plan to attack Poland, had already foreshadowed the slave-labor program as one of its corollaries when he cryptically pointed out to defendants Göring, Raeder, Keitel, and others that the Polish population "will be available as a source of labor."[94] This was the part of the plan made good by Frank, who, as Governor General notified Göring that he would supply "at least one million male and female agricultural and industrial workers to the Reich,"[95] and by Sauckel, whose impressments throughout occupied territory aggregated numbers equal to the total population of some of the smaller nations of Europe.

Here also comes to the surface the link between war labor and concentration camps, a manpower source that was increasingly used and with increasing cruelty. An agreement between Himmler and the Minister of Justice Thierack in 1942 provided for "the delivery of anti-social elements from the execution of their sentence to the Reichsführer SS to be worked to death."[96] An SS directive provided that bedridden prisoners be drafted for work to be performed in bed.[97] The Gestapo ordered forty-five thousand Jews arrested to increase the "recruitment of manpower into the concentration camps."[98] One hundred thousand Jews were brought from Hungary to augment the camps' manpower.[99] On the initiative of the defendant Dönitz, concentration-camp labor was used in the construction of submarines.[100] Concentration camps were thus geared into war production on the one hand, and into the administration of justice and the political aims of the Nazis on the other.

The use of prisoner-of-war labor as here planned also grew with German needs. At a time when every German soldier was needed at the front and forces were not available at home, Russian prisoners of war were forced to man antiaircraft guns against Allied planes. Field Marshal Milch reflected the Nazi merriment at this flagrant violation of International Law, saying,

> This is an amusing thing, that the Russians must work the guns.[101]

The orders for the treatment of Soviet prisoners of war were so ruthless that Admiral Canaris, pointing out that they would "result in arbitrary mistreatments and killings," protested to the OKW against them as breaches of International Law. The reply of Keitel was unambiguous:

> The objections arise from the military conception of chivalrous warfare! This is the destruction of an ideology! Therefore I approve and back the measures.[102]

The Geneva Convention would have been thrown overboard openly except that Jodl objected because he wanted the benefits of Allied observance of it while it was not being allowed to hamper the Germans in any way.[103]

Other crimes in the conduct of warfare were planned with equal thoroughness as a means of insuring the victory of German arms. In October 1938, almost a year before the start of the war, the large-scale violation of the established rules of warfare was contemplated as a policy, and the Supreme Command circulated a most secret list of devious explanations to be given by the Propaganda Minister in such cases.[104] Even before this time commanders of the armed forces were instructed to employ any means of warfare so long as it facilitated victory.[106] After the war was in progress the orders increased in savagery. A typical Keitel order, demanding use of the "most brutal means," provided that:

> It is the duty of the troops to use all means without restriction, even against women and children, so long as it insures success.[106]

The German naval forces were no more immune from the infection than the land forces. Raeder ordered violations of the accepted rules of warfare wherever necessary to gain strategic successes.[107] Dönitz urged his submarine crews not to rescue survivors of torpedoed enemy ships in order to cripple merchant shipping of the Allied nations by decimating their crews.[108]

Thus, the war crimes against Allied forces and the crimes

against humanity committed in occupied territories are incontestably part of the program of making the war because, in the German calculations, they were indispensable to its hope of success.

Similarly, the whole group of pre-war crimes, including the persecutions within Germany, fall into place around the plan for aggressive war like stones in a finely wrought mosaic. Nowhere is the whole catalogue of crimes of Nazi oppression and terrorism within Germany so well integrated with the crime of war as in that strange mixture of wind and wisdom which makes up the testimony of Hermann Göring. In describing the aims of the Nazi program before the seizure of power, Göring said:

> The first question was to achieve and establish a different political structure for Germany which would enable Germany to obtain against the Dictate [of Versailles], and not only a protest, but an objection of such a nature that it would actually be considered.[109]

With these purposes, Göring admitted that the plan was made to overthrow the Weimar Republic, to seize power, and to carry out the Nazi program by whatever means were necessary, whether legal or illegal.[110]

From Göring's cross-examination we learn how necessarily the whole program of crime followed.[111] Because they considered a strong state necessary to get rid of the Versailles Treaty, they adopted the *Führerprinzip*. Having seized power, the Nazis thought it necessary to protect it by abolishing parliamentary government and suppressing all organized opposition from political parties.[112] This was reflected in the philosophy of Göring that the opera was more important than the Reichstag.[113] Even the "opposition of each individual person was not tolerated unless it was a matter of unimportance." To insure the suppression of opposition a secret political police was necessary. In order to eliminate incorrigible opponents, it was necessary to establish concentration camps and to resort to the device of protective custody. Protective custody, Göring testified, meant that

> People were arrested and taken into protective custody who had committed no crime but who one might expect, if they remained in freedom, would do all sorts of things to damage the German state.[114]

The same purpose was dominant in the persecution of the Jews. In the beginning, fanaticism and political opportunism played a principal part, for anti-Semitism and its allied scapegoat mythology were a vehicle on which the Nazis rode to power. It was for this reason that the filthy Streicher and the blasphemous Rosenberg were welcomed to a place at Party rallies and made leaders and officials of the state or Party. But the Nazis soon regarded the Jews as foremost amongst the opposition to the police state with which they planned to put forward their plans of military aggression. Fear of their pacifism and their opposition to strident nationalism was given as the reason that the Jews had to be driven from the political and economic life of Germany.[115] Accordingly, they were transported like cattle to the concentration camps, where they were utilized as a source of forced labor for war purposes.

At a meeting held on November 12, 1938, two days after the violent anti-Jewish pogroms instigated by Goebbels and carried out by the Party Leadership Corps and the SA, the program for the elimination of the Jews from the German economy was mapped out by Göring, Funk, Heydrich, Goebbels, and other top Nazis. The measures adopted included confinement of the Jews in ghettos, cutting off their food supply, "aryanizing" their shops, and restricting their freedom of movement.[116] Here another purpose behind the Jewish persecutions crept in, for it was the wholesale confiscation of their property which helped finance German rearmament. Although Schacht's plan to have foreign money ransom the entire race within Germany was not adopted, the Jews were stripped to the point where Göring was able to advise the Reich Defense Council that the critical situation of the Reich exchequer, due to rearmament, had been relieved "through the billion Reichsmark fine imposed on Jewry, and through profits accrued to the Reich in the aryanization of Jewish enterprises."[117]

A glance over the dock will show that, despite quarrels among themselves, each defendant played a part which fitted in with every other, and that all advanced the common plan. It contradicts experience that men of such diverse backgrounds and talents should so forward each other's aims by coincidence.

The large and varied role of Göring was half militarist and half gangster. He stuck a pudgy finger in every pie. He used his SA musclemen to help bring the gang into power. In order to entrench that power he contrived to have the Reichstag burned, established the Gestapo, and created the concentration camps. He was equally adept at massacring opponents and at framing scandals to get rid of stubborn generals. He built up the Luftwaffe and hurled it at his defenseless neighbors. He was among the foremost in harrying the Jews out of the land. By mobilizing the total economic resources of Germany he made possible the waging of the war which he had taken a large part in planning. He was, next to Hitler, the man who tied the activities of all the defendants together in a common effort.

The parts played by the other defendants, although less comprehensive and less spectacular than that of the Reichsmarshal, were nevertheless integral and necessary contributions to the joint undertaking, without any one of which the success of the common enterprise would have been in jeopardy. There are many specific deeds of which these men have been proven guilty. No purpose would be served—nor indeed is time available—to review all the crimes which the evidence has charged up to their names. Nevertheless, in viewing the conspiracy as a whole and as an operating mechanism it may be well to recall briefly the outstanding services which each of the men in the dock rendered to the common cause.

The zealot HESS, before succumbing to wanderlust, was the engineer tending the Party machinery, passing orders and propaganda down to the Leadership Corps, supervising every aspect of Party activities, and maintaining the organization as a loyal and ready instrument of power. When apprehensions abroad threatened the success of the Nazi scheme for conquest, it was the duplicitous RIBBENTROP, the salesman of deception, who was detailed to pour wine on the troubled waters of suspicion by preaching the gospel of limited and peaceful intentions. KEITEL, weak and willing tool, delivered the armed forces, the instrument of aggression, over to the Party and directed them in executing its felonious designs.

KALTENBRUNNER, the grand inquisitor, took up the bloody mantle of Heydrich to stifle opposition and terrorize compliance, and buttressed the power of National Socialism on a foundation of guiltless corpses. It was ROSENBERG, the intellectual high priest of the "master race," who provided the doctrine of hatred which gave the impetus for the annihilation of Jewry, and who put his infidel theories into practice against the eastern occupied territories. His woolly philosophy also added boredom to the long list of Nazi atrocities. The fanatical FRANK, who solidified Nazi control by establishing the new order of authority without law, so that the will of the Party was the only test of legality, proceeded to export his lawlessness to Poland, which he governed with the lash of Cæsar and whose population he reduced to sorrowing remnants. FRICK, the ruthless organizer, helped the Party to seize power, supervised the police agencies to insure that it stayed in power, and chained the economy of Bohemia and Moravia to the German war machine.

STREICHER, the venomous vulgarian, manufactured and distributed obscene racial libels which incited the populace to accept and assist the progressively savage operations of "race purification." As Minister of Economics FUNK accelerated the pace of rearmament, and as Reichsbank President banked for the SS the gold teeth fillings of concentration camp victims—probably the most ghoulish collateral in banking history. It was SCHACHT, the façade of starched respectability, who in the early days provided the window-dressing, the bait for the hesitant, and whose wizardry later made it possible for Hitler to finance the colossal rearmament program, and to do it secretly.

DÖNITZ, Hitler's legatee of defeat, promoted the success of the Nazi aggressions by instructing his pack of submarine killers to conduct warfare at sea with the illegal ferocity of the jungle. RAEDER, the political admiral, stealthily built up the German navy in defiance of the Versailles Treaty, and then put it to use in a series of aggressions which he had taken a large part in planning. VON SCHIRACH, poisoner of a generation, initiated the German youth in Nazi doctrine, trained them in legions for service in the SS and Wehrmacht, and delievered them up to the Party as fanatic, unquestioning executors of its will.

SAUCKEL, the greatest and cruelest slaver since the Pharaohs of Egypt, produced desperately needed manpower by driving foreign peoples into the land of bondage on a scale unknown even in the ancient days of tyranny in the kingdom of the Nile.

JODL, betrayer of the traditions of his profession, led the Wehrmacht in violating its own code of military honor in order to carry out the barbarous aims of Nazi policy. VON PAPEN, pious agent of an infidel regime, held the stirrup while Hitler vaulted into the saddle, lubricated the Austrian annexation, and devoted his diplomatic cunning to the service of Nazi objectives abroad.

SEYSS-INQUART, spearhead of the Austrian fifth column, took over the government of his own country only to make a present of it to Hitler, and then, moving north, brought terror and oppression to the Netherlands and pillaged its economy for the benefit of the German juggernaut. VON NEURATH, the old-school diplomat, who cast the pearls of his experience before Nazis, guided Nazi diplomacy in the early years, soothed the fears of prospective victims, and as Reich Protector of Bohemia and Moravia, strengthened the German position for the coming attack on Poland. SPEER, as Minister of Armaments and War Production, joined in planning and executing the program to dragoon prisoners of war and foreign workers into German war industries, which waxed in output while the laborers waned in starvation. FRITZSCHE, radio propaganda chief, by manipulation of the truth goaded German public opinion into frenzied support of the regime and anesthetized the independent judgment of the population so that they did without question their masters' bidding. And BORMANN, who has not accepted our invitation to this reunion, sat at the throttle of the vast and powerful engine of the Party, guiding it in the ruthless execution of Nazi policies, from the scourging of the Christian church to the lynching of captive Allied airmen.

The activities of all these defendants, despite their varied backgrounds and talents, were joined with the efforts of other conspirators not now in the dock, who played still other essential roles. They blend together into one consistent and militant pattern animated by a common objective to reshape the map of Europe by force of arms. Some of these defendants were ardent members of the Nazi movement from its birth. Others, less fanatical, joined the common enterprise later, after successes had made participation attractive by the promise of rewards. This group of latter-day converts remedied a crucial defect in the ranks of the original true believers, for as Dr. Seimers has pointed out in his summation:

> There were no specialists among the National Socialists for the particular tasks. Most of the National Socialist collaborators did not previously follow a trade requiring technical education.[118]

It was the fatal weakness of the early Nazi band that it lacked technical competence. It could not from among its own ranks make up a government capable of carrying out all the projects necessary to realize its aims. Therein lies the special crime and betrayal of men like Schacht and von Neurath, Speer and von Papen, Raeder and Dönitz, Keitel and Jodl. It is doubtful whether the Nazi master plan could have succeeded without their specialized intelligence which they so willingly put at its command.[119] They did so with knowledge of its announced aims and methods, and continued their services after practice had confirmed the direction in which they were tending. Their superiority to the average run of Nazi mediocrity is not their excuse. It is their condemnation.

The dominant fact which stands out from all the thousands of pages of the record of this trial is that the central crime of the whole group of Nazi crimes—the attack on the peace of the world—was clearly and deliberately planned. The beginning of these wars of aggression was not an unprepared and spontaneous springing to arms by a population excited by some current indignation. A week before the invasion of Poland Hitler told his military commanders:

> I shall give a propagandist cause for starting war——never mind whether it be plausible or not. The victor shall not be asked later on whether we told the truth or not. In starting and making a war, not the right is what matters, but victory.[120]

The propagandist incident was duly provided by dressing concentration camp inmates in Polish uniforms, in order to create the appearance of a Polish attack on a German frontier radio station.[121] The plan to occupy Belgium, Holland, and Luxembourg first appeared as early as August 1938 in connection with the plan for attack on Czechoslovakia.[122] The intention to attack became a program in May 1939, when Hitler told his commanders that:

> The Dutch and Belgian air bases must be occupied by armed forces. Declarations of neutrality must be ignored.[123]

Thus, the follow-up wars were planned before the first was launched. These were the most carefully plotted wars in all history. Scarcely a step in their terrifying succession and progress failed to move according to the master blueprint or the subsidiary schedules and timetables until long after the crimes of aggression were consummated.

Nor were the war crimes and the crimes against humanity unplanned, isolated, or spontaneous offenses. Aside from our undeniable evidence of their plotting, it is sufficient to ask whether six million people could be separated from the population of several nations on the basis of their blood and birth, could be destroyed and their bodies disposed of, except that the operation fitted into the general scheme of government. Could the enslavement of five millions of laborers, their impressment into service, their transportation to Germany, their allocation to work where they would be most useful, their maintenance—if slow starvation can be called maintenance—and their guarding have been accomplished if it did not fit into the common plan? Could hundreds of concentration camps located throughout Germany, built to accommodate hundreds of thousands of victims, and each requiring labor and materials for construction, manpower to operate and supervise, and close gearing into the economy—could such efforts have been expended under German autocracy if they had not suited the plan? Has the Teutonic passion for organization become famous for its toleration of nonconforming activity? Each part of the plan fitted into every other. The slave-labor program meshed with the needs of industry and agriculture, and these in turn synchronized with the military machine. The elaborate propaganda apparatus geared with the program to dominate the people and incite them to a war their sons would have to fight. The armament industries were fed by the concentration camps. The concentration camps were fed by the Gestapo. The Gestapo was fed by the spy system of the Nazi Party. Nothing was permitted under the Nazi iron rule that was not in accordance with the program. Everything of consequence that took place in this regimented society was but a manifestation of a premeditated and unfolding purpose to secure the Nazi state a place in the sun by casting all others into darkness.

COMMON DEFENSES AGAINST THE CHARGE OF COMMON RESPONSIBILITY

The defendants meet this overwhelming case, some by admitting a limited responsibility,[124] some by putting the blame on others,[125] and some by taking the position, in effect, that while there have been enormous crimes there are no criminals. Time will not permit me to examine each individual and peculiar defense, but there are certain lines of defense common to so many cases that they deserve some consideration.

Counsel for many of the defendants seek to dismiss the conspiracy or common-planning charge on the ground that the pattern of the Nazi plan does not fit the concept of conspiracy applicable in German law to the plotting of a highway robbery or a burglary.[126] Their concept of conspiracy is in the terms of a stealthy meeting in the dead of night, in a secluded hideout, in which a group of felons plot every detail of a specific crime. The Charter forestalls resort to such parochial and narrow concepts of conspiracy taken from local law by using the additional and nontechnical term, "common plan." Omitting entirely the alternative term of "conspiracy," the Charter reads that "leaders, organizers, instigators, and accomplices participating in the formulation or execution of a common plan to commit" any of the described crimes "are responsible for all acts performed by any persons in execution of such plan."

The Charter concept of a common plan really represents the conspiracy principle in an international context. A common plan or conspiracy to seize the machinery of a state, to commit crimes against the peace of the world, to blot a race out of existence, to enslave millions, and to subjugate and loot whole nations cannot be thought of in the same terms as the plotting of petty crimes, although the same underlying principles are applicable. Little gangsters may plan which will carry a pistol and which a stiletto, who will approach a victim from the front and who from behind, and where they will waylay him. But in planning a war the

147

pistol becomes a Wehrmacht, the stiletto a Luftwaffe. Where to strike is not a choice of dark alleys, but a matter of world geography. The operation involves the manipulation of public opinion, the law of the state, the police power, industry, and finance. The baits and bluffs must be translated into a nation's foreign policy. Likewise, the degree of stealth which points to a guilty purpose in a conspiracy will depend upon its object. The clandestine preparations of a state against international society, although camouflaged to those abroad, might be quite open and notorious among its own people. But stealth is not an essential ingredient of such planning. Parts of the common plan may be proclaimed from the housetops, as anti-Semitism was, and parts of it kept undercover, as rearmament for a long time was. It is a matter of strategy how much of the preparation shall be made public, as was Göring's announcement in 1935 of the creation of an air force, and how much shall be kept covert, as in the case of the Nazis' use of shovels to teach "labor corps" the manual of arms.[127] The forms of this grand type of conspiracy are amorphous, the means are opportunistic, and neither can divert the law from getting at the substance of things.

The defendants contend, however, that there could be no conspiracy involving aggressive war because: (1) none of the Nazis wanted war;[128] (2) rearmament was only intended to provide the strength to make Germany's voice heard in the family of nations;[129] and (3) the wars were not in fact aggressive wars but were defensive against a "Bolshevik menace."[130]

When we analyze the argument that the Nazis did not want war it comes down, in substance, to this: "The record looks bad indeed—objectively—but when you consider the state of my mind —subjectively I hated war. I knew the horrors of war. I wanted peace." I am not so sure of this. I am even less willing to accept Göring's description of the General Staff as pacifist.[131] However, it will not injure our case to admit that as an abstract proposition none of these defendants liked war.[132] But they wanted things which they knew they could not get without war. They wanted their neighbors' lands and goods. Their philosophy seems to be that if the neighbors would not acquiesce, then they are the aggressors and are to blame for the war. The fact is, however, that war never became terrible to the Nazis until it came home to them, until it exposed their deceptive assurances to the German people that German cities, like the ruined one in which we meet, would be invulnerable. From then on war was terrible.

But again the defendants claim: "To be sure we were building guns. But not to shoot. They were only to give us weight in negotiating." At its best this argument amounts to a contention that the military forces were intended for blackmail, not for battle. The threat of military invasion which forced the Austrian *Anschluss*, the threats which preceded Munich, and Göring's threat to bomb the beautiful city of Prague if the President of Czechoslovakia did not consent to the Protectorate,[133] are examples of what the defendants have in mind when they talk of arming to back negotiation.

But from the very nature of German demands, the day was bound to come when some country would refuse to buy its peace, would refuse to pay Danegeld—

> For the end of that game is oppression and shame,
> And the nation that plays it is lost.

Did these defendants then intend to withdraw German demands, or was Germany to enforce them and manipulate propaganda so as to place the blame for the war on the nation so unreasonable as to resist? Events have answered that question, and documents such as Admiral Carls's memorandum, quoted earlier, leave no doubt that the events occurred as anticipated.[134]

But some of the defendants argue that the wars were not aggressive and were only intended to protect Germany against some eventual danger from the "menace of Communism," which was something of an obsession with many Nazis.

At the outset this argument of self-defense falls because it completely ignores this damning combination of facts clearly established in the record: first, the enormous and rapid German preparations for war; second, the repeatedly avowed intentions of the German leaders to attack, which I have previously cited; and third, the fact that a series of wars occurred in which German forces struck the first blows, without warning, across the borders of other nations.

149

Even if it could be shown—which it cannot be—that the Russian war was really defensive, such is demonstrably not the case with those wars which preceded it.

It may also be pointed out that even those who would have you believe that Germany was menaced by Communism also compete with each other in describing their opposition to the disastrous Russian venture.[135] Is it reasonable that they would have opposed that war if it were undertaken in good faith self-defense?

The frivolous character of the self-defense theory on the facts it is sought to compensate, as advocates often do, by resort to a theory of law. Dr. Jahrreiss, in his scholarly argument for the defense, rightly points out that no treaty provision and no principle of law denied Germany, as a sovereign nation, the right of self-defense. He follows with the assertion, for which there is authority in classic International Law, that:

> . . . every state is alone judge of whether in a given case it is waging a war of self-defense.[136]

It is not necessary to examine the validity of an abstract principle which does not apply to the facts of our case. I do not doubt that if a nation arrived at a judgment that it must resort to war in self-defense, because of conditions affording reasonable grounds for such an honest judgment, any tribunal would accord it great and perhaps conclusive weight, even if later events proved that judgment mistaken.

But the facts in this case call for no such deference to honest judgment because no such judgment was even pretended, much less honestly made.

In all the documents which disclose the planning and rationalization of these attacks, not one sentence has been or can be cited to show a good-faith fear of attack. It may be that statesmen of other nations lacked the courage forthrightly and fully to disarm. Perhaps they suspected the secret rearmament of Germany. But if they hesitated to abandon arms, they did not hesitate to neglect them. Germany well knew that her former enemies had allowed their armaments to fall into decay, so little did they contemplate another war. Germany faced a Europe that not only was unwilling to attack, but was too weak and pacifist even adequately to defend, and went to the very verge of dishonor, if not beyond, to buy its peace. The minutes we have shown you of the Nazis' secret conclaves identify no potential attacker. They bristle with the spirit of aggression and not of defense. They contemplate always territorial expansion, not the maintenance of territorial integrity.

Minister of War von Blomberg, in his 1937 directive prescribing general principles for the preparation for war of the armed forces, has given the lie to these feeble claims of self-defense. He stated at that time:

> The general political situation justifies the supposition that Germany need not consider an attack on any side. Grounds for this are, in addition to the lack of desire for war in almost all nations, particularly the Western Powers, the deficiencies in the preparedness for war in a number of states and of Russia in particular.

Nevertheless, he recommended

> . . . a continuous preparedness for war in order to (a) counterattack at any time, and (b) to enable the military exploitation of politically favorable opportunities should they occur.[137]

If these defendants may now cynically plead self-defense, although no good-faith need of self-defense was asserted or contemplated by any responsible leader at the time, it reduces nonaggression treaties to a legal absurdity. They become only additional instruments of deception in the hands of the aggressor, and traps for well-meaning nations. If there be in nonaggression pacts an implied condition that each nation may make a *bona fide* judgment as to the necessity for self-defense against imminent, threatened attack, they certainly cannot be invoked to shelter those who never made any such judgment at all.

In opening this case I ventured to predict that there would be no serious denial that the crimes charged were committed, and that the issue would concern the responsibility of particular defendants. The defendants have fulfilled that prophecy. Generally, they do not deny that these things happened, but it is contended that they "just happened," and that they were not the result of a common plan or conspiracy.

One of the chief reasons the defendants say there was no conspiracy is the argument that conspiracy was impossible with a dictator.[138] The argument runs that they all had to obey Hitler's orders, which had the force of law in the German state, and hence obedience cannot be made the basis of a criminal charge. In this way it is explained that while there have been wholesale killings, there have been no murderers.

This argument is an effort to evade Article 8 of the Charter, which provides that the order of the government or of a superior shall not free a defendant from responsibility but can only be considered in mitigation. This provision of the Charter corresponds with the justice and with the realities of the situation, as indicated in defendant Speer's description of what he considered to be the common responsibility of the leaders of the German nation:

> . . . with reference to utterly decisive matters, there is total responsibility. There must be total responsibility insofar as a person is one of the leaders, because who else could assume responsibility for the development of events, if not the immediate associates who work with and around the head of the state? [139]

And again he told the Tribunal:

> . . . it is impossible after the catastrophe to evade this total responsibility. If the war had been won, the leaders would also have assumed total responsibility.[140]

Like much of the defense counsel's abstract arguments, the contention that the absolute power of Hitler precluded a conspiracy crumbles in face of the facts of record. The *Führerprinzip* of absolutism was itself a part of the common plan, as Göring has pointed out.[141] The defendants may have become slaves of a dictator, but he was *their* dictator. To make him such was, as Göring has testified, the object of the Nazi movement from the beginning. Every Nazi took this oath:

> I pledge eternal allegiance to Adolf Hitler. I pledge unconditional obedience to him and the Führers appointed by him.[142]

Moreover, they forced everybody else in their power to take it. This oath was illegal under German law, which made it criminal to become a member of an organization in which obedience to "unknown superiors or unconditional obedience to known superiors is pledged." [143] These men destroyed free government in Germany and now plead to be excused from responsibility because they became slaves. They are in the position of the fictional boy who murdered his father and mother and then pleaded for leniency because he was an orphan.

What these men have overlooked is that Adolf Hitler's acts are their acts. It was these men among millions of others, and it was these men leading millions of others, who built up Adolf Hitler and vested in his psychopathic personality not only innumerable lesser decisions but the supreme issue of war or peace. They intoxicated him with power and adulation. They fed his hates and aroused his fears. They put a loaded gun in his eager hands. It was left to Hitler to pull the trigger, and when he did they all at that time approved. His guilt stands admitted, by some defendants reluctantly, by some vindictively. But his guilt is the guilt of the whole dock, and of every man in it.

But it is urged that these defendants could not be in agreement on a common plan or in a conspiracy because they were fighting among themselves or belonged to different factions or cliques. Of course, it is not necessary that men should agree on everything in order to agree on enough things to make them liable for a criminal conspiracy. Unquestionably there were conspiracies within the conspiracy, and intrigues and rivalries and battles for power. Schacht and Göring disagreed, but over which of them should control the economy, not over whether the economy should be regimented for war.[144] Göring claims to have departed from the plan because through Dahlerus he conducted some negotiations with men of influence in England just before the Polish war. But it is perfectly clear that this was not an effort to prevent aggression against Poland but to make that aggression successful and safe by obtaining English neutrality.[145] Rosenberg and Göring may have had some differences as to how stolen art should be distributed but they had none about how it should be stolen. Jodl and Goebbels may have disagreed about whether to denounce the Geneva Convention, but they never disagreed about violating it. And so it goes through the whole long and sordid story. Nowhere do we find an instance where any one of the defendants stood up against the rest and said: "This thing is wrong and I will not go along with it." Wherever they differed, their differences were as to method or disputes over jurisdiction, but always within the framework of the common plan.

Some of the defendants also contend that in any event there was no conspiracy to commit war crimes or crimes against humanity because cabinet members never met with the military to plan these acts. But these crimes were only the inevitable and incidental results of the plan to commit the aggression for *Lebensraum* purposes. Hitler stated, at a conference with his commanders, that:

> The main objective in Poland is the destruction of the enemy and not the reaching of a certain geographical line.[146]

Frank picked up the tune and suggested that when their usefulness was exhausted,

> . . . then, for all I care, mincemeat can be made of the Poles and Ukrainians and all the others who run around here—it does not matter what happens.[147]

Reichskommissar Koch in the Ukraine echoed the refrain:

> I will draw the very last out of this country. I did not come to spread bliss. . . .[148]

This was *Lebensraum* on its seamy side. Could men of their practical intelligence expect to get neighboring lands free from the claims of their tenants without committing crimes against humanity?

The last stand of each defendant is that even if there was a conspiracy, he was not in it. It is therefore important in examining their attempts at avoidance of responsibility to know, first of all, just what it is that a conspiracy charge comprehends and punishes.

In conspiracy we do not punish one man for another man's crime. We seek to punish each for his own crime of joining a common criminal plan in which others also participated. The measure of the criminality of the plan and therefore of the guilt of each participant is, of course, the sum total of crimes committed by all in executing the plan. But the gist of the offense is participation in the formulation or execution of the plan. These are rules which every society has found necessary in order to reach men, like these defendants, who never get blood on their own hands but who lay plans that result in the shedding of blood. All over Germany today, in every zone of occupation, little men who carried out these criminal policies under orders are being convicted and punished. It would present a vast and unforgivable caricature of justice if the men who planned these policies and directed these little men should escape all penalty.[149]

These men in this dock, on the face of the record, were not strangers to this program of crime, nor was their connection with it remote or obscure. We find them in the very heart of it. The positions they held show that we have chosen defendants of self-evident responsibility. They are the very top surviving authorities in their respective fields and in the Nazi state. No one lives who, at least until the very last moments of the war, outranked Göring in position, power, and influence. No soldier stood above Keitel and Jodl, and no sailor above Raeder and Dönitz. Who can be responsible for the duplicitous diplomacy if not the Foreign Ministers, von Neurath and Ribbentrop, and the diplomatic handy man, von Papen? Who should be answerable for the oppressive administration of occupied countries if Gauleiters, Protectors, Governors, and Commissars such as Frank, Seyss-Inquart, Frick, von Schirach, von Neurath, and Rosenberg are not? Where shall we look for those who mobilized the economy for total war if we overlook Schacht, and Speer, and Funk? Who was the master of the great slaving enterprise if it was not Sauckel? Where shall we find the hand that ran the concentration camps if it is not the hand of Kaltenbrunner? And who whipped up the hates and fears of the public, and manipulated the Party organizations to incite these crimes, if not Hess, von Schirach, Fritzsche, Bormann, and the unspeakable Julius Streicher? The list of defendants is made up of men who played indispensable and reciprocal parts in this tragedy. The photographs and the films show them again and again together on important occasions. The documents show them agreed on policies and on methods, and all working aggressively for the expansion of Germany by force of arms.

Each of these men made a real contribution to the Nazi plan. Every man had a key part. Deprive the Nazi regime of the functions performed by a Schacht, a Sauckel, a von Papen, or a Göring, and you have a different regime. Look down the rows of fallen men and picture them as the photographic and documentary evidence shows them to have been in their days of power. Is there one whose work did not substantially advance the conspiracy along its bloody path towards its bloody goal? Can we assume that the great effort of these men's lives was directed towards ends they never suspected?

To escape the implications of their positions and the inference of guilt from their activities, the defendants are almost unanimous in one defense. The refrain is heard time and again: these men were without authority, without knowledge, without influence, indeed without importance. Funk summed up the general self-abasement of the dock in his plaintive lament that,

> I always, so to speak, came up to the door. But I was not permitted to enter.[150]

In the testimony of each defendant, at some point there was reached the familiar blank wall: nobody knew anything about what was going on. Time after time we have heard the chorus from the dock:

> I only heard about these things here for the first time.[151]

These men saw no evil, spoke none, and none was uttered in their presence. This claim might sound very plausible if made by one defendant. But when we put all their stories together, the impression which emerges of the Third Reich, which was to last a thousand years, is ludicrous. If we combine only the stories from the front bench, this is the ridiculous composite picture of Hitler's government that emerges. It was composed of:

> A number two man who knew nothing of the excesses of the Gestapo which he created, and never suspected the Jewish extermination program although he was the signer of over a score of decrees which instituted the persecutions of that race;
>
> A number three man who was merely an innocent middleman transmitting Hitler's orders without even reading them, like a postman or delivery boy;
>
> A Foreign Minister who knew little of foreign affairs and nothing of foreign policy;

A Field Marshal who issued orders to the armed forces but had no idea of the results they would have in practice;

A security chief who was of the impression that the policing functions of his Gestapo and SD were somewhat on the order of directing traffic;

A Party philosopher who was interested in historical research, and had no idea of the violence which his philosophy was inciting in the twentieth century;

A Governor General of Poland who reigned but did not rule;

A Gauleiter of Franconia whose occupation was to pour forth filthy writings about the Jews, but who had no idea that anybody would read them;

A Minister of the Interior who knew not even what went on in the interior of his own office, much less the interior of his own department, and nothing at all about the interior of Germany;

A Reichsbank President who was totally ignorant of what went in and out of the vaults of his bank;

And a Plenipotentiary for the War Economy who secretly marshaled the entire economy for armament, but had no idea it had anything to do with war.

This may seem like a fantastic exaggeration, but this is what you would actually be obliged to conclude if you were to acquit these defendants.

They do protest too much. They deny knowing what was common knowledge. They deny knowing plans and programs that were as public as *Mein Kampf* and the Party program. They deny even knowing the contents of documents they received and acted upon.

Nearly all the defendants take two or more conflicting positions. Let us illustrate the inconsistencies of their positions by the record of one defendant—one who, if pressed, would himself concede that he is the most intelligent, honorable, and innocent man in the dock. That is Schacht. And this is the effect of his own testimony—but let us not forget that I recite it not against him alone, but because most of its self-contradictions are found in the testimony of several defendants:

Schacht did not openly join the Nazi movement until it had won, nor openly desert it until it had lost. He admits that he never gave it public opposition, but asserts that he never gave it private loyalty. When we demand of him why he did not stop the criminal course of the regime in which he was a minister, he says he had not a bit of influence. When we ask why he remained a member of the criminal regime, he tells us that by sticking on he expected to moderate its program. Like a Brahmin among untouchables, he could not bear to mingle with the Nazis socially, but never could he afford to separate from them politically. Of all the Nazi aggressions by which he now claims to have been shocked,[152] there is not one that he did not support before the world with the weight of his name and prestige. Having armed Hitler to blackmail a continent, his answer now is to blame England and France for yielding.

Schacht always fought for his position in a regime he now affects to despise. He sometimes disagreed with his Nazi confederates about what was expedient in reaching their goal, but he never dissented from the goal itself. When he did break with them in the twilight of the regime, it was over tactics, not principles. From then on he never ceased to urge others to risk their positions and their necks to forward his plots, but never on any occasion did he hazard either of his own. He now boasts that he personally would have shot Hitler if he had had the opportunity, but the German newsreel shows that even after the fall of France, when he faced the living Hitler, he stepped out of line to grasp the hand he now claims to loath and hung upon the words of the men he now says he thought unworthy of belief. Schacht says he steadily "sabotaged" the Hitler government.[153] Yet, the most relentless secret service in the world never detected him doing the regime any harm until long after he knew the war to be lost and the Nazis doomed. Schacht, who dealt in hedges all his life, always kept himself in a position to claim that he was in either camp. The plea for him is as specious on analysis as it is persuasive on first sight. Schacht represents the most dangerous and reprehensible type of opportunism—that of the man of influential position who is ready to join a movement that he knows to be wrong because he thinks it is winning.

These defendants, unable to deny that they were the men in the very top ranks of power, and unable to deny that the crimes I have outlined actually happened, know that their own denials are incredible unless they can suggest someone who is guilty.

The defendants have been unanimous, when pressed, in shifting the blame on other men, sometimes on one and sometimes on another. But the names they have repeatedly picked are Hitler, Himmler, Heydrich, Goebbels, and Bormann. All of these are dead or missing. No matter how hard we have pressed the defendants on the stand, they have never pointed the finger at a living man as guilty. It is a temptation to ponder the wondrous workings of a fate which has left only the guilty dead and only the innocent alive. It is almost too remarkable.

The chief villain on whom blame is placed—some of the defendants vie with each other in producing appropriate epithets—is Hitler. He is the man at whom nearly every defendant has pointed an accusing finger.

I shall not dissent from this consensus, nor do I deny that all these dead or missing men shared the guilt. In crimes so reprehensible that degrees of guilt have lost their significance they may have played the most evil parts. But their guilt cannot exculpate the defendants. Hitler did not carry all responsibility to the grave with him. All the guilt is not wrapped in Himmler's shroud. It was these dead whom these living chose to be their partners in this great conspiratorial brotherhood, and the crimes that they did together they must pay for one by one.

It may well be said that Hitler's final crime was against the land that he had ruled. He was a mad Messiah who started the war without cause and prolonged it without reason. If he could not rule he cared not what happened to Germany. As Fritzsche has told us from the stand, Hitler tried to use the defeat of Germany for the self-destruction of the German people.[154] He continued the fight when he knew it could not be won, and continuance meant only ruin. Speer, in this courtroom, has described it as follows:

> The sacrifices which were made on both sides after January 1945 were without sense. The dead of this period will be the accusers of the man responsible for the continuation of that fight, Adolf Hitler, just as much as the destroyed cities, destroyed in that last phase, who had lost tremendous cultural values and tremendous numbers of dwellings. . . . The German people remained faithful to Adolf Hitler until the end. He has betrayed them knowingly. He has tried to throw it into the abyss. . . .[155]

Hitler ordered every one else to fight to the last and then retreat into death by his own hand. But he left life as he lived it, a deceiver; he left the official report that he had died in battle. This was the man whom these defendants exalted to a Führer. It was they who conspired to get him absolute authority over all of Germany. And in the end he and the system they created for him brought the ruin of them all. As stated by Speer on cross-examination:

. . . the tremendous danger, however, contained in this totalitarian system only became abundantly clear at the moment when we were approaching the end. It was then that one could see what the meaning of the principle was, namely, that every order should be carried out without any criticism. Everything . . . you have seen in the way of orders which were carried out without any consideration, did after all turn out to be mistakes. . . . This system—let me put it like this—to the end of the system it has become clear what tremendous dangers are contained in any such system, as such, quite apart from Hitler's principle. The combination of Hitler and this system, then, brought about this tremendous catastrophe to this world.[156]

But let me for a moment turn devil's advocate. I admit that Hitler was the chief villain. But for the defendants to put all blame on him is neither manly nor true. We know that even the head of a state has the same limits to his senses and to the hours of his day as do lesser men. He must rely on others to be his eyes and ears as to most that goes on in a great empire. Other legs must run his errands; other hands must execute his plans. On whom did Hitler rely for such things more than upon these men in the dock? Who led him to believe he had an invincible air armada if not Göring? Who kept disagreeable facts from him? Did not Göring forbid Field Marshal Milch to warn Hitler that in his opinion Germany was not equal to the war upon Russia? [157] Did not Göring, according to Speer, relieve General Gallant of his air force command for speaking of the weaknesses and bungling of the air force? [158] Who led Hitler, utterly untraveled himself, to believe in the indecision and timidity of democratic peoples if not Ribbentrop, von Neurath, and von Papen? Who fed his illusion of German invincibility if not Keitel, Jodl, Raeder and Dönitz? Who kept his hatred of the Jew inflamed more than

Streicher and Rosenberg? Who would Hitler say deceived him about conditions in concentration camps if not Kaltenbrunner, even as he would deceive us? These men had access to Hitler, and often could control the information that reached him and on which he must base his policy and his orders. They were the Prætorian Guard, and while they were under Cæsar's orders, Cæsar was always in their hands.

If these dead men could take the witness stand and answer what has been said against them, we might have a less distorted picture of the parts played by these defendants. Imagine the stir that would occur in the dock if it should behold Adolf Hitler advancing to the witness box, or Himmler with an armful of dossiers, or Goebbels, or Bormann with the reports of his Party spies, or the murdered Röhm or Canaris. The ghoulish defense that the world is entitled to retribution only from the cadavers, is an argument worthy of the crimes at which it is directed.

We have presented to this Tribunal an affirmative case based on incriminating documents which are sufficient, if unexplained, to require a finding of guilt on Count One against each defendant. In the final analysis, the only question is whether the defendants' own testimony is to be credited as against the documents and other evidence of their guilt. What, then, is their testimony worth?

The fact is that the Nazi habit of economizing in the use of truth pulls the foundations out from under their own defenses. Lying has always been a highly approved Nazi technique. Hitler, in *Mein Kampf*, advocated mendacity as a policy. Von Ribbentrop admits the use of the "diplomatic lie." [159] Keitel advised that the facts of rearmament be kept secret so that they could be denied at Geneva.[160] Raeder deceived about rebuilding the German navy in violation of Versailles.[161] Göring urged Ribbentrop to tell a "legal lie" to the British Foreign Office about the *Anschluss*, and in so doing only marshaled him the way he was going.[162] Göring gave his word of honor to the Czechs and proceeded to break it.[163] Even Speer proposed to deceive the French into revealing the specially trained among their prisoners.[164]

Nor is the lie direct the only means of falsehood. They all speak with a Nazi doubletalk with which to deceive the unwary. In the Nazi dictionary of sardonic euphemisms "final solution" of the Jewish problem was a phrase which meant extermination;

"special treatment" of prisoners of war meant killing; "protective custody" meant concentration camp; "duty labor" meant slave labor; and an order to "take a firm attitude" or "take positive measures" meant to act with unrestrained savagery. Before we accept their word at what seems to be its face, we must always look for hidden meanings. Göring assured us, on his oath, that the Reich Defense Council never met "as such." [165] When we produced the stenographic minutes of a meeting at which he presided and did most of the talking, he reminded us of the "as such" and explained this was not a meeting of the Council "as such" because other persons were present.[166] Göring denies "threatening" Czechoslovakia—he only told President Hácha that he would "hate to bomb the beautiful city of Prague." [167]

Besides outright false statements and doubletalk, there are also other circumventions of truth in the nature of fantastic explanations and absurd professions. Streicher has solemnly maintained that his only thought with respect to the Jews was to resettle them on the island of Madagascar.[168] His reason for destroying synagogues, he blandly said, was only because they were architecturally offensive.[169] Rosenberg was stated by his counsel to have always had in mind a "chivalrous solution" to the Jewish problem.[170] When it was necessary to remove Schuschnigg after the *Anschluss*, Ribbentrop would have had us believe that the Austrian Chancellor was resting at a "villa." It was left to cross-examination to reveal that the "villa" was Buchenwald Concentration Camp.[171] The record is full of other examples of dissimulations and evasions. Even Schacht showed that he, too, had adopted the Nazi attitude that truth is any story which succeeds. Confronted on cross-examination with a long record of broken vows and false words, he declared in justification:

> I think you can score many more successes when you want to lead someone if you don't tell them the truth than if you tell them the truth.[172]

This was the philosophy of the National Socialists. When for years they have deceived the world, and masked falsehood with plausibilities, can anyone be surprised that they continue the habits of a lifetime in this dock? Credibility is one of the main issues of this trial. Only those who have failed to learn the bitter lessons of the last decade can doubt that men who have always played on the unsuspecting credulity of generous opponents would not hesitate to do the same now.

It is against such a background that these defendants now ask this Tribunal to say that they are not guilty of planning, executing, or conspiring to commit this long list of crimes and wrongs. They stand before the record of this trial as blood-stained Gloucester stood by the body of his slain King. He begged of the widow, as they beg of you: "Say I slew them not." And the Queen replied, "Then say they were not slain. But dead they are. . . ." If you were to say of these men that they are not guilty, it would be as true to say there has been no war, there are no slain, there has been no crime.

NOTES ON CLOSING ADDRESS

[1] English transcript, p. 5844.

[2] Göring, *Reconstruction of a Nation*, 1934 (2344–PS, USA–233, Tr. p. 1399).

[3] "Prime Minister Göring's Press Conference," published in *Völkischer Boebachter*, Berlin edition, July 23–24, 1933, p. 1 (2494–PS, USA–F, Tr. p. 255). Göring has admitted excesses in connection with the seizure of power (Tr. p. 5838).

[4] Law about changing rules of Criminal Law and Criminal Procedure of April 24, 1934, 1934 *Reichsgesetzblatt*, Part I, p. 34 (2548–PS, USA–F, Tr. p. 255; Tr. p. 6051).

[5] Decree of the Reich President for protection against treacherous attacks on the government of the Nationalist movement, March 21, 1933. 1933 *Reichsgesetzblatt*, Part I, p. 135 (1652–PS, USA–F, Tr. p. 255).

[6] Decree of the Reich President for the Protection of the People and State, February 28, 1933, 1933 *Reichsgesetzblatt*, Part I, p. 83 (1390–PS, USA–B, Tr. p. 255): "Sections 114, 115, 117, 118, 123, 124, and 153 of the Constitution of the German Reich are suspended until further notice. Thus, restrictions on personal liberty, on the right of free expression of opinion, including freedom of the press, on the right of assembly and the right of association, and violations of the privacy of postal, telegraphic, and telephonic communications, and warrants for house-searches, orders for confiscations as well as restrictions on property, are also permissible beyond the legal limits

otherwise prescribed. . . . Whoever provokes or incites to an act contrary to public welfare is to be punished with a penitentiary sentence, under mitigating circumstances, with imprisonment of not less than three months."

[7] Law to change the Penal Code of June 28, 1935, 1935 *Reichsgesetzblatt*, Part I, p. 839 (1962–PS, USA–F, Tr. p. 255): "Any person who commits an act which the law declares to be punishable or which is deserving of penalty according to the fundamental conceptions of the penal law and sound popular feeling, shall be punished. If there is no penal law directly covering an act it shall be punished under that law which most closely fits, in regards to fundamental conception."

[8] Extract from "Germany's Road to Freedom," as published in *Documents of German Politics*, Vol. 3 (2549–PS, USA–F, Tr. p. 255): "National Socialism substitutes for the conception of formal wrong the idea of factual wrong, it considers every attack against the welfare of the people's community, every violation of the requirements of the life of a nation as a wrong. Therefore wrong may be committed in the future in Germany even in cases when no law threatens it with punishment. Even without the threat of punishment every violation of the goals of life which the community sets up for itself is a wrong."

[9] Affidavit of Dr. Hans Anschuetz, November 17, 1945 (2967–PS, USA–756, Tr. p. 255). Ten years of Security Police and SD (1680–PS, USA–477, Tr. p. 1892).

[10] Transcript p. 6073. This bureau was camouflaged under the name of "Research Office of the Airforce" (Tr. p. 5880).

[11] Decree of the Reich President for the Protection of the People and State, February 28, 1933, 1933 *Reichsgesetzblatt*, Part I, p. 83 (1390–PS, USA–F, Tr. p. 255). *Supra*, Note 5.

[12] *Organizationbuch der NSDAP*, 1943 edition, pp. 99–104 (1893–PS, USA–323, Tr. p. 1578).

[13] "Meaning and Tasks of the Secret State Police," published in *The Archives*, January 1936, Vol. 23-4, p. 1342 (1956–PS, USA–F, Tr. p. 255).

[14] Original Protective Custody Order served on Dr. R. Kempner, March 15, 1935 (2499–PS, USA–232, Tr. p. 1399). Extract from article "Legislation and Judiciary in Third Reich" from *Journal of the Academy for German Law*, 1936, pp. 141-2 (2533–PS, USA–F, Tr. p. 255).

[15] Law on the Secret State Police of February 10, 1936, Prussian *Gesetzemmhung*, p. 21. "Orders in matters of the Secret State Police are not subject to review of the administrative courts" (2107–PS, Tr.

p. 1904). Summary of decisions of the Supreme Administrative Court, 1935 *Reichsverwaltungsblatt*, Vol. 56, No. 29, pp. 577-8, July 20, 1935 (2347–PS, Tr. p. 1904).

[16] Affidavit of Dr. Hans Anschuetz, November 17, 1945 (2967–PS, USA–756, Tr. p. 255).

[17] Letter from Gürtner to Mutschmann, January 18, 1935, concerning charges against members of camp personnel of Protective Custody Camp Hohnstein (783–PS, USA–731, Tr. p. 255). Letters from Minister of Justice to Hess and SA Chief of Staff, June 5, 1935, concerning penal proceedings against merchant and SA Leader and 22 companions because of inflicting bodily injury on duty (784–PS, USA–732, Tr. p. 255). Memorandum of Gürtner concerning legal proceedings against the camp personnel of Concentration Camp Hohnstein (785–PS, USA–733, Tr. p. 255). Minister of Justice memorandum, November 29, 1935, concerning pardon of those sentenced in connection with mistreatment in Hohnstein Concentration Camp (786–PS, USA–734, Tr. p. 255).

[18] Affidavit of Dr. Hans Anschütz, November 17, 1945 (2967–PS, USA–756, Tr. p. 255).

[19] Affidavit of Dr. Hans Anschütz, November 17, 1945 (2967–PS, USA–756, Tr. p. 255). Law amending regulations of criminal law and criminal procedure, April 24, 1934, 1934 *Reichsgesetzblatt*, Part I, p. 341 (2014–PS, USA–C, Tr. p. 255). Law on People's Court and on 25th Amendment to Salary Law of April 18, 1936, 1936 *Reichsgesetzblatt*, Part I, p. 169 (2342–PS, USA–C, Tr. p. 255).

[20] *The Nazi Plan*, excerpt of script of a motion picture composed of captured German film (3054–PS, USA–167, Tr. p. 1264).

[21] Decree of the Government concerning formation of Special Courts, March 21, 1933, 1933 *Reichsgesetzblatt*, Part I, pp. 136–7 (2076–PS, USA–C, Tr. p. 255). Decree concerning the extension of the Jurisdiction of Special Courts, November 20, 1938, 1938 *Reichsgesetzblatt*, Part I, p. 1632 (2056–PS, USA–C, Tr. p. 255). Affidavit of Dr. Hans Anschütz, November 17, 1945 (2967–PS, USA–756, Tr. p. 255).

[22] Extract from *German Justice*, a legal periodical, 10th year, Edition A, No. 42, October 16, 1942. "The judge is therefore not the supervisor of, but the direct assistant in the Administration of the State. He is responsible to the leadership of the State (*Staatsführung*) within his sphere of duty for the conservation of the national community. By protecting the national values (*Völkische Werte*) and eliminating [dangerous elements from the community of the people] he is, in this respect akin to the political leader, the pro-

mulgator of national self preservation (*Völkische Selbsterhaltung*). This point of view must be decisive for the judge. The judge taking it for his guiding principle will find many a decision which seemed very difficult to be solved at first, facilitated" (2482–PS, USA–C, Tr. p. 255). Extract from pamphlet, *Judges Letters,* concerning judgment of Lower Court, April 24, 1942, on concealment of Jewish identification (D–229, USA–C, Tr. p. 255).

23 Lecture of Major General Thomas delivered May 24, 1939, at the Foreign Office (EC–28, USA–760, Tr. pp. 275, 5124).

24 The treaties and assurances applicable to each are specified in Appendix C of the Indictment and remain uncontradicted.

25 English transcript p. 5980. "The Hague Convention was for land warfare. When I scanned it over on the eve of the Polish campaign, I was reading the Articles and I was sorry that I had not studied them much sooner. If I had done so I would have told the Führer that with these rules as they had been put down, paragraph by paragraph, a modern war could not be waged, but that in a modern war, with its technical improvements, the stipulations of 1906 and 1907 would have to be changed in order to have a new type of warfare."

26 English transcript p. 6016.

27 Memorandum of September 15, 1941, from Canaris to Keitel concerning an OKW Order regulating the treatment of Soviet prisoners of war (EC–338, USSR–366, Tr. p. 4441). "The Geneva Convention for the treatment of prisoners of war is not binding in the relationship between Germany and the U.S.S.R., therefore only the principles of general international law on the treatment of prisoners of war apply. Since the eighteenth century these have gradually been established along the lines that war captivity is neither revenge nor punishment, but solely protective custody (*Sicherheitsschaft*) the only purpose of which is to prevent the prisoners of war from a further participation in the war. This principle was developed in accordance with the view held by all armies that it is contrary to military tradition to kill or injure helpless people; this is also in the interest of all belligerents in order to prevent mistreatment of their own soldiers in case of capture. . . . The instructions are very general. But if one considers their basic principles the expressly approved measures will result in arbitrary mistreatments and killings, the formal prohibition of arbitrary action notwithstanding."

28 Hitler Commando Order, October 18, 1942 (498–PS, USA–501, Tr. pp. 1944, 2173). Night and Fog Decrees, December 7 and 12, 1942 (L–90, USA–503, Tr. p. 1945). Minister of Labor Order on employment of French prisoners of war in armament industry, August

1941 (3005–PS, USA–213, Tr. p. 3010). Himmler Order to protect lynchers of Allied fliers, August 10, 1943 (R–110, USA–333, Tr. p. 1624).

[29] Decree appointing Sauckel General Plenipotentiary for Manpower, March 21, 1942, and decree of Göring conferring certain powers on Sauckel, March 27, 1942, 1942 *Reichsgesetzblatt*, Part I, pp. 179-80 (1666–PS, USA–208, pp. 1337, 4063).

[30] Speer's conference minutes of Central Planning Board, 1942–4, concerning labor supply. "Our best new engine is made 88% by Russian prisoners of war and the other 12% by German men and women. . . . The list of the shirkers should be entrusted to Himmler's trustworthy hands who will make them work all right" (Milch, p. 26) (R–124, USA–179, Tr. pp. 1313, 1320).

[31] Top secret memorandum signed by Brautigam, October 25, 1942, concerning conditions in Russia (294–PS, USA–185, Tr. p. 1293).

[32] Speer's conference minutes of Central Planning Board, 1942–4, concerning labor supply (R–124, p. 22, USA–179, Tr. pp. 1286, 1293, 1309, 2989). By an official directive, "Estates of those who refuse to work are to be burned, their relatives are to be arrested as hostages and to be brought to forced labor camps," and the burning of homes in connection with labor conscription was therefore not considered culpable. Letter from Rosenberg Ministry, November 12, 1943, concerning burning of houses in Mueller's district (290–PS, USA–189, Tr. p. 1304). The burning-down of houses was a method used to force citizens in occupied territories into Reich labor. Letter from Rabb to Reichsminister for Occupied Eastern Territories, June 7, 1944, concerning burning of houses in Wassilkow district (254–PS, USA–188, Tr. p. 1300). Forced-labor agents caught persons attending churches and theaters and transported them to the Reich. Lammers report to Himmler, April 12, 1943, concerning the situation in the Government General (2220–PS, USA–175, Tr. p. 1275).

[33] Report to Reich Ministry for Occupied Eastern Territories, October 7, 1942, concerning treatment of Ukrainian Specialists (054–PS, USA–198, Tr. p. 1314). Interdepartmental report of Ministry for Occupied Eastern Territories, September 30, 1942, concerning status of eastern laborers. "In this train women gave birth to babies who were thrown out of the windows during the journey, people having tuberculosis and venereal diseases rode in the same car, dying people lay in freight cars without straw, and one of the dead was thrown on the railroad embankment. The same must have occurred in other returning transports" (084–PS, USA–199, Tr. p. 1317).

[34] Sauckel's Labor Mobilization Program, April 20, 1942. "Apart

from the prisoners of war still in the occupied territories, we must, therefore, requisition skilled or unskilled male and female labor from the Soviet territory from the age of 15 up for the labor mobilization" p. 7 (016–PS, USA–168, Tr. p. 1319).

[35] Affidavit of Edward L. Deuss, November 1, 1945, concerning approximate number of foreign workers for German War Effort in Old Reich (2520–PS, USA–197, Tr. p. 1312).

[36] Memorandum to Mr. Hupe, March 14, 1942, concerning employment of Russians (D–316, USA–201, Tr. p. 1320).

[37] Affidavit of Dr. Wilhelm Jaeger, October 15, 1945. "Conditions in all of those camps were extremely bad. The camps were greatly overcrowded. In some camps there were twice as many people in a barrack as health conditions permitted. . . . Camp Humboldstrasse has been inhabitated by Italian prisoners of war. After it had been destroyed by an air raid, the Italians were removed and 600 Jewish females from Buchenwald Concentration Camp were brought in to work at the Krupp factories. Upon my first visit at Camp Humboldstrasse, I found these females suffering from open festering wounds and other diseases. I was the first doctor they had seen for at least a fortnight. There was no doctor in attendance at the camp. There were no medical supplies in the camp. They had no shoes and went about in their bare feet. The sole clothing of each consisted of a sack with holes for their arms and head. Their hair was shorn. The camp was surrounded by barbed wire and closely guarded by SS guards" pp. 1, 5 (D–288, USA–202, Tr. p. 1322).

[38] Secret Order of Reichsführer SS, February 20, 1942, concerning commitment of manpower from the east. "In severe case, that is in such cases where the measures at the disposal of the leader of the guard do not suffice, the state police office has to act with its means. Accordingly, they will be treated, as a rule, only with strict measures, that is with transfer to a concentration camp or with special treatment. . . . Special treatment is hanging" (3040–PS, USA–207, Tr. p. 1336).

[39] Order signed Christiansen, March 19, 1943, to all group leaders of Security Service, and record of telephone conversations signed by Stapj, March 11, 1943 (3012–PS, USA–190, Tr. pp. 1304, 12200). Letter of Terboven to Göring, dated May 1, 1942 (R. 134, RD–293, Tr. p. 6235). Göring has admitted the excesses in occupied territories: "I do not in any way wish to dispute that things took place which may be debated as far as international law is concerned, and other things occurred which under every circumstance may be considered and must be considered as excesses" (Tr. p. 5932).

CLOSING ADDRESS

[40] Excerpts from Frank's Diary (USSR–223) (English translation p. 43).

[41] Stenographic report on conference between Göring and Reich Commissioners for Occupied Territories, August 8, 1942 (USSR–170, Tr. p. 5720; EC–317, Tr. pp. 5903, 5904).

[42] Report to Führer regarding confiscated art treasures, March 20, 1941 (014–PS, USA–784, Tr. p. 6213). Field Marshal Kesselring, Göring's subordinate, testified that his method of punishing the small-scale looting of common soldiers under his command was by shooting on the spot (Tr. p. 5775).

[43] Hague Convention IV, Articles 43, 46, 47, 50, 52.

[44] Affidavit of Dr. Rudolf Kastner, former President of the Hungarian Zionist Organization, September 13, 1945 (2605 PS, USA 242, Tr. pp. 1408, 1409).

[45] Affidavit of Dr. Wilhelm Hoettl, November 5, 1945 (2738–PS, Tr. p. 1502). Affidavits of Hermann Graebe. "Moennikes and I went direct to the pits. Nobody bothered us. Now I heard rifle shots in quick succession, from behind one of the earth mounds. The people who had got off the trucks—men, women, and children of all ages—had to undress upon the orders of an SS-man, who carried a riding or dog whip. They had to put down their clothes in fixed places, sorted according to shoes, top clothing. I saw a heap of shoes of about 800 to 1,000 pairs, great piles of under-linen and clothing. Without screaming or weeping these people undressed, stood around in family groups, kissed each other, said farewells, and waited for a sign from another SS-man, who stood near the pit, also with a whip in his hand. During the 15 minutes that I stood near the pit I heard no complaint or plea for mercy. I watched a family of about 8 persons, a man and woman, both about 50 with their children of about 1, 8, and 10, and two grown-up daughters of about 20 to 24. An old woman with snow-white hair was holding the one-year-old child in her arms and singing to it, and tickling it. The child was cooing with delight. The couple were looking on with tears in their eyes. The father was holding the hand of a boy about 10 years old and speaking to him softly; the boy was fighting his tears. The father pointed toward the sky, stroked his head, and seemed to explain something to him. At that moment the SS-man at the pit shouted something to his comrade. The latter counted off about 20 persons and instructed them to go behind the earth mound. Among them was the family which I have mentioned. I well remember a girl, slim and with black hair, who, as she passed close to me, pointed to herself and said, "23." I walked around the mound, and found myself confronted by a tremendous grave.

People were closely wedged together and lying on top of each other so that only their heads were visible. Nearly all had blood running over their shoulders from their heads. Some of the people shot were still moving. Some were lifting their arms and turning their heads to show that they were still alive. The pit was already two-thirds full. I estimated that it already contained about 1000 people. I looked for the man who did the shooting. He was an SS-man, who sat at the edge of the narrow end of the pit, his feet dangling into the pit. He had a Tommy gun on his knees and was smoking a cigarette. The people, completely naked, went down some steps which were cut in the clay wall of the pit and clambered over the heads of the people lying there, to the place to which the SS-man directed them. They lay down in front of the dead or injured people; some caressed those who were still alive and spoke to them in a low voice. Then I heard a series of shots. I looked into the pit and saw that the bodies were twitching or the heads lying already motionless on top of the bodies that lay before them. Blood was running from their necks. I was surprised that I was not ordered away, but I saw that there were two or three postmen in uniform nearby. The next batch was approaching already. They went down into the pit, lined themselves up against the previous victims and were shot. When I walked back, round the mound I noticed another truckload of people which had just arrived. This time it included sick and infirm persons. An old, very thin woman with terribly thin legs was undressed by others who were already naked, while two people held her up. The woman appeared to be paralyzed. The naked people carried the woman around the mound. I left with Moennikes and drove in my car back to Dubno" (2992–PS, pp. 2, 3; USA–494, Tr. p. 1922).

[46] SD Inspector Bierkamp's letter, December 12, 1941, to RSHA, enclosing copy of secret decree signed by Bormann, entitled, "Relationship of National Socialism and Christianity" (D–75, USA–348, Tr. p. 1637).

[47] Extracts from *The Myth of the 20th Century,* by Alfred Rosenberg, 1941. "A German religious movement which would like to develop into a folk-church will have to declare that the idea of neighborly love is unconditionally to be subordinated to the idea of national honor, that no act of a German church may be approved which does not primarily serve the safeguarding of the folkdom," p. 608 (2349–PS, USA–352, Tr. p. 1642).

[48] Documents on RSHA meeting concerning the study and treatment of church positions (1815–PS, USA–510, Tr. p. 1956).

[49] Secret letter, April 21, 1942, from SS to all concentration camp

commanders, concerning treatment of priests (1164–PS, USA–736, Tr. p. 255). Report from the Bavarian Political Police to the Gestapo, Berlin, August 24, 1934, concerning National mourning on occasion of death of von Hindenburg (1521–PS, USA–740, Tr. p. 255). Letter from Kerrl to Minister of State, July 23, 1938, with enclosures dealing with persecution of Bishop Sproll (849–PS, USA–354, Tr. p. 1644). Gestapo telegram from Berlin to Nürnberg, July 24, 1938, dealing with demonstrations against Bishop Sproll in Rottenburg (848–PS, USA–353, Tr. p. 1642). Göring has admitted the policy of sending clergymen to concentration camps (Tr. p. 5853).

⁵⁰ Gestapo order, January 20, 1938, dissolving and confiscating property of Catholic Youth Women's Organizations in Bavaria (1481–PS, USA–737, Tr. p. 255). (See also Tr. p. 584.)

⁵¹ Order of Frick, November 6, 1934, addressed *inter alios* to Prussian Gestapo, prohibiting publication of Protestant Church announcements (1498–PS, USA–739, Tr. p. 255).

⁵² Bormann's letter to Rosenberg, enclosing copy of letter, January 24, 1939, to Minister of Education, requesting restriction or elimination of theological faculties (116–PS, USA–685, Tr. p. 2792). Bormann's letter to Rosenberg, April 17, 1939, enclosing copy of Minister of Education letter, April 6, 1939, on elimination of theological faculties in various universities (122–PS, USA–362, Tr. p. 1658).

⁵³ Secret letter, July 20, 1933, to provincial governments and the Prussian Gestapo from Frick, concerning Confessional Youth Organizations (1482–PS, USA–758, Tr. p. 255). Gestapo order January 20, 1938, dissolving and confiscating property of Catholic Youth Women's Organizations in Bavaria (1481–PS, USA–737, Tr. p. 255). State Police Order, May 28, 1934, at Dusseldorf, signed Schmid, concerning sanction of denominational youth and professional associations and distribution of publications in churches (R–145, USA–745, Tr. p. 255).

⁵⁴ Report by Headquarters, Third United States Army June 21, 1945, concerning Flossenburg Concentration Camp (2309–PS, USA–245, Tr. pp. 1398, 1412). Affidavit of Hans Marsalak, April 8, 1946, concerning Mauthausen Concentration Camp and dying statement of Franz Ziereis, the Commandant (3870–PS, USA–797, Tr. p. 7699). American concentration camp films (2430–PS, USA–79, Tr. p. 593). Soviet atrocity films (USSR–81, Tr. p. 4673). Affidavit of Rudolf Franz Ferdinand Hoess, April 5, 1946: ". . . I commanded Auschwitz until December 1, 1943, and estimate that at least 2,500,000 victims were executed and exterminated there by gassing and burning, and at least another half million succumbed to starvation and disease

making a total dead of about 3,000,000. This figure represents about 70% or 80% of all persons sent to Auschwitz as prisoners, the remainder having been selected and used for slave labor in the concentration camp industries. Included among the executed and burned were approximately 20,000 Russian prisoners of war (previously screened out of prisoner of war cages by the Gestapo) who were delivered at Auschwitz in Wehrmacht transports operated by regular Wehrmacht officers and men. The remainder of the total number of victims included about 100,000 German Jews, and great numbers of citizens, mostly Jewish from Holland, France, Belgium, Poland, Hungary, Czechoslovakia, Greece, or other countries. We executed about 400,000 Hungarian Jews alone at Auschwitz in the summer of 1944. . . . I visited Treblinka to find out how they carried out their extermination. The camp commandant at Treblinka told me that he had liquidated 80,000 in the course of half a year. He was principally concerned with liquidating all the Jews from the Warsaw Ghetto. He used monoxide gas, and I did not think that his methods were very efficient. So when I set up the extermination building at Auschwitz, I used Cyclon B, which was a crystallized Prussic Acid which we dropped into the death chamber from a small opening. It took from 3 to 15 minutes to kill the people in the death chamber depending upon climatic conditions. We knew when the people were dead because their screaming stopped. We usually waited about half an hour before we opened the doors and removed the bodies. After the bodies were removed our special commandos took off the rings and extracted the gold from the teeth of the corpses.

"Another improvement we made over Treblinka was that we built our gas chambers to accommodate 2,000 people at one time, whereas at Treblinka their 10 gas chambers only accommodated 200 people each. The way we selected our victims was as follows: we had two SS doctors on duty at Auschwitz to examine the incoming transports of prisoners. The prisoners would be marched by one of the doctors who would make spot decisions as they walked by. Those who were fit for work were sent into the camp. Others were sent immediately to the extermination plants. Children of tender years were invariably exterminated since by reason of their youth they were unable to work. Still another improvement we made over Treblinka was that at Treblinka the victims almost always knew that they were to be exterminated, and at Auschwitz we endeavored to fool the victims into thinking that they were to go through a delousing process. Of course, frequently they realized our true intentions and we sometimes had riots and difficulties due to that fact. Very frequently women would hide their children under their clothes but of course when we found them we would send the children to be exterminated. We were required to carry out these exterminations in secrecy but of course the foul and nauseating stench from the continuous burning of bodies permeated the entire area and all of the people living in the surrounding communities knew that exterminations were going on at Auschwitz" (3868–PS, USA–819, Tr. p. 7810).

[55] Testimony of witness Blaha (Tr. pp. 2592, 2636). Testimony of witness Hoess (Tr. pp. 7785, 7820).

[56] Testimony of the defendant Funk. ". . . And when these measures of terror and violence against Jews were put up to me, I suffered a nervous breakdown because at the moment it came to my mind with all clearness that from here on the catastrophe took its course all the way up to the terrible and atrocious things about which we have heard here and about which I knew only in part from the time of my captivity. I felt ashamed and the feeling of guilt at that moment and I do feel the same way today, but too late" (Tr. pp. 9042-3). Von Schirach has testified that "Hitler's racial policy was a crime" (Tr. p. 10295) and that Auschwitz "is the greatest and most devilish mass murder of history" (Tr. p. 10293).

[57] Testimony of Frank. ". . . I myself have never installed an extermination camp for Jews or demanded that they should be installed, but if Adolf Hitler personally has turned that dreadful responsibility over to these people of his, then it must be mine too" (Tr. p. 8099).

[58] English transcript p. 13116.

[59] Hitler, *Mein Kampf.* "In regard to this point I should like to make the following statement: To demand that the 1914 frontiers should be restored is a glaring political absurdity that is fraught with such consequences as to make the claim itself appear criminal. The confines of the Reich as they existed in 1914 were thoroughly illogical. . . . We National Socialists must stick firmly to the aim that we have set for our foreign policy, namely, that the German people must be assured the territorial area which is necessary for it to exist on this earth. . . . The territory on which one day our German peasants will be able to bring forth and nourish their sturdy sons will justify the blood of the sons of the peasants that has to be shed today" (GB–128, Tr. pp. 2281-2).

[60] Hitler, *Mein Kampf* (GB–128, Tr. p. 2285).

[61] Hitler, *Mein Kampf.* "The soil on which we now live was not a gift bestowed by Heaven on our forefathers. But they had to conquer it by risking their lives. So also in the future our people will not obtain

territory, and therewith the means of existence, as a favor from any other people, but will have to win it by the power of a triumphant sword" (GB–128, Tr. p. 2278).

[62] English transcript, pp. 6068-9.

[63] English transcript, p. 6071.

[64] Affidavit of Schnitzler, November 10, 1945 (EC–439, USA–618, Tr. pp. 282, 283, 2532).

[65] Letter from Krupp to Hitler, April 25, 1933, with enclosure (D–157, USA–765, Tr. pp. 299, 5124).

[66] Krupp speech, "Thoughts about the Industrial Enterpriser," January 1944. ". . . I have already often repeated orally as well as in writing, and today I also want to restate to this group that, according to the terms of the Dictate of Versailles [Diktat] Krupp had to destroy and demolish considerable quantities of machines and utensils of all kinds. It is the one great merit of the entire German war economy that it did not remain idle during those bad years, even though its activity could not be brought to light for obvious reasons. Through years of secret work, scientific and basic ground work was laid, in order to be ready again to work for the German Armed Forces at the appointed hour, without loss of time or experience" (D–317, USA–770, Tr. p. 289).

[67] "The Fifth Day of the Party Congress," from Völkischer Beobachter, Munich (Southern German) Edition, Issue 258, September 14, 1936 (2283–PS, USA–337, Tr. p. 255). The Social Life of the New Germany with Special Consideration of the German Labor Front, containing principal parts of two NSDAP orders directing seizure of unions in 1933, pp. 51-4 (392–PS, USA–326, Tr. p. 1600). Organization Book of the NSDAP, the NSBO, p. 185 (2271–PS, USA–328, Tr. p. 255). Affidavits of Josef Simon, Chairman of German Shoemakers Union in 1933 (2335–PS, USA–749, Tr. p. 255). Affidavits of Lorenz Hagan, Chairman of Local Committee, German Trade Unions, Nürnberg (2334–PS, USA–238, Tr. p. 1405). Affidavit of Mathias Lex, deputy president of the German Shoemakers Union (2928–PS, USA–239, Tr. pp. 1405, 2258). Affidavit, October 17, 1945, of Gustav Schiefer, Chairman of General German Trade Union Association, Local Committee, Munich, 1933 (2277–PS, USA–748, Tr. p. 255). Death certificate, Flossenburg Concentration Camp, concerning union leader Staimer and official letter to his wife, December 22, 1941 (2332–PS, Tr. p. 255). Death certificate, Flossenburg Concentration Camp, concerning union leader Hermann, and official letter to his wife, December 29, 1941 (2333–PS, USA–744, Tr. p. 255).

[68] National Socialist Party Correspondence, release of May 2, 1933, p. 1 (2224-PS, USA-364, Tr. pp. 1662-4). *Völkischer Beobachter* (*People's Observer*) Munich edition, May 17, 1933, Führer Edict, p. 1 (1940-PS, Tr. p. 255). *The German Labor Front, Nature, Goal, Means,* official publication of the German Labor Front, footnote on p. 11 (2275-PS, Tr. p. 255).

[69] Law concerning trustees of labor, May 19, 1933, 1933 *Reichsgesetzblatt,* Part I, p. 285 (405-PS, Tr. p. 255).

[70] Speech by Ley published in *Forge of the Sword,* with an introduction by Marshal Göring, pp. 14-7 (1939-PS, Tr. p. 255).

[71] Minutes of second session of Working Committee of the Reich Defense Council held on April 26, 1933 (EC-177, USA-390, Tr. pp. 1699, 1727).

[72] Minutes of conference of sixth session of Working Committee of Reich Defense Council, held on January 23 and 24, 1934 (EC-404, USA-764, Tr. pp. 291, 5124).

[73] Directive from Blomberg to Supreme Commanders of Army, Navy, and Air Forces, June 24, 1935; accompanied by copy of Reich Defense Law of May 21, 1935 and copy of Decision of Reich Cabinet of May 12, 1935 on the Council for defense of the Reich (2261-PS, USA-24, Tr. pp. 277, 292).

[74] Memorandum report about the Four Year Plan and preparation of the war economy, December 30, 1936 (EC-408, USA-579, Tr. pp. 279, 281, 287, 5874, 6083).

[75] Report on state of preparation for war economic mobilization as of September 30, 1934 (EC-128, USA-623, Tr. pp. 295, 2537).

[76] Law against Economic Sabotage, 1936 *Reichsgesetzblatt,* Part I, p. 999.

[77] Affidavit of Puhl, November 2, 1945 (EC-436, USA-620, Tr. pp. 255, 2535).

[78] Minutes of meeting of council of ministers on May 27, 1936 (1301-PS, p. 15, USA-123, Tr. p. 299).

[79] English transcript, p. 8342.

[80] English transcript, p. 2135.

[81] Excerpts from Diary kept by General Jodl, January 1937 to August 1939 (1780-PS, USA-72, Tr. pp. 556, 1157).

[82] Notes on a conference with Hitler in the Reich Chancellory, Berlin, November 5, 1937, signed by Hitler's Adjutant, Hossbach, and dated November 10, 1937 (386-PS, USA-25, Tr. pp. 336, 735, 2137).

[83] File of papers on *Case Green* (the plan for the attack on Czechoslovakia) kept by Schmundt, Hitler's Adjutant, April–October 1938

(388–PS, USA–26, Tr. pp. 735, 741-8, 760-5, 769-76, 793, 789-807).

84 Excerpts from Diary kept by General Jodl, January 1937 to August 1939 (1780–PS, USA–72, Tr. pp. 556, 1157).

85 File of papers on *Case Green* (the plan for the attack on Czechoslovakia) kept by Schmundt, Hitler's Adjutant, April-October 1938 (388–PS, USA–26, Tr. p. 744).

86 Documents found in official Navy files containing notes year by year, from 1927 to 1940, on reconstruction of the German Navy, and dated February 18, 1938, March 8, 1938, September 1938 (C–23, USA–49, Tr. p. 449).

87 "Germany neither intends nor wishes to interfere in the internal affairs of Austria, to annex Austria, or to unite with Austria." (Berlin, May 21, 1935, *Völkischer Beobachter*, May 22, 1935.) "Immediately after the *Anschluss*, I informed Yugoslavia that the frontier in common with that country would henceforth be regarded as unalterable by Germany and that we wished to live with her in peace and friendship." (Berlin, Oct. 6, 1939, *Völkischer Beobachter*, October 7, 1939.) "I have given binding declarations to a number of states. None of these can complain that even a trace of a demand contrary thereto has ever been made to them by Germany. None of the Scandinavian statesmen, for example, can contend that the German government or that German public opinion has ever made a demand which was incompatible with the sovereignty and integrity of their state." (Berlin, April 28, 1939, *Völkischer Beobachter*, April 29, 1939.) "We have given guarantees to the states in the west and have guaranteed to all contiguous neighbors the inviolability of their territory as far as Germany is concerned. That is not a phrase; that is our sacred will." (Berlin, September 26, 1938, *Völkischer Beobachter*, September 27, 1938.) "Without taking the past into account, Germany has concluded a nonaggression pact with Poland. This is more than a valuable contribution to European peace, and we shall adhere to it unconditionally. We only hope that it will be renewed and continued uninterruptedly and that it will deepen the friendly relations between the two countries. With the understanding and heartfelt friendship of genuine nationalists, we recognize Poland as the home of a great and nationally conscious people." (Berlin, May 21, 1935, *Völkischer Beobachter*, May 22, 1935.) "Germany has steadily given her assurance, and I solemnly repeat this assurance here, that between ourselves and France, for example, there are no grounds for quarrel that are humanly thinkable." (Berlin, January 30, 1937, *Völkischer Beobachter*, January 31, 1937.)

CLOSING ADDRESS

[88] Notes on conference between Göring, Mussolini, and Ciano, April 15, 1939 (1874–PS, USA–125, Tr. p. 929).

[89] Note for Reichsminister, August 26, 1938 (TC–76, GB–31, Tr. p. 980).

[90] Speech of Führer at a conference, November 23, 1933, to which all Supreme Commanders were ordered (789–PS, USA–23, Tr. pp. 275, 931).

[91] Minutes of conference with Göring at the Air Ministry, October 14, 1938, concerning acceleration of rearmament (1301–PS, USA–123, Tr. pp. 295, 296, 299, 300, 2555, 2556, 2558, 2559, 5126). Notes on conference with Göring in Westerland on July 26, 1939, signed Mueller, dated Berlin, July 27, 1939 (R–133, USA–124, Tr. p. 928).

[92] Minutes of conference, May 23, 1939 "Indoctrination on the Political Situation and Future Aims" (L–79, USA–27, Tr. pp. 359, 408, 930).

[93] Minutes of Second Meeting of Reich Defense Council, June 23, 1939 (3787–PS, USA–782, Tr. pp. 6167, 6406, 12875–12886).

[94] Minutes of conference, May 23, 1939, "Indoctrination on the Political Situation and Future Aims" (L–79, USA–27, Tr. pp. 359, 408, 930).

[95] Letter from Frank to Göring, January 25, 1940 (1375–PS, USA–172, Tr. p. 1273).

[96] Thierack's notes, September 18, 1942, on discussion with Himmler concerning delivery of Jews to Himmler for extermination through work (654–PS, USA–218, Tr. pp. 1350, 1950). Letter from Minister of Justice to Prosecutors, April 1, 1944, concerning Poles and Jews who are released from Penal institutions of Department of Justice (701–PS, USA–497, Tr. p. 1940).

[97] Directive of April 27, 1943 to Commanders of Concentration Camps, regarding executions of prisoners (1933–PS, USA–459, Tr. p. 1844).

[98] Copy of telegram from Mueller to Himmler, December 16, 1942, concerning recruiting Jewish labor (1472–PS, USA–279, Tr. p. 1454). Mueller's order, December 17, 1942, concerning prisoners qualified for work to be sent to concentration camps (1063–D–PS, USA–219, Tr. p. 1354).

[99] Speer's conference minutes of Central Planning Board, 1942–4, concerning labor supply, p. 36 (R–124, USA–179, Tr. pp. 1286, 1293, 1309, 2989).

[100] Report signed by Dönitz, 1944, giving support to Navy and Merchant Marine (C–195, GB–211, Tr. p. 2709).

[101] Speer's conference minutes of Central Planning Board, 1942–4, concerning labor supply (R–124, USA–179, p. 32, Tr. pp. 1286, 1293, 1309).

[102] Memorandum of September 15, 1941 from Canaris to Keitel concerning an OKW Order regulating the treatment of Soviet prisoners of war (EC–338, USSR–356, Tr. p. 4441).

[103] English transcript, p. 6016.

[104] Examples of violations of International Law and proposed counterpropaganda, issued by OKW, October 1, 1938 (C–2, USA–90, Tr. p. 2959).

[105] OKW circular entitled Direction of War as Problem of Organization, April 19, 1938 (L–211, GB–161, Tr. p. 2397).

[106] English transcript p. 5786.

[107] Report by Raeder to Hitler, October 16, 1939 (C–157, GB–224, Tr. p. 2734).

[108] Extract from *Befehlshaber der U-bootes;* Secret Standing Order No. 154 signed by Dönitz (D–642, GB–196, Tr. p. 2663). Operation Order "Atlantic" No. 56 for U-boats in Atlantic, October 7, 1943 (D–663, GB–200, Tr. p. 2666).

[109] English transcript, p. 6069.

[110] English transcript, p. 5843.

[111] English transcript, pp. 6050-2.

[112] Extracts from testimony of Göring: "As soon as we had come into power we were decided to keep that power under all circumstances . . . we could not leave this to the play of coincidence by way of elections and parliamentary majorities. . . ." (Tr. p. 5824.) "The Laender Parliaments . . . I considered entirely superfluous. . . . I could not understand why so many different authorities should exist which, with their unnecessary frictions, discussions, arguments, could only prevent constructive work. . . . A further point in the strengthening of power was the elimination of the Reichstag as a parliament. . . . In some cases we suggested to the former parties they dissolve themselves, because they had no purpose, and those who would not dissolve themselves were dissolved by us" (Tr. p. 5828). ". . . Towards the further strengthening of power, those laws were established which : . . did away with the so-called freedoms. . . ." (Tr. p. 5829.) (See also Tr. pp. 6049, 6051.) Frick accurately predicted the Nazi method of dealing with political opponents when he declared to an opposing member of the Reichstag in 1932, "Don't worry, when we are in power, we shall put all of you guys into concentration camps" (Affidavit of Gebhart H. Seger, L–83, USA–234).

[113] English transcript, p. 6064.

[114] English transcript, p. 6054.

[115] English transcript, p. 5860.

[116] Stenographic report of the meeting on The Jewish Question, under the Chairmanship of Field Marshal Göring, November 12, 1938 (1816–PS, USA–261, Tr. p. 1440).

[117] Memorandum, November 19, 1938, concerning meeting of Reich Defense Council (3575–PS, USA–781, Tr. pp. 6157, 6406). (See also Tr. p. 5846.) For similar reasons Göring preferred the destruction of Jews rather than of their property (1816–PS).

[118] English transcript, p. 15706.

[119] Other factors were not overlooked. One of the reasons for von Nourath's selection as Foreign Minister at the beginning of the Nazi regime was his excellent connections abroad (Tr. p. 6024).

[120] Hitler's speech to Commanders in Chief, August 22, 1939 (1014–PS, USA–30, Tr. p. 377).

[121] Affidavit of Alfred Helmut Naujocks, November 20, 1945 (2751–PS, USA–482, Tr. p. 1907). Likewise, Jodl noted in his diary a few weeks before the planned invasion of Norway that the Führer was still looking for an excuse for the operation (1809–PS, GB–88, Tr. pp. 1088, 2403).

[122] *Case Green* with wider implications, report of Intelligence Division, Luftwaffe General Staff, August 25, 1938 (375–PS, USA–84, Tr. p. 752).

[123] Minutes of conference, May 23, 1939, "Indoctrination on the political situation and future aims" (L–79, USA–27, Tr. pp. 359, 408, 930).

[124] Göring has accepted responsibility for the Nürnberg Laws, which he signed (Tr. p. 5871), for the Austrian *Anschluss* (Tr. p. 5895), and for the use of prisoners of war in armament industries (Tr. p. 6219). Von Schirach has admitted responsibility for the training of the Hitler Youth: "It is my guilt that I educated the German youth for a man who committed murders million-fold. I believed in that man. That is all that I can say as an explanation for my attitude. But that guilt is my own, my personal guilt. I had the responsibility for the youth. I carried the authority of command; and so I alone carry the guilt for that youth" (Tr. p. 10295). Frank has admitted: "I feel a terrible guilt within me" (Tr. p. 8092).

[125] Göring blamed persecution of the churches on Himmler and Bormann (Tr. p. 5856). Von Schirach blamed extermination of the Jews on Hitler and Himmler: "The murder was ordered by Adolf Hitler

. . . he and Himmler together committed that crime, which of all times is the darkest spot in our history. It is a crime which is shameful to every German" (Tr. p. 10293).

[126] Final argument of Dr. Stahmer, counsel for Göring (Tr. p. 12973 et seq.).

[127] *The Nazi Plan*, excerpt of script of a motion picture composed of captured German film (3054–PS, USA–167, Tr. p. 1264).

[128] Göring testified: "No, I did not want any war. . . ." (Tr. p. 6087.) Ribbentrop testified: "The Führer has—and then I have upon his orders, and I believe I may be a good witness for it myself—always tried to solve these problems in a diplomatic way" (Tr. p. 6826).

[129] Göring testified: ". . . to set aside Versailles, the state had to be strong, for a weak state was never listened to; that we knew from experience" (Tr. p. 6070).

[130] Göring testified: "I told the Führer that in spite of this principal point of view I oversaw a menace threatening from Russia; I still would ask him to rather let this menace continue to exist and, if it was at all possible, to try to direct the interests of Russia against England" (Tr. p. 5957).

[131] English transcript, p. 6048.

[132] English transcript, pp. 5894-5, 6036, 6069.

[133] English transcript, p. 5998.

[134] Other defendants admitted that the wars were aggressive. Schacht testified: "Q. Well, we found something we agree on, Doctor. You knew of the invasion of Poland? A. Yes. Q. As an unqualified act of aggression on Hitler's part? A. Absolutely. Q. And of Holland? A. Absolutely. Q. And of Denmark? A. Absolutely. Q. And of Norway? A. Absolutely. Q. And of Yugoslavia? A. Absolutely. Q. And of Russia? A. Absolutely, sir; and Norway and Belgium, which you left out" (Tr. p. 8910).

[135] Göring testified: "I urged him not at that moment or an even short time thereafter to start any war against Russia" (Tr. p. 5956.) (See also Tr. p. 6056). Keitel testified that he wrote a memorandum to Hitler opposing the attack on Russia. He said: "But I did in that memorandum most certainly refer to the fact that the Non-aggression Pact existed" (Tr. p. 7096).

[136] English transcript, p. 12929.

[137] OKW Directive for Unified Preparation for War 1937–1938, with covering letter from von Blomberg, June 24, 1937 (C–175, USA–69, Tr. p. 547). Yet it was in this period that Göring was trying out the strength of his Luftwaffe in the Spanish Civil War (Tr. p.

5871). Göring has admitted the nondefensive nature of the Luftwaffe (Tr. p. 5869).

138 Final argument of Dr. Stahmer, counsel for Göring. "Therefore, a conspiracy with a dictator at its head is a contradiction in itself. A dictator does not enter into a conspiracy with his followers, he does not make any agreement with them, he dictates" (Tr. p. 12970).

139 English transcript, p. 12155.

140 English transcript, p. 12183.

141 English transcript, pp. 5854, 6036, 6056.

142 Extracts from *Organization Book of the NSDAP*, 1943 edition (1893–PS, USA–323, Tr. p. 1578).

143 Criminal Code, 1871, Sec. 128 (never repealed).

144 Göring testified: "In the case of Schacht he was a very strong personality and whilst not wanting to overemphasize my importance and disregarding whether we were friends or not, on the basis of the two positions we had to get into difficulties and one or the other had to cede finally" (Tr. p. 6082).

145 "Q. Mr. Dahlerus, will you tell me whether I got all of your last answer to Dr. Stahmer correctly? Did you say that 'I then realized that it was on September 26, that his, [Göring's] aim, had been to split Poland and grab and occupy Poland with the consent of Great Britain'? Is that right? A. Yes, it is correct, but I should like to say it was the German Government's, including Göring's, aim" (Tr. p. 6119). The Führer informed Göring some time before the attack on Poland was launched that the task was to "eliminate British intervention" (TC–90, GB–64).

146 Hitler's speech to Commanders in Chief, August 22, 1939 (1014–PS, USA–30, Tr. p. 376).

147 Frank Diary. Tagebuch. January 1, 1944 to February 28, 1944. Entries of January 14, January 15, February 8, 1944 (2233–BB–PS, USA–295, Tr. p. 1501).

148 Note, April 11, 1943, and report of speech of Koch in Kiev on March 5, 1943, concerning treatment of civilian population in Ukraine (1130–PS, USA–169, Tr. p. 1269).

149 Frank testified: "Q. Did you ever participate in the destruction of Jews? A. I say yes, and the reason why I say yes is because, being under the impression of these five months of this trial, and particularly under the impression of the statements made by the witness Hoess, I cannot allow it before my conscience that responsibility for all this should be handed over to these small people alone. I myself have never installed an extermination camp for Jews or demanded that

they should be installed, but if Adolf Hitler personally has turned that dreadful responsibility over to these people of his, then it must be mine too. We have fought against Jewry; we have fought against it for years; and we have allowed ourselves to make utterances, and my own diary has become a witness against me in this connection—utterances which are terrible. It is my duty—my only duty—therefore, to answer your question in this connection with yes. A thousand years will pass and this guilt of Germany will still not be erased" (Tr. p. 8099).

[150] Funk explained that he did not hold "the position of minister as one would generally think of it" (Tr. p. 9014).

[151] Ribbentrop, Tr. p. 6857, 6823; Keitel, Tr. p. 7157; Funk, Tr. p. 9118; Göring, Tr. p. 6247.

[152] English transcript, p. 8910, *supra*, note 121.

[153] English transcript, pp. 8808, 8814-17, 8923-5.

[154] "The fact was that Hitler tried to use this defeat for the self-destruction of the German people, as Speer has testified and confirmed, in a most terrible way, and as I could observe in the last phase of the conflict in Berlin when, under the pretense of a false hope, fifteen-year-old, fourteen-year-old, and thirteen-year-old boys were equipped for war with hand firearms and called into battle—boys who perhaps might have been the hope for the period of reconstruction. Hitler fled into death, and he left the decree and the order to keep on fighting. He also left the official report that he had died in battle. I learned that he had committed suicide, and my last public statement, on May 2, 1945, was the publication of the fact of this suicide, for I wanted to kill a Hitler legend in the bud" (Tr. p. 12547). Dahlerus has recorded his impression of Hitler before the war as "a completely abnormal person" (Tr. p. 6125).

[155] English transcript, p. 12080.

[156] English transcript, p. 12117.

[157] Milch testified: "My offer that I would try to speak to Hitler against war once more was rejected by the Reichsmarshal as absolutely hopeless" (Tr. p. 5576).

[158] English transcript, p. 12118

[159] English transcript, p. 6881.

[160] Minutes of second session of Working Committee of the Reich Defense Council held on April 26, 1933 (EC-177, USA-390, Tr. pp. 1699, 1727).

[161] Raeder testified: "That is the circumvention of the Versailles Treaty as far as that was necessary to improve our defenses, which I

explained during the recent days here. It was a matter of honor for every man to do it" (Tr. p. 9919).

162 Göring testified: "During a conversation which I had with Foreign Minister von Ribbentrop who was in London at that time, I stressed that the ultimatum had not been put by ourselves but by Seyss-Inquart. That was absolutely true. Legally, in fact, of course I put it, but that telephone conversation was heard on the English side and I had to conduct a diplomatic conversation, and I have never heard yet that diplomats in such cases say later how it was in fact, but they always stress how it was *de jure*, and why should I be an exception there?" (Tr. p. 5801.) But the transcript of the telephone conversation between Göring and Seyss-Inquart which led to the capitulation of Austria shows Göring saying: "Now, remember the following: You go immediately together with Lt. General Muff and tell the Federal President that if the conditions which are known to you are not accepted immediately, the troops who are already stationed in and advancing to the frontier will march in tonight along the whole line, and Austria will cease to exist." Transcript of telephone calls from Air Ministry, March 11–14, 1938 (2949–PS, USA–76, Tr. p. 566).

163 German assurance to Czechoslovakia of March 11, 1938 (TC–27, GB–21, Tr. p. 962).

164 Speer's conference minutes of Central Planning Board, 1943–4, concerning labor supply (R–124, USA–179, Tr. pp. 1286, 1293, 1309, 2989).

165 English transcript, p. 5878.

166 English transcript, p. 6150.

167 English transcript, p. 5900; see also Tr. p. 5998.

168 English transcript, p. 8527.

169 English transcript, pp. 8516-19.

170 English transcript, p. 13276.

171 English transcript, p. 6857.

172 Examples of the application of this philosophy may be found in Göring's explanation of his art looting: he had intended to put his pictures in a gallery which he intended to construct for the German people—some day (Tr. p. 5934); his statement that he had always held that captured enemy airmen were to be treated as "comrades" (Tr. p. 5979); and his attempt to minimize his words advocating harsh treatment of the Jews, as the result of conversational excitement (Tr. p. 6192).

VI

EXCERPTS FROM CROSS-EXAMINATION OF DEFENDANTS

HERMANN GÖRING

Herman Göring, next to Hitler, was the dominant figure in Germany during a large part of the Nazi regime. He was designated to succeed Hitler as head of the German state and of the Nazi Party in case of Hitler's death. He was a member of the Nazi Party, a member and President of the Reichstag, Chief of the Prussian Secret State Police, Trustee of the Four Year Plan for rearmament of Germany, Reich Minister for Air, Commander in Chief of the Air Force, President of the Council of Ministers for the Defense of the Reich, Member of the Secret Cabinet Council and head of the Hermann Göring Industrial Combine.

※　※　※

Hermann Göring, defendant, appearing as a witness in his own behalf was cross-examined for the United States by Mr. Justice Jackson:

Q. You are perhaps aware that you are the only living man who can expound to us the true principles of the Nazi Party and the inner workings of its leadership?

A. I am perfectly clear on that subject.

Q. You, from the very beginning, together with those who were associated with you, intended to overthrow, and later did overthrow, the Weimar Republic?

A. That was my firm intention.

Q. And upon coming into power, you immediately abolished parliamentary government in Germany?

A. It was no longer necessary. But I should like to emphasize the fact that we were also the strongest party parliamentarily speaking; yet you are correct that the parliamentary government was disbanded.

HERMANN GÖRING ON THE WITNESS STAND FOR HIMSELF

"So far as opposition is concerned in any form, the opposition
of each individual person was not tolerated unless it was a
matter of unimportance."

"The German people were not asked. They were notified of
the fact and of the reasons for that fact." (War against Russia.)

Q. You established the leadership principle which you have described as a system under which authority exists only at the top and is passed downward and is imposed on the people below; is that correct?

A. In order to avoid any misunderstanding, I should like to explain it once more as I understand it. In previous German parliaments, the responsibility resided in the highest offices and it represented the anonymous power of the whole. In the Führer principle we arranged for the opposite of that, and the authority went from above to below and the permission was given from the lowest to the above.

Q. In other words, you did not believe in and did not permit government as we do, in which the people, through their representatives, are the possessors of power and authority?

A. That is not entirely correct. We repeatedly called on the population from time to time to express their opinion of our system, only by a different way than was previously used, and in a different way than is used in other countries. We also were of the point of view that, of course, the Government could maintain itself through the Führer principle that had some sort of confidence in its population. If it no longer had such confidence, then it had to rule with bayonets, and the Führer was always of the opinion that that was impossible in the long run.

Q. You did not permit the election by the people of those who should act with authority, but they were designated from the top, were they not?

A. The conduct of the government was entirely up to the Führer. The individual representatives were not chosen by the people, but their leaders were.

Q. Now, was this leadership principle supported and adopted by you in Germany because you believed that no people is capable of self-government, or because you believed that the German people are not—that no matter whether some of us are capable of using our own system, it should not be allowed in Germany?

A. I didn't quite understand the question, but I could perhaps answer it as follows: The Führer's principle proved to be necessary because the conditions previous to his leadership had brought Germany to the verge of ruin. I might in this case remind you that your own President Roosevelt, so far as I can recall—I don't want to quote it verbatim—said that democracy had produced men who were too weak to give their people work and bread. To correct this it would be best for the people to abolish democracy. There is much truth in that statement. Democracy ruined Germany, and accordingly, only a strong leadership could bring back order. Let it be understood that the Führer was not brought into power against the will of the people, but only by many elections during the course of time which was more and more strongly expressed.

Q. The principles of the government which you set up required, as I understand you, that there should be no opposition by political parties which might oppose the policy of the Nazi Party?

A. Let us understand this correctly. We lived long enough through that period of opposition. It was now time not to have a party of opposition, but to build up.

Q. After you came to power, you believed it necessary in order to maintain power to suppress all opposition parties?

A. We found it necessary that we permit no opposition to us.

Q. And you also held the theory that you should suppress all individual opposition lest it should develop a party of opposition?

A. So far as opposition is concerned in any form, the opposition of each individual person was not tolerated unless it was a matter of unimportance.

Q. Now, in order to make sure that you suppressed the parties and individuals also, you found it necessary to have a secret political police to detect opposition?

A. I have already stated that I knew that to be necessary just as previously the political police existed. Only, we did this to a stronger and larger degree.

Q. And upon coming into power, you also considered it immediately necessary to establish concentration camps to take care of all incorrigible opponents?

A. I have already stated that the idea of the concentration camps did not arise in such a way. One might say that there were a number of people in opposition to us who should be taken into custody. The idea arose as an immediate measure against the

Communists who were attacking us in thousands, and we could not accommodate them in prisons, so it was necessary to erect camps.

Q. But you are explaining, as a high authority in this system, to men who don't understand the system at all, and I want you to tell us what was necessary to run the kind of system you set up; and you, as one of the powers, should be able to tell us what was necessary, as you saw it.

A. I am afraid that was disorderly translated, but I can still answer you. You asked me if it was necessary to establish camps in order to eliminate opposition, is that correct?

Q. Your answer is yes, I take it?

A. Yes.

Q. You may state also, in explaining this system, what persons were entitled to public trials. You issued an order that acts of your political police would not be subject to court review or to court orders, did you not?

A. You must discriminate between two categories; those who had committed any act of treason against the new state, of course, were turned over to the courts. The cases, however, of those from whom one could expect such acts, were taken into protective custody and those were the ones who went into concentration camps. I am now speaking of the beginning. If for any cause someone was taken into custody for political reasons, this could not be reviewed by any court. Later, when people were taken into custody for no political reasons, but because they—

Q. Let's omit that. I have not asked for that. I just want you to answer my question. Your counsel will have a chance to bring out any explanation that is necessary.

You did prohibit all court review, and considered it necessary to prevent court review of the reasons for taking people into what is called "protective custody"?

A. That I answered very clearly, but I would like to make an explanation in connection with my answer.

* * *

The President: Mr. Justice Jackson, the Tribunal feels that the witness should be allowed to make whatever explanation he cares to make in answer to this question.

Mr. Justice Jackson: The Tribunal feels that you may be permitted to explain your answers.

The President: I did not mean that to apply generally to his answers. I meant it to apply to this particular answer.

The Witness: In connection with your question that these persons could not be reviewed by the court, I want to say that was an order by the Führer that those who were turned over to concentration camps were to be informed of the reasons that they were there after twenty-four hours had elapsed; and after forty-eight hours, or after a short period of time, they should have the right of attorney. But this by no means rescinded the order that a review by courts of political arrests was not permissible. I simply wanted to give these people the right to express their own opinions on what had happened to them.

* * *

Q. And protective custody meant you were taking people into custody who had not committed any crime but who you thought might possibly commit a crime?

A. Yes. People were arrested and taken into protective custody who had committed no crime, but of whom one could expect that if they remained in freedom they would do all sorts of things to damage the German state.

Q. Now, it is also a necessity in that kind of state that you have some kind of organization to carry propaganda down to the people and to get their reactions and inform the leadership of it, is it not?

A. Of course we carried on propaganda, and for that reason organized a propaganda department.

Q. You carried that on through the Leadership Corps of the Nazi Party?

A. The Leadership Corps was there to inform the people of the propaganda and our attitude.

Q. Through your system of Gauleiters and Kreisleiters, down to Blockleiters, commands and information went down from the higher authority, and information as to the people's reactions came back to the leadership, didn't it?

A. That is correct. The orders that were given for propaganda or other purposes were passed down the line as far as necessary. On the other hand, it was a matter of course that the reactions on the part of the people were again transmitted up through the various offices, in order to keep us informed of the mood of the people.

Q. And you also had to have certain organizations to carry out orders—executive organizations, organizations to fight for you, if necessary, did you not?

A. Administrative organizations were, of course, necessary. I don't understand exactly what organizations you mean. For what fights?

Q. Well, if you wanted certain people killed you have to have some organization that would kill them, didn't you? Röhm and the rest of them were not killed by Hitler's own hands nor by yours, were they?

A. Röhm—I explained that that was a matter of state necessity.

Q. But whether it was state necessity to kill somebody, you had to have somebody to do it, didn't you?

A. I also know other states where it is called secret service or something else.

Q. And the SA, the SS, and the SD—organizations of that kind —were the organizations that carried out the orders and dealt with people on a physical level, were they not?

A. The SA never received such an order to kill people. The SA in my time did not. Later on I had no influence. The only orders that were carried out without court order that were given were against a few people in the Röhm *Putsch*, and this was carried out by the police or by a state organ.

Q. What police?

A. So far as I recall, through the Gestapo. At any rate, it received the order to fight against enemies of the state.

Q. And the SS was for the same purpose, was it not?

A. At this time, in north Germany, not; what the case was in south Germany I don't know.

Q. Well, the SS carried out arrests and carried out the transportation of people to concentration camps, didn't it? You were arrested by the SS, weren't you?

A. Yes, but I said later.

Q. At what time did the SS perform this function of acting as an executor of the Nazi policy?

A. After the seizure of power the police came to be more and more in the hands of Himmler, and it can no longer be understandable to somebody outside this picture where the SS was active and where the Gestapo was active. They worked very closely, hand in hand. It is known that the SS guarded concentration camps later.

Q. And carried out other functions in the camps?

A. What functions do you refer to?

Q. All of the functions of the camps, didn't they?

A. If an SS unit was guarding a camp and an SS leader was in charge of it, then it could only be that unit that carried out all the functions necessary in the camp.

Q. Now, this system was not a secret system. This entire system was openly avowed, its merits were publicly advocated by yourself and others, and every person entering into the Nazi Party was enabled to know the kind of system of government you were going to set up, wasn't he?

A. Every member of the Party knew that we embraced the Führer principle, knew the specific measure we wanted to carry out, so far as they were stated in the program, but every member of the Party did not know what was going to happen up to the most minute details.

Q. But this system was set up openly and was well known, if not as to every one of its details? As to organization, for example, everybody knew who the Gestapo was, did they not?

A. Yes, everyone knew who the Gestapo was.

Q. And what its program was, in general, not in detail?

A. I explained that program in detail. At the beginning I described that publicly, and I also spoke publicly of the tasks of the Gestapo, and also those in foreign countries.

Q. And there was nothing secret about the establishment of a Gestapo as a political police, about the fact that people were taken into protective custody, about the fact that there were concentration camps? Nothing secret about those things, was there?

A. There was nothing secret about that at all.

Q. As a matter of fact, part of the effectiveness of a secret police and a part of the effectiveness of concentration camp penalties is that the people do know that there are such agencies, isn't it?

A. It is true that if everyone knows that if he acts against the state he will end up in a concentration camp or will be accused before a court of high treason—that is to our advantage. But the original reason why concentration camps were created was to handle enemies of the state.

Q. Now, that type of government—the government which we have just been describing—is the only type of government which you think is possible to govern Germany?

A. I should not like to say that the basic characteristic of this government—and what was most necessary about it—was the immediate organization of the Gestapo and the concentration camps in order to receive our opponents. Over and above that, we had much more important things to take care of. These were not the basic foundations of our government.

Q. But all of these things were necessary things, as I understood you?

A. Yes. These things were all necessary because of the opposition that was present.

Q. And I assume that that is the only kind of government that you think can function in Germany under present conditions?

A. Under conditions then, that was, in my opinion, the only possible form, and we also demonstrated that Germany could be raised in a short time from its miserable poverty to relative prosperity.

Q. You have related to us the manner in which you and others co-operated in concentrating all authority in the German state in the hands of the Führer, is that right?

A. I was speaking about myself and how far I was connected in this direction.

Q. Now, I want to call your atention to the fruits of this system. You, as I understand it, were informed in 1940 of an impending attack by the German Army on Soviet Russia?

A. I have already mentioned just how far I was informed of these matters.

Q. You believed the attack not only to be unnecessary but also to be unwise from the point of view of Germany itself?

A. At that time I was of the opinion that this attack should be postponed in order to take care of more important tasks.

Q. You didn't see any military necessity for an attack at that time even from the point of view of Germany?

A. I saw the effort of Russia in the direction of a mobilization, but hoped to put through measures which would be useful, and thought that time would prevent a danger toward Germany. Later on I was of the opinion that perhaps at any time this period of danger for Germany would arrive and might arrive at any later moment.

Q. I will repeat my question, which I think you have not answered: Did you at that time see any military necessity for an attack by Germany on Soviet Russia?

A. I personally believed that at that period of time, the danger had not reached its zenith; therefore, at that time, the attack might not be necessary, but I emphasize that that was my personal view.

Q. And you were the number two man at that time in all Germany?

A. It has nothing to do with my position of second importance. Two points of view were contradictory. The Führer saw one danger, and the Führer was the number one man, and if you wish to put it that way, had I wished to put another strategic measure through and if my plans had gone through, then I would have become the number one man, but since the number one man was of a different opinion and I was only the second man, his opinion naturally prevailed.

Q. I have understood from your testimony—and I think you can answer this yes or no, and I would greatly appreciate it if you would—I have understood from your testimony that you were opposed, and told the Führer that you were opposed, to an attack upon Russia at that time. Am I right or wrong?

A. That is correct.

Q. Now, you were opposed to it because you thought that it was a dangerous move for Germany to make; is that correct?

A. Yes, I was of the opinion that the moment—and I emphasize again that at that time the decisive moment—had not come and that more expedient measures should have been taken for Germany.

Q. And, again, because of the Führer system, as I understand you, you could give no warning to the German people; you could bring no pressure of any kind to bear to prevent that step; and you could not even resign to protect your own place in history.

A. There are quite a few questions coming together at one time, and I would like to answer the first one. The first question was to the effect, I believe, whether I took no occasion to tell the German people about this danger. I had no responsibility in that connection. We were in the war and at war, and any difference of opinion, as far as strategic problems were concerned, could not be brought before the public during the course of a war. I believe that never in the course of history has anything like that happened. As far as my resignation is concerned, I do not wish to debate about that, for during a war I was an officer, a soldier, and I was not concerned with whether I shared an opinion or not. I had to serve my country as a soldier. Point three: It was not my task to tell a man whom I had given my oath of loyalty to, and to separate myself from him if he was not of my opinion. If that had been the case, I would not have had to bind myself to him, and it never occurred to me to leave the Führer.

Q. As far as you know, the German people were led into the war, attacking Soviet Russia, under the belief that you favored it?

A. The German people knew about the declaration of war on Russia after the war on Russia had started. The German people cannot be brought in in this connection. The German people were not asked. They were notified of the fact and of the reasons for that fact.

Q. At what time did you know that the war, so far as achieving the objectives that you had in mind, was a lost war?

A. It is extraordinarily difficult to say that. According to my conviction, relatively late—and by that I mean at a late period of time—the conviction grew within me that the war had been lost. Previous to that time, I thought we would have a chance, and I was hoping for a chance.

Q. Well, in November 1941 the offensive in Russia broke down, did it not?

A. That is not right at all. We had reverses because of adverse weather, and the aims that we had set out for were not won. The push-through of 1943 proved that a military collapse is not even to be thought of. Some corps which had advanced were thrown back, or were taken back, and the frost that set in before we expected it was the cause of all of this.

Q. You see, "relatively late," the expression you used, does not tell me anything because I do not know what you regard as relatively late. Will you fix in terms either of events or of time when it was that the conviction came to you that the war was lost?

A. When the push-through of the Russian offensive of January 12, 1945, advanced as far as the Oder, and simultaneously the Ardennes offensive was not successful, at that period of time I thought—and I could not think otherwise—that slowly, in all possibility, a defeat would result. Before that period of time, I had always hoped that perhaps either at Weichsel—the position would change toward the East or perhaps towards the West Wall and could be held until new weapons would be put in production and used in such strength so that the American air war could be weakened.

Q. Now, will you fix that by date? You told us when it was by events.

A. I just said January 1945—middle or end of January 1945. At that point I saw no hope any longer.

Q. Do you want it understood that as a military man you did not realize until January 1945 that Germany could not be successful in the war?

A. I have already said that we must differentiate between two methods: to end the war successfully and to end it otherwise. At the period of time when we could do that there are two separate points. The fact that a defeat would take place—and I am concerned with the collapse of the date that I just mentioned.

Q. For some period before that, you knew that a successful termination of the war could only be accomplished if you could come to some kind of terms with the enemy; was that not true?

A. Yes, of course. A termination of a war is only to be considered successful if I either conquer the enemy or through negotiations come to such a conclusion that I am successful. That I would call a successful conclusion. The remaining conclusion is if I come to terms with the enemy through negotiations and I do not achieve the result which victory would have brought but which precludes a defeat on my part. That is an ending without victorious or conquered people.

Q. But you knew that it was Hitler's policy never to negotiate and you know that as long as he was head of the government, the enemy would not negotiate with Germany, did you not?

A. Hostile propaganda emphasized that they would never negotiate with Hitler; that fact I knew. That Hitler did not wish to negotiate under any circumstances—that also was known to me, but not in the same connection. Hitler wanted to negotiate if negotiations would have given him an opportunity, but negotiating which would be completely without success, he did not wish. Through the declaration of the Western Powers after the landing in Africa that under no circumstances would they negotiate with Germany but were interested in forcing an unconditional victory, the resistance of Germany was stiffened to the utmost and had to be organized as such. If I have no chance to conclude a war through negotiations, then negotiations are senseless, and I must try by using weapons to bring about a change in these conditions.

Q. By the time of January 1945 you also knew that you were unable to defend the German cities against the air attacks of the Allies, did you not?

A. The defense of German cities against Allied bomb attacks —I will try to give you a picture of the possibility.

Q. Can you not answer my question? Time may not mean quite as much to you as it does to the rest of us. Can you not answer yes or no? Did you then know, at the same time that you knew that the war was lost, that the German cities could not successfully be defended against air attack by the enemy? Can you not tell us yes or no?

A. I can say that I knew that at that period of time it was not possible.

Q. And after that time, the air attacks which were continued against England were well known to you that they could not turn the tide of war and were designed solely to effect a prolongation of what you then knew was a hopeless conflict?

A. I believe you are mistaken. After January there were no

195

attacks, except perhaps a plane at a time, because at that time I needed all of my fighters for defense. If I had had any bombers and oil, then, of course, I would have used them up until the last minute to attack as reprisals for attacks which were being carried out on German cities. It would not have had anything to do with our chances.

Q. What about robot attacks? Were there any robot attacks after January 1945?

A. Thank heavens, we still had weapons—one weapon—that we could use. I have just set forth that as long as the fight was going on, we had to give return blows and as a soldier I can only regret that we did not have enough of these V-1's and V-2's, for this was the only means which perhaps would bring about an easing of the situation of the enemy attacks on our cities, if we were able to use reprisals against them.

Q. And there was no way to prevent the war going on as long as Hitler was the head of the German government, was there?

A. As long as Hitler was the Führer of the German people, he determined solely and alone the war leadership. As long as the enemy threatened us with the fact that he would accept only unconditional capitulation, I fought up until the last breath, for that was the only thing that was left to me to perhaps have a chance to turn fate, even though it looked hopeless.

Q. Well, the people of Germany who thought it was time for the slaughter to stop had no means to stop it except revolution or assassination of Hitler, did they?

A. A revolution changes a situation—that is, if the revolution is successful. The murder or assassination of Hitler at that period of time, say January 1945, would have brought about my succession. If the opponent had given me the same answer, an unconditional surrender, and those terrible conditions which had been handed out, I would have continued fighting under all circumstances.

Q. There was an attack on Hitler's life on July 20, 1944?

A. Unfortunately, yes.

Q. And there came a time in 1945 when Hitler made a will in Berlin whereby he turned over the presidency to your code-fendant Admiral Dönitz. You know about that?

A. That is correct. I read of this testament here.

Q. And in so making his will and turning over the government of Germany to Admiral Dönitz, I call your attention to this statement:

> Göring and Himmler, quite apart from their disloyalty to my person, have done immeasurable harm to the country and the whole nation by secret negotiations with the enemy which they conducted without my knowledge and against my wishes and by illegally attempting to seize power in the state for themselves.

And by that will he expelled you and Himmler from the Party and from all offices of the state.

A. I can only reply for myself. What Himmler did I do not know. I neither betrayed the Führer nor did I at that period of time negotiate with even one foreign soldier. This will, or this document, of the Führer's rests on an unfortunate mistake and a mistake which grieves me: that the Führer could believe in his last hours that I would ever be disloyal to him. It all rests on a mistake of the transmission and perhaps on a wrong picture which Bormann gave to the Führer. I never thought for a minute to take over power illegally or to act against the Führer in any way.

Q. In any event you were arrested and expected to be shot?

A. That is correct.

Q. Now, in tracing the rise to power of the Party, you have omitted some things as for example, the Reichstag fire of February 27, 1933. There was a great purge following that fire, was there not, in which many people were arrested and many people were killed?

A. I am not familiar with one case, where even one man was killed because of the Reichstag fire other than those who were convicted through a court. The other two were exonerated, and it was not as you believed the other day, that we incriminated Thälmann as a Communist leader. He was also exonerated, as well as a Bulgarian man by the name of Dimitrov. Arrests did take place in connection with the Reichstag fire, but they were comparatively few. The arrests which you refer to are the arrests of Communist functionaries, and I have stated repeatedly, and wish to emphasize at this point, they were completely independent of this fire and would have been arrested nevertheless;

the fire just accelerated their arrest, and some of the functionaries escaped.

Q. In other words, you had lists of Communists already prepared at the time of the Reichstag fire of persons who should be arrested, did you not?

A. We had lists of Communist functionaries who were to be arrested. We had established these lists prior to, and they were entirely independent of, the Reichstag fire.

Q. They were immediately put into execution—the arrests, I mean—after the Reichstag fire?

A. Contrary to my intention to delay these actions for a few days and have them go through regular channels, the Führer wished to take care of those matters during the night and immediately have all those arrests made at that time.

Q. You and the Führer met at the fire, did you not?

A. Yes, that is right.

Q. And then and there you decided to arrest all the Communists that you had theretofore listed?

A. I would like to emphasize again the decision for the arrests had been established several days prior, but the action of immediate arrest took place that same night. I would rather have waited a few days, then some of the more important men would not have been able to escape.

Q. And the next morning the decree was presented to President von Hindenburg suspending the (civil liberty) provisions of the constitution which we have discussed here, was it not?

A. I believe, yes.

❋   ❋   ❋

Q. The Röhm purge you have left a little indefinite. What was it that Röhm did for which he was shot? What acts did he commit?

A. Röhm wanted an act against the state in which the Führer was to be killed. Also, he wished to start a revolution which was chiefly concerned against the Army, the Officer Corps, and everything else which he considered to be reactionary.

Q. And you had evidence of that fact?

A. We had sufficient evidence to that effect.

Q. But he was never tried in any court where he would have a chance to tell his story as you are telling yours, was he?

A. That is correct. He wanted to bring about an act of a revolutionary nature, and the Führer considered it correct and right to choke back this thing in its beginning; not through a court, but through a beating-down of this revolt from the beginning.

Q. Were the names of the people who were killed in that purge, following the arrest of Röhm, ever published?

A. Some of the names, yes, but not all of them, I believe.

Q. Among those who were killed were von Schleicher and his wife, who was one of your political opponents, was he not?

A. That is right.

Q. And also Erich Klausner, who had been chief of the Catholic Action Party of Germany?

A. Klausner was among those who were shot, and the case of Klausner motivated my requesting the Führer to stop this action, for in my opinion Klausner was not innocently—

Q. And Strasser, who had been the former number two man to Hitler and had disagreed with him in December 1932—Strasser was killed, was he not?

A. Strasser was not, as we say, the second man after Hitler. He had an extraordinary important role before the taking over of power, that is, within the Party, but before the taking over of power he was banned from the Party. Strasser was participating in this revolt, and he was also shot.

Q. When you met Hitler, as I understand your testimony, you found a man with a serious and definite aim, as you said, in that he was not content with the defeat of Germany in the previous war and was not content with the Versailles Treaty.

A. I believe you did not quite understand me correctly, for I did not say things in that order. I did set forth that I noted that Hitler had a definite view of the impotency of protest; and as a second point that he was of the opinion that Germany should be freed from the peace of Versailles. It was not only Adolf Hitler —every German, every patriotic German had the same feeling, and since I was a glowing patriot, as a glowing patriot I felt that the shame of Versailles was unbearable; and I identified myself with the man who thought the same as I, who saw the results which would come through Versailles, and that he perhaps would take the right way to set this Treaty of Versailles aside. But everything that was said in the Treaty of Versailles, if I may say so, was just empty chatter.

Q. So that if I understand you, from the very beginning, publicly and notoriously, it was the position of the Nazi Party that the Versailles Treaty must be set aside and that protest was impotent for that purpose?

A. From the beginning, it was the aim of Adolf Hitler, and for those of us in his movement, to free Germany of the shock of Versailles; by that we meant, not from the total Treaty but from those terms which were strangling Germany and which were to strangle Germany in the future.

Q. And to do it by war, if necessary?

A. We did not even debate about those things at that time. We debated only about the first condition; whether everyone else talked about the peace of Versailles, but we Germans always speak about the Dictate of Versailles. The first question was to achieve and establish a different political structure for Germany which would enable Germany to object against the Dictate, and not only a protest—an objection—but objection of such a nature that it would actually be considered.

Q. That is, the means was the reorganization of the German state, but your aim was to get rid of what you call the Dictate of Versailles?

A. The freeing from those terms of the Dictate of Versailles which for a continued period of time would make German life impossible and that was the aim; and in that connection, we did not say we shall have to have a war and defeat our enemies; this was the aim, and the methods had to be adapted to the political situation.

* * *

Q. If you would answer three or four questions for me yes or no, then I will be quite willing to let you give your version of this thing. In the first place, you wanted a stronger German state to overcome the conditions of Versailles.

A. Yes, we wanted a strong government regardless of Versailles, but to set aside Versailles, the state had to be strong, for a weak state was never listened to; that, we knew from experience.

Q. And the Führer's principle you adopted because you thought it would serve the ends of a strong state?

A. Correct.

Q. And this aim, which was one of the aims of the Nazi Party, to modify the conditions of Versailles was a public and notorious aim in which the people generally joined—it was one of your best means of getting people to join with you, was it not?

A. The Dictate of Versailles was of such a nature that every German, in my opinion, was for its modification and there was no doubt that this was a strong inducement for joining the Party.

Q. Now, a number of the men who took part in this movement are not here. There is no doubt in your mind, is there, that Adolf Hitler is dead?

A. I believe there is no doubt in that connection.

Q. And the same is true of Goebbels?

A. Goebbels—I have no doubt about that, for I know someone, whom I trust completely, who told me that he witnessed Goebbels' death.

Q. And you have no doubt of the death of Himmler, have you?

A. I am not exactly certain but I believe that you should be all the more certain, for he died in your internment. I was not there.

Q. You have no doubt of the death of Heydrich, have you?

A. I am definitely certain about that.

Q. And probably of Bormann?

A. I am not absolutely certain in this connection. I have no proof. I do not know but I assume so.

Q. And those are the chief persons in your testimony, who have been mentioned as being responsible—Hitler for everything; Goebbels for inciting riot against the Jews; and Himmler, who deceived Hitler (this morning); and Bormann who misled him about his will?

A. His influence on the Führer varied with time. The chief influence on the Führer, if I may mention influence on the Führer at all, was up until the end of 1941 or the beginning of 1942; and that chief influence was I. Then my influence gradually decreased up until 1943, and from 1943 on it decreased speedily. All in all, I do not believe anyone had anywhere near the influence on the Führer that I had, beyond or outside of myself. If there was influence from the beginning—in certain directions Goebbels, with whom the Führer was together quite a good deal—this influence varied temporarily and would be light at certain points and was increasingly large in the last four years. A certain influence before the taking-over of power, Hess had influence before the taking-over of power and after the taking-over of power, and that is in his special field only. In the course of years Himmler's influence grew; after the end of 1944 this influence decreased rapidly, and the decisive influence during the war on the person of Hitler, and especially from the year 1942 on after Hess had been eliminated in 1941, and after a year had elapsed, was the influence of Bormann—but this was a disastrously strong influence. It was possible only since July 20, the Führer had a very strong mistrust and Bormann was with him constantly and told him everything, pictured everything to him. Thus, in a rather sketchy way, I have described the personalities who had influence on Hitler at one time or another temporarily.

Q. Now, the Four Year Plan (of which you were head) had as its purpose to put the entire economy in a state of readiness for war, did it not?

A. I have explained that it had two tasks: first to assure German economy against crises, that is to say to make it independent of difficulties of export and nutrition problems; second, to establish it as independent of any blockade, that is to say, based on the experience of the first World War, to make sure that any blockade would not have the disastrous consequences that the first one had. But that the Four Year Plan in this respect was a basic prerequisite for the re-establishment of the armament industry goes without saying. Without it rearmament could not have taken place. The armament industry could not have been reorganized.

Q. To get a specific answer did you not say in a letter to Schacht, dated December 18, 1936, that you saw it to be your task, using these words: "within four years to put the German economy in a state of readiness for war"? Did you say that or didn't you?

A. Of course I said.

Q. Now, do you recall the report of Minister of War Blomberg in 1937? You may examine, if you wish, Document C–175, in which he starts by saying:

The general political position justifies the supposition that Germany need not consider an attack from any side?

(*Document shown to witness*)

A. That may have been probable for that moment. The situation of Germany in 1937 I considered the most quiet one. At that period—at that time the general situation was quite peaceful. But that had nothing to do with the fact that I felt obliged, independent of changing difficulties and differences, to make the German economy ready against crises or blockades which could have been brought about by war, and one year later incidents of a different nature occurred.

Q. Well, now, doesn't General Blomberg continue:

Grounds for this are, in addition to the lack of desire for war in almost all nations, particularly the western powers, the deficiencies in the preparedness for war of a number of states and of Russia in particular?

That was the situation in 1937, was it not?

A. That is the way Herr von Blomberg saw the situation. Concerning the readiness for war in Russia, Herr von Blomberg in the same way as all the representatives of our Reichswehr, our Armed Forces, was in error and contrary to the opinions which had been given from other sides concerning the armament in Russia. This is only the opinion of von Blomberg, not the Führer's not mine or not the opinion of other people.

Q. That, however, was the report of the Commander in Chief of the Armed Forces on June 24, 1937, was it not?

A. That is correct.

Q. Well, at all events, you continued your efforts to rearm and on the 8th of November 1943, you made a speech describing those efforts to the Gauleiters in the Führer Building at Munich, is that right?

A. I don't know the date, but around that time I made a short speech in connection with other speeches made to the Gauleiters. As far as I remember it was about the situation in the air and also maybe the armament situation. I do not remember the words of that speech because I have not been asked about it since, but the fact is so.

Q. Well, let me remind you that you used these terms—refresh your recollection.

> Germany, at the beginning of the war, was the only country in the world possessing an operative fighting air force. The other countries had split their air arms up into army and navy air forces and had considered the air arm primarily as a necessary and important auxiliary of the other branches of the forces. In consequence, they relaxed the instrument which is alone capable of dealing concentrated and effective blows, namely, the operative air force. In Germany we had gone ahead on those lines from the very outset, and the main body of the air force was disposed so that it could thrust deep into the hostile areas with strategic effect, while a lesser portion of the air force, consisting of Stukas and, of course, fighter planes, went into action on the front line in the battlefields. You all know what great results were achieved by these tactics and what superiority we attained at the very beginning of the war through this modern kind of air force.

A. That is definitely true. I said that under all circumstances, and what is still more decisive, I acted like that too. But in order to be sure that this is understood correctly, I would like to explain it briefly. In this statement I dealt with two separate opinions of air strategy which are still debated today and not quite clear, that is to say: shall the air force be an auxiliary of army and navy and part of either the army or navy, or should it be a separate part of the armed forces? I have explained that nations with a very large navy find it desirable if such a distribution takes place between army and navy, but we, consequently and quite correctly, had chosen the path that besides army and navy we had built a strong air force; and I underlined the word strong, and I explained what part we had taken, how we came to an operative air force. As an expert I still am of the opinion that only operative air forces can bring about decisions. I have also explained as to the proportion between two and four-motored planes, that at first I was satisfied with the two-motored planes because, first, I did not have four-motored, and then because the operating radius of the four-motored bombers was not large enough. I further pointed out that the quick termination of the campaign in Poland and in the west proved in an extraordinary way the effectiveness of the air force. That is quite correct.

Q. I remind you of the testimony of the witness Milch sworn in your behalf, as to a subject on which I have not heard you express yourself. He said:

> I have been under the impression that already at the time of the occupation of the Rhineland, he—Göring—was worried that Hitler's policies would lead to war.

Do you remember that?
A. Yes.

*　*　*

Q. And it is true, as Milch said, that you were worried that Hitler's policies would lead to war at the time of the occupation of the Rhineland?
A. Excuse me. I just understood that you asked whether it is also my opinion today that only a nation that is armed can have peace. That is what I meant to answer with my last statement. You referred to the statement by Milch, that I was worried that the policy of the Führer could lead to war. I would like to say that I was worried that war as such would come, and if possible I wanted to avoid it, not in the sense that the policy of the Führer would lead to it, because the Führer also desired to carry out his program by agreements and diplomatic action. On the question of the Rhineland occupation, I was worried temporarily about the reactions, repercussions. Just the same, it was necessary.

*　*　*

Q. Now, I want to review with you briefly what the prosecution understands to be public acts taken by you in reference to the Jewish question. From the very beginning you regarded the elimination of the Jew from the economic life of Germany as one phase of the Four Year Plan under your jurisdiction, did you not?
A. The elimination, yes; that is right in part. The elimination as far as the large concerns were concerned because there continually disturbances were created by pointing out that there were large industries, also armament industries, still under Jewish

directors or with Jewish shareholders, and that caused serious disturbances about the industries.

Q. Do I understand that you want the Tribunal to believe that all you were concerned about was the big Jewish enterprises? That is the way you want to be understood?

A. I was not at first disturbed by the small stores.

Q. When did you become disturbed with the small stores?

A. When trade had to be limited, then it was pointed out that this could be done first by closing the Jewish stores.

Q. Now, let us go through the public acts which you performed on the Jewish question. First, did you proclaim the Nürnberg racial laws?

A. As President of the Reichstag, yes; I have already stated that.

Q. What date was that?

A. 1935, I believe, in Nürnberg in September.

Q. That was the beginning of the legal measures taken against the Jews, was it not?

A. No, I believe that the elimination from various phases of civil employment was before. I could not state the exact date, but I believe that happened in 1933.

Q. Then on the first day of December 1936, you promulgated an act making a death penalty for Germans to transfer property abroad or leave it abroad; the property of a culprit to be forfeited to the state, and the "People's Court" given jurisdiction of such cases, did you not?

A. That is correct, the act to protect foreign currency. That is to say, whoever without the permission of the government established an account in a foreign country.

Q. Then, your third public act was on April 22, 1939, when you published penalties for veiling the character of a Jewish enterprise within the Reich, was it not?

A. Yes.

Q. Then on July 28, 1939, you published certain prescriptions on the competence of the regular courts to handle those matters?

A. Please, would you kindly read the law to me? I do not know it.

Q. I will not take time reading it. Do you deny that you published *Reichsgesetzblatt* Law, 1939, found on page 1370, referring to the competence of the courts to handle penalties against the law? If you do not remember, say so.

A. Yes, I say that I cannot remember the law. If it was in the *Reichsgesetzblatt* and has my name under it, then, of course, it is so, but I do not remember the contents.

Q. On April 26, 1938, you, under the Four Year Plan, published a decree providing for the registration of Jewish property which provided that Jews inside and outside Germany must register their property, did you not?

A. I assume so. I do not remember it any more, but if you have the decree there and if it is signed by me, there cannot be any doubt.

Q. On April 26, 1938, you published a decree under the Four Year Plan, did you not, that all acts of disposal of Jewish enterprises required the permission of the authorities?

A. That I remember.

Q. Then you published on November 12, 1938, a decree also under the Four Year Plan, imposing a fine of a billion marks for atonement on all Jews?

A. I have already explained that, that all the decrees of that time were signed by me, and I assumed responsibility for them.

Q. Then on November 12, 1938, you also signed a decree that, under the Four Year Plan, all damage caused to Jewish property by the riots of 1938 must be repaired immediately by the Jews, and at their own expense, and their insurance claims were forfeited to the Reich. Did you personally sign that law?

A. A similar law I signed. Whether it was exactly the same as you have just read, I could not say.

Q. You agree that that was the substance of the law, do you?
A. Yes.

Q. And on November 12, 1938, did you not also personally sign a decree, also under the Four Year Plan, that Jews may not own retail stores or engage independently in handicrafts or offer goods or services for sale at markets, fairs, or exhibitions, or be leaders of enterprises or members of co-operatives. Do you recall all of that?

A. Yes. These are all parts of the decrees for the elimination of Jewry from economic life.

Q. On February 21, 1939, you personally signed a degree, did you not, that the Jews must surrender all precious metals and jewels to a public officer within two weeks?

A. I do not remember that, but I am sure, without doubt, that that is correct.

Q. Did you not also, on March 3, 1939, sign a further decree concerning the period within which items of jewelry must be surrendered by Jews—*Reichsgesetzblatt,* Volume I, 1939, page 387?

A. I assume that was the decree of execution concerning the decree mentioned before. A law sometimes requires regulations of execution as a consequence of the law. Seen together, this is just one measure.

Q. Did you not also sign personally a decree on September 17, 1940, ordering the sequestration of Jewish property in Poland?

A. Yes. I stated that once before. In that part of Poland, if I may point that out, which had been previously an old German province. It was to return to Germany.

Q. Did you not also, on November 30, 1940, personally, in the capacity of President of the Reich Defense Council, sign a decree which provided that the Jews should receive no compensation for damages caused by enemy attacks or by German Forces? I refer to *Reichsgesetzblatt,* Volume I, 1940, page 1547.

A. If you have it there before you, then it must be correct.

Q. You have no recollection of that?

A. Not concerning all details of law and decrees. That is impossible.

Q. Then it was you, was it not, who signed, on July 31, 1941, a decree asking Himmler and the chief of security police and the SS *Gruppenführer* Heydrich to make the plans for the complete solution of the Jewish question?

A. No, that is not correct. This decree I know very well.

Q. I ask to have you shown document 710–PS, US–509.

(*A document was handed to the witness*)

That document is signed by you, is it not?

A. That is correct.

Q. And it is addressed to the chief of the security police and the security service and to SS *Gruppenführer* Heydrich, isn't it?

A. That is also correct.

FROM CROSS-EXAMINATION OF GÖRING

Q. That we may have no difficulty about the translation of this, you correct me if I am wrong:

Completing the task that was assigned to you on January 24, 1939—

A. That is a mistake already. It says

In completion of the task which has been transferred to you,

not as it was translated to me before.

Q. Very well, I will accept that.

Which dealt with arriving at, through furtherance of emigration and evacuation, a solution of the Jewish problem, as advantageous as possible, I hereby charge you with making all necessary preparations in regard to organizational and financial matters for bringing about a complete solution of the Jewish question in the German sphere of influence in Europe.

Am I correct so far?

A. No, that is in no way correctly translated into the German.

Q. Give us your translation of it.

A. May I read it as it is written here?

In completion of the task which has been conferred upon you already on the 24th, 1939, to solve the Jewish problem in the form of emigration and evacuation and to bring to the best possible solution, according to present conditions, I charge you herewith to make all necessary preparations in the way of organization and material matters.

Now comes the decisive word which has been mistranslated:

For a collective solution,

not

for a final solution—

For an entire, a collective solution of the Jewish question within the area of German influence in Europe. As far as here the competency of other agencies would be touched, they are to participate. I charge you further to submit to me soon your total plan concerning it in the way of organization and materials, in order to be able to carry out the desired solution of the Jewish question, in completing the task which has been turned over to you on January 24, 1939.

That is to say, at a time when no war had started or was to be expected.

* * *

Q. Now, at the time that you conferred this power on Heydrich you had received complete reports as to the 1938 riots and Heydrich's part in them, hadn't you?

A. As far as the participation of Heydrich was concerned, I did not have the information about it at that time—only the report by Heydrich about the riots which I had demanded.

Q. All right. Now we will show you Exhibit No. 3058–PS, in evidence as United States' Exhibit 508.

(*A document was handed to the witness*)

That is the report of Heydrich which you say you had received, dated November 11, 1938, was it not?

A. That is correct.

Q. And it recited to you the looting of Jewish shops, the arrest of 174 persons for looting, the destruction of 815 shops, 171 dwellings set on fire or destroyed, and that those indicated only a fraction of the actual damage caused; 191 synagogues were set on fire, and another 76 completely destroyed; in addition, 11 parish halls, cemetery chapels, and similar buildings were set on fire, and 3 more completely destroyed; 20,000 Jews were arrested; also 7 Aryans and 3 foreigners. The latter were arrested for their own safety. 36 deaths were reported, and those seriously injured were also numbered at 36. Those killed and injured are Jews. 1 Jew is still missing. The Jews killed include 1 Polish national, and those injured include 2 Poles.

You had that report on or about November 11, 1938, did you not?

A. That is correct. That is the report which I have mentioned which I had requested from the police, because I wanted to know what had happened up to then.

* * *

Q. Did you receive a report from the chief Party adjutant of the Nazi Party, dated Munich, February 13, 1939, of the Party Supreme Court proceedings about these matters?

A. That is correct. Much later I received that report.

* * *

FROM CROSS-EXAMINATION OF GÖRING

Q. In the first place, the Party court reported that it was probably understood—I quote—

by all of the Party leaders present, from oral instructions of the Reich Propaganda Director, that the Party should not appear outwardly as the originator of the demonstrations but in reality should organize and execute them.

Was that the report of the Party court?

A. The Party court, as a result of its investigation, established that the Propaganda Chief Goebbels had given these directives.

❁ ❁ ❁

Q. Did the court—the Party court—not also report this to you:

The Supreme Party Court has reserved for itself the investigation of the killings, severe mistreatment and moral crimes and that it would request the Führer to quash proceedings against any persons that the Party court did not find guilty of excesses.

A. That is correct.

Q. And the Party court was made up of Gauleiters and group leaders of the Party?

❁ ❁ ❁

A. Yes, that is a matter of course that the jurors of the Party court were always taken from these categories according to their importance.

Q. In the cases of killing Jews (contrary to orders) I will not go through those in detail, but is it not a fact that only minor punishments were pronounced by the Supreme Court of the Party for such killing of Jews?

A. Yes, that is correct.

❁ ❁ ❁

Q. And one further question. It was also reported to you, was it not in that report?

The public down to the last man realizes that political drives, like those of November 9, were organized and directed by the Party, whether this is admitted or not. When all the synagogues burned down in one night, it must have been organized in some way and could only have been organized by the Party.

That also was in the report of the Supreme Party Court?

A. Yes, I just found it.

Q. Now, the *Völkischer Beobachter* of March 12, 1933 quotes a speech of yours delivered at Essen on March 11, 1933, including the following—and I refresh your recollection by calling it to your attention:

I am told that I must employ the police. Certainly I shall employ the police, and quite ruthlessly, whenever the German people are hurt, but I refuse the notion that the police are protective troops for Jewish stores. No, the police protect whoever comes into Germany legitimately, but it does not exist for the purpose of protecting usurers.

Did you say that on March 11, 1933, in a speech at Essen—that or that in substance?

A. That is correct, but there was a different connection with the speech.

Q. After the riot of November 9 and 10, you have testified that you called a meeting on November 12 and ordered all officials concerned to be present, and that the Führer had insisted on Goebbels being present?

A. Yes.

Q. Will you please name them by name so we won't have any mistake about who was there at that time?

A. I can quote only from memory. Present were, to report all events: The Leader of the Secret Police for Berlin, Heydrich; Minister of the Interior, Dr. Frick; Dr. Goebbels you have mentioned already; the Minister of Economy, Funk; Finance Minister, Count Schwerin-Krosigk; from the Eastern Province, Fischboeck for the Ostmark. These are the only names of personalities I can recall at present, although there may be a few others who were there too.

Q. Part of the time, Hilgard, representing the insurance companies was also present, was he not?

A. He was called in, was waiting, and was heard on special questions.

Q. You have been shown the stenographic minutes of that meeting which are in evidence as United States' Exhibit 261, being document 1816–PS, have you not, in your interrogation?

A. Yes.

Q. I will ask that they be shown to you now so that we may have no misunderstanding about the translations. This is the meeting held on November 12, 1938, at the office of the Reich Ministry for Air. That is correct, is it not?

A. Yes, that is correct.

Q. You opened the meeting:

Gentlemen, today's meeting is of a decisive nature. I have received a letter written on the Führer's orders by the Stabsleiter of the Führer's Deputy Bormann, requesting that the Jewish question be now, once for all, co-ordinated and solved one way or another.

Is that correct?

A. Yes, that is correct.

Q. Further down, I find this by you:

Because, gentlemen, I have had enough of these demonstrations. They don't harm the Jews, but me, who is the last authority for co-ordinating the German economy. If today a Jewish shop is destroyed, if goods are thrown into the street, the insurance company will pay for the damages which the Jew does not even have, and furthermore, goods of the consumer, goods belonging to the people, are destroyed. If, in the future, demonstrations which are necessary occur, then I pray that they be directed so as not to hurt us.

Am I correct?

A. Yes, quite correct.

Q. Skipping two or three paragraphs, I come to this—

I shouldn't want to leave any doubt, gentlemen, as to the aim of today's meeting. We have not come together merely to talk again, but to make decisions, and I implore the competent agencies to take all measures for the elimination of the Jew from German economy and to submit them to me as far as is necessary.

A. That is correct.

Q. I then skip a considerable portion, unless there is more that you wish to put in, and come to this statement:

The trustee of the state will estimate the value of the property and decide what amount the Jew shall receive. Naturally, this amount is to be set as low as possible. The representative of the state shall then turn the establishment over to the Aryan proprietor, that is, the property shall be sold according to its real value.

There begin the difficulties. It is easily understood that strong attempts will be made to get all these stores to Party members and to let them have some kind of compensation. I have witnessed terrible things in the past; little chauffeurs of Gauleiters have profited so much by these transactions that they have now about half a million. You gentlemen know it. Is that correct?

And they assented?

A. Yes I said that.

Q. I will quote another portion:

In other words, an ordinary business transaction is to be sought, one merchant selling, the other one buying a business. If there are Party members among the contenders, they are to be preferred—that is, if they have the same qualifications. First shall come the one who has had the most damage; secondly, selection should be according to ranks of Party membership.

I skip a line or two:

This Party member should have a chance to buy the store for as cheap a price as possible. In such a case, the state will not receive the full price, but only the amount the Jew received.

Is that correct?

A. Just a moment, please. I believe we skipped something.

Q. Yes, we did. If you want to put it in, you may read it.

A. No, I might just say briefly, regarding the substance; I said what you have already said, that if there is any consideration to be given, the Party member is to be preferred, first of all the one who had been hurt previously in that his business concessions had been taken away from him just because he had been a Party member, and then follows the paragraph which you read and which is correct as it was read.

Q. You then take up at considerable length the method by which you shall Aryanize Jewish stores, is that right?

A. Yes.

Q. And then you take up the Aryanization of Jewish factories?

A. Yes.

Q. You take up the smaller factories first?

A. Yes.

Q. Quoting:

As for the smaller and medium ones, two things shall have to be made clear: First, which factories do I not need at all, which are the ones where production could be suspended? Could they not be put to another use? If not, the factories will be razed immediately.

Second, in case the factory should be needed, it will be turned over to Aryans in the same manner as the stores.

That is correct, is it?

A. Yes.

Q. Now, we will pass to the conversation between yourself and Heydrich. You inquired how many synagogues were actually burned, and Heydrich replied:

Altogether there were 101 synagogues destroyed by fire, 76 synagogues demolished, and 7,500 stores ruined in the Reich.

Have I quoted that correctly?

A. Yes.

Q. Then Dr. Goebbels raised the question of Jews traveling on railway trains?

A. Yes.

Q. And see if I quote the dialogue between you and Dr. Goebbels correctly on that subject. That Dr. Goebbels said:

Furthermore, I advocate that Jews be eliminated from all positions in public life in which they may prove to be provocative. It is still possible today that a Jew shares a compartment in a sleeping car with a German; therefore, we need a decree by the Reich Ministry for Communications stating that separate compartments for Jews shall be available. In cases where compartments are filled up, Jews cannot claim a seat. They shall be given separate compartments only after all Germans have secured seats. They shall not mix with the Germans, and if there is no more room, they shall have to stand in the corridor.

Is that right?

A. Yes, that is correct.

Q.

Göring: In that case I think it would make more sense to give them separate compartments. Goebbels: Not if the train is overcrowded.

Göring: Just a moment. There will be only one Jewish coach. If that is filled up the other Jews will have to stay at home. Goebbels: Suppose though there won't be many Jews going on an express train to Munich. Suppose there will be two Jews in a train, and the other compartments would be overcrowded; those two Jews would then have a compartment all by themselves; therefore, Jews may claim a seat only after all Germans have secured a seat. Göring: I would give the Jews one coach, or one compartment, and should a case like you mentioned arise, and the train be overcrowded, believe me, we won't need a law. We will kick him out, and he will have to sit alone in the toilet all the way.

Is that correct?

A. Yes. I had become a little nervous when Goebbels had had important matters that were brought forward in certain particulars, and in this connection I gave out no decrees or no laws. Of course, today it is very pleasant for the prosecution to present it, but I wish to state that it was a very lively session, in which Goebbels made demands which were as I say in a radical scope, and in a radical criminal scope, and in accordance with my demeanor I expressed myself.

* * *

Q. Then you made a statement to Mr. Hilgard when he appeared:

The following is our case. Because of the justified anger of the people against the Jews, the Reich has suffered a certain amount of damage. Windows were broken, goods were damaged, and people hurt; synagogues burned and so forth. I suppose that Jews, many of them are also insured against damage committed by public disorder. Hilgard: Yes. Göring: If that is so the following situation arises. The people in their justified anger meant to harm the Jews, but these German insurance companies are to compensate the Jews for the damage. This situation is simple enough. I only have to issue a decree to that effect, that damage resulting from these risks shall not have to be paid by the insurance company.

Is that what you said?

A. Yes, I said all of that.

Q. Yes, and Hilgard pointed out that:

Incidentally the amount of damage equals about half of a whole year's production of the Belgian glass industry. We believe that half a year will be necessary for the manufacturers to deliver the glass.

Do you recall that?

A. Yes.

Q. Now, Hilgard objected to your plan of relieving the insurance companies from paying the claims, did he not?

A. Yes, that is right also.

Q. And he gave these reasons:

Hilgard: If I may give reasons for this request, I would like to say that it simply has to do with the fact that we carry out to a large extent quite a number of international transactions. We have a very good international basis for our business transactions and in the interests of the equilibrium of the foreign exchange in Germany we have to make sure that the confidence in German insurance shall not be ruined. If we now refuse to honor clear-cut obligations imposed upon us through a lawful contract, it would be a black spot on the shield of honor of German insurance.

Göring: It would not be the minute I issue a decree, a law sanctioned by the state.

Am I quoting correctly?

A. Yes, and Hilgard's reply—and that was the reply I am concerned with—he meant without a basis in law they could not refuse to pay their claims but if the sovereign state made a law that the insurance claims may be taken over in favor of the state, then the insurance company in itself is not responsible for any action thereafter.

Q. Now, I suggest to you that that is not correct but that even though you proposed to issue a decree absolving the German insurance companies, the companies insisted on meeting their obligations and then Heydrich interposed and said:

The insurance may be granted but as soon as it is to be paid it will be confiscated. In that way we will have saved our face.

Correct?

A. No, I did not support Heydrich. I made a law that the insurance claims that were to go to Jews were to be redirected to the Ministry of Finance. I did not agree with Heydrich that insurance was to be paid and on the quiet be confiscated. I went a definite, legal way and was not afraid to make the law and to take the responsibility that these claims were to be paid to the state, that is to the Finance Minister.

Q. And the number of stores destroyed—Heydrich reported 7,500, is that right?

A. Yes.

Q. Now, I call your attention to the following conversation:

Daluege: One more question ought to be cleared up. Most of the goods in the stores were not the property of the owner but were kept on the books of other firms which had delivered them. Then there are the unpaid-for deliveries by other firms which definitely are not all Jewish but Aryan—those goods that were delivered on the basis of commission.

Hilgard: We will have to pay for them too.

Göring: I wish you had killed two hundred Jews and not destroyed such valuables.

Do I read that correctly?

A. Yes, it was an utterance of spontaneous excitement.

Q. Spontaneously sincere, wasn't it?

A. It was not meant seriously as I emphasized. It was a spontaneous and momentary excitement about the proceedings, about the destruction of valuables and the difficulties which had arisen for me. Of course, if every word you utter during the course of twenty-five years in intimate circles—if you put them into balance, I admit these utterances assume another nature.

Q. Hilgard returned again to the subject of the profit of the insurance companies, did he not?

A. Yes, of course.

Q. And you made this statement, did you not?

The Jews shall have to report the damage. He will get the refund from the insurance company but the refund will be confiscated. If it is all said and done, there will remain some profit to the insurance companies, since they do not have to make good for all the damage. Mr. Hilgard you may enjoy yourself.

Hilgard: I have no reason for that. The fact that we won't have to pay all the damage is called profit!

Göring: Just a moment. If you are compelled under the law to pay five million, and all of a sudden there appears an angel in my somewhat corpulent form before you and tells you you may keep one million, why can't that be called making a profit? I should actually split with you or whatever you would call it. I can see it looking at you, your whole body grins, you made a big profit.

Am I quoting correctly?

A. Yes, of course, I said all of that.

Q. There was a representative of Austria present at this meeting, was there not?

A. Yes.

Q. And I ask you whether he did not report to your meeting as follows:

Your Excellency, in this matter we have already a very complete plan for Austria. There are 12,000 Jewish artisans and 5,000 Jewish retail shops in Vienna. Before the national revolution we had already a definite plan for tradesmen regarding this total of 17,000 stores, of the shops of the 12,000 artisans, about 10,000 were to be closed definitely and 2,000 were to be kept open. 4,000 of the 5,000 retail stores should be closed and 1,000 kept open, that is, were to be Aryanized. According to this plan, between 3,000 and 3,500 of the total of 17,000 stores would be kept open, all others closed. This was decided following investigations in every single branch and according to local needs in agreement with all competent authorities and is ready for publication as soon as we shall receive the law with we requested in September. This law shall empower us to withdraw licenses from artisans quite independently of the Jewish question.

Göring: I shall have this decree issued today.

A. Yes, of course. This had to do with the law for the limitation of the retail trade which without connection with the Jewish question would have required a limitation in numbers. That can be seen from the minutes.

Q. Please go on down two paragraphs to where this was reported:

This way I believe that fewer than 100 stores would be left and by the end of the year we would have liquidated all the Jewish-owned businesses which so far have been obvious as such in the eyes of the public.

Göring: That would be excellent.

A. Yes, yes, that was the sense—the reason for that meeting.

Q.

Out of 17,000 stores 12,000 or 14,000 would be shut down and the remainder Aryanized or handed over to the Bureau of Trustees, which is operated by the store.

Göring: I have to say that this proposal is grand. This way the whole affair would be wound up in Vienna, one of the Jewish capitals, so to speak, by Christmas or by the end of the year.

Funk: We can do the same thing here. I have prepared a law elaborating that. Effective January 1, 1939, Jews shall be prohibited from operating retail stores and wholesale establishments, as well as independent artisan shops. They shall be further prohibited from keeping employees or offering any ready products on the market. Whenever a Jewish shop is operated the police shall shut it down.

From January 1, 1939 a Jew can no longer be employed as an enterpriser, as stipulated in the law for the organization of national labor from January 20, 1934. If a Jew has a leading position in an establishment without being enterpriser, his contract may be declared void within six weeks by the enterpriser. With the expiration of the contract all claims of the employee, including all claims to maintenance, become obliterated. That is always very disagreeable and a great danger.

A Jew cannot be a member of a corporation. Jewish members of corporations shall have to be retired by December 31, 1938. A special authorization is unnecessary. The competent ministers of the Reich are being authorized to issue the provision necessary for execution of this law.

Göring: I believe we can agree with this law.

A. Yes.

*　　*　　*

Q. Toward the close of that meeting you used these words, didn't you?

I shall close the meeting this way: That German Jewry shall as a punishment for their abominable [and so forth and so forth] have to make a contribution of one billion. That will work. The pigs won't commit another murder. Incidentally, I would like to say again that I wouldn't like to be a Jew in Germany.

A. I have told you exactly how it came to the fine of one billion.

Q. You have pointed out that the chauffeurs of Gauleiters must be stopped from getting anything out of the aryanization of the Jewish property, right?

A. Yes.

Q. We will now take up the subject of art. . . . Did you know a Dr. Bunjes?

A. Bunjes, B-u-n-j-e-s, yes.

Q. I will ask to have you shown, so that you can follow me, Document 2523–PS, USA–783, a letter from Dr. Bunjes, and ask you if this refreshes your recollection of certain events.

On Tuesday, February 4, 1941, at 1830 o'clock, I was ordered for the first time to report to the Reichsmarshal at the Quai d'Orsay. Field Commander von Behr of the Special Purpose Staff Rosenberg was present at the report. It is, of course, difficult to describe in words the cordial tone in which the conversation was held.

Do you recall such a meeting?

A. No, it would not have been so important that I should have remembered it, but I will not deny it, of course.

Q. We'll see if this refreshes your recollection:

The Reichsmarshal dropped the subject of Turner for the time being and asked for the report of the present state of the seizure of Jewish art property in the occupied western territories. On this occasion he gave Mr. von Behr the photographs of these objects of art that the Führer wants to bring into his possession. In addition, he gave Mr. von Behr the photographs of those objects of art that the Reichsmarshal wants to acquire for himself.

A. I cannot follow here.

Q. You mean you do not find these words, or you do not recall the events?

A. No, I haven't found the passage yet, and I would like to have a little time to see the connection in this letter which was neither written by me nor addressed to me.

Q. Let me call your attention to a further paragraph of it and see if it doesn't refresh your recollection:

THE NÜRNBERG CASE

On Wednesday, February 5, 1941, I was ordered to the Joue de Pomme by Reichsmarshal. At 1500 o'clock, the Reichsmarshal, accompanied by General Hannesse, Mr. Angerer, and Mr. Hofer, visited the exhibit of Jewish art treasures newly set up there.

A. Yes, I have stated before that at Joue de Pomme I selected the art treasures which were exhibited there, that's right.

Q. That's right; now we are getting there.

Then, with myself as his guide, the Reichsmarshal inspected the exhibited art treasures and made a selection of these works of art which were to go to the Führer and those which were to be placed in his own collection.

During this confidential conversation, I again called the Reichsmarshal's attention to the fact that a note of protest had been received from the French government against the activity of the *Einsatzstab* Rosenberg, with reference to the Hague Rules on Land Warfare recognized by Germany at the armistice of Compiègne, and I pointed out that General von Stülpnagel's interpretation of the manner in which the confiscated Jewish art treasures are to be treated was apparently contrary to the Reichsmarshal's interpretation. Thereupon, the Reichsmarshal asked for a detailed explanation and gave the following orders:

"First, my orders are decisive. You will act directly according to my orders. The art objects collected in the Joue de Pomme are to be loaded into a special train immediately and taken to Germany on orders of the Reichsmarshal. Those art objects which are to go into the Führer's possession and those art objects which the Reichsmarshal claims for himself will be loaded into two railroad cars which will be attached to the Reichsmarshal's special train, and upon his departure for Germany, at the beginning of next week, will be taken along to Berlin. *Feldführer* von Behr will accompany the Reichsmarshal in his special train on the trip to Berlin."

When I made the objection that the jurists would probably be of a different opinion and that protests would most likely be made by the military commander in France, the Reichsmarshal answered, saying verbatim as follows, "Dear Bunjes, let me worry about that; I am the highest jurist in the state."

The Reichsmarshal promised to send from his headquarters by courier to the Chief of the Paris Military Administrative District on Thursday, February 6, the written order for the transfer to Germany of the confiscated Jewish art treasures.

Now, does that fresh your recollection?

A. It is not at all in contradiction to what I have said with respect to the art treasures with the exception of one sentence; the notion which is expression here is the fact that it alleges that I said that I was the highest jurist in the state because that, thank God, I was not. That is an expression which Mr. Bunjes used, and I cannot be held responsible for each expression which anyone may have made to somebody else without my having any possibility of correcting it. The rest, however, is according to the explanation which I gave the other day.

Q. Now, the art then was loaded in the cars and shipped to Berlin, was it not?

A. In part, yes.

Q. I now call your attention to, and ask to have you shown, Document 104–PS, USA–784. Now, I ask you to refresh your recollection by following this report to the Führer, and tell me if this conforms with your testimony:

I report the arrival—

A. (interposing) I would like to point out that this report did not come from me.

Q. I understand that. I am asking if it is right or wrong.

I report the arrival of the principal shipment of ownerless Jewish cultural property in the salvage location Neuschwanstein by special train on Saturday the 15th of this month. It was secured by my Staff for Special Purposes, *Einsatzstab*, in Paris. The special train, arranged for by Reichsmarshal Hermann Göring, comprised 25 express baggage cars filled with the most valuable paintings, furniture, Gobelins, works of artistic craftsmanship, and ornaments. The shipment consisted of the most important parts of the collections of Rothschild, Seligman

—and half a dozen others.

Have you found that and is it correct?

A. Whether this is correct I could not say because the report did not come from me. The only thing that I remember is that I had been asked by the *Einsatzstab* to take care to see to it that they should have sufficient special cars, box cars, in order to ship the art treasures, since Joue de Pomme was not at all a safe place in case of bombing attacks, nor was Neuschwanstein, south of Munich, and they were the objects which went to the Führer.

I should like, however, to emphasize the next sentence of this document, which was not written by me, and that goes as follows:

> The action of confiscation by my *Einsatzstab*, which took place on the basis of your order, my Führer, started in October 1940 in Paris.

That proves again what I have said in my previous statements.

Q. And would you care to read further?

A. You mean:

> Outside of this special train, already before the main art objects which the Reichsmarshal had selected, mainly from the collection of the Rothschilds, had been brought in two special cars to Munich and were there put into the air raid shelter of the Führer Building.

Those were the ones that at first I had selected following the wish of the Führer—the most precious objects which should have been sent to the air raid shelter—and they have nothing to do with mine, but I did not dispute the fact. I have explained it in detail.

      *   *   *

Q. Who was the Reichskommissar for Norway?

A. In Norway the Gauleiter Terboven was Reichskommissar.

Q. Terboven—he was also a Gauleiter you say?

A. He was Gauleiter at Essen.

Q. And he was there from January 1940 until January 1945?

A. I believe that is correct.

Q. Now, I will ask to have you shown Document R–134, communication from Terboven to you.

(*The document was handed to the witness*)

That is a communication of May 1, 1942, is it not?

A. I noted the date, yes.

Q. And that reports to you as follows, does it not—it is addressed to you as Reichsmarshal: "My esteemed Reichsmarshal," is that right?

A. Yes.

Q. Omitting the first paragraph, unless you care to give it:

> Several days ago on an island west of Bergen we have flushed out a Norwegian sabotage unit which was trained by the Secret Service,

and have found that during this, extensive stores of sabotage instruments, some of them of a new kind, among which poison and bacteria can probably be found, and which so far as they are known have been forwarded to the Reich Security Main Office for closer examination. Besides other tasks, this sabotage unit was to begin with their sabotage work with the explosive devices of which a sample is available on Sola and Herdla. This can be constructed from finely written directives. Since it must be assumed that similar actions are under way on air fields of the remaining European coast, and assuming that a means of sabotage actually unknown until now is in question here, I forward it to you by the fastest means in order to give you the opportunity to be sure to issue the appropriate warning order. Unfortunately, two especially deserving officers of the Security Police were killed in the fight against the sabotage unit. We buried them this morning at about 1000 hours in the Heroes' Cemetery in Bergen. On the same day and at the same hour eighteen Norwegians were shot on my order. These had been captured some time previously in the attempt to go to England illegally. Also, on the same day, the entire community which granted a hiding place to the sabotage unit was burned down and the population was deported. All males were sent to a German concentration camp without their families receiving any notification about it. The women were sent to a female forced-labor camp in Norway, and the children not capable of working to a children's home. *Heil Hitler!* Yours obediently, Terboven.

Is that correct?

A. It says so in the letter, of which I have just seen a copy.

Q. Terboven remained after that report until 1945, didn't he?

A. That's correct.

Q. Well, you adopted later in the same year the same means as Terboven, didn't you, in substance?

A. I—where?

Q. Well, I will ask that you be shown Document 1742–PS. (*Document USA–789 handed to the witness*)

Now, this is a decree of October 1942, by Göring. I ask you to follow me:

Simultaneously with the intensified combating of gang activity ordered by the Führer and the cleaning-up of the hinterland, in particular that behind the Army Group Middle, I request that the following aspects are taken into consideration and that the deductions drawn therefrom are put into practice:

One, during the combating of the Underground and the combing-through of the areas contaminated by them, all available cattle stock there must simultaneously be driven off to safe areas. Food supplies are to be evacuated and protected similarly, so that there will be no more accessible to the bands.

Second, all masculine and feminine labor which can be considered for some kind of employment must be seized by force and transported to the Plenipotentiary, chief of the labor exchange, who will then employ them in safe areas of the hinterland or at home. The accommodation of the children in the hinterland camps is to be regulated separately.

Is that right?

A. Absolutely. We were concerned with those areas of bands, and no man could demand of me that I leave foodstuffs and cattle for the bands who harassed us so tremendously and bands—those people who might have been used if band-activity had to be taken into regions which were assured us and had to be used for manpower. I would like to emphasize that this is an absolute necessity of life for the security of the fighting forces. But I would like to emphasize again that you said I decreed the same which you read from the letter of Terboven. I did not ask for the shooting of hostages. We are concerned with two diametrically opposed matters.

✿　✿　✿

HJALMAR SCHACHT

Schacht was credited with being the financial wizard whose resourcefulness enabled a bankrupt Germany to finance her huge rearmament program. He was Reich Minister of Economics and President of the Reichsbank. In 1935 by secret decree he was appointed General Plenipotentiary for the War Economy. Schacht quarreled with Göring and eventually lost favor. He remained President of the Reichsbank until 1939 when he was dismissed, having previously given up his other positions. He remained in the Hitler government however as Minister without Portfolio until 1943. At the time of the surrender of Germany he was in a concentration camp.

HJALMAR SCHACHT TESTIFYING IN HIS OWN BEHALF

"I think you can score many more successes when you want to lead someone if you don't tell them the truth than if you tell them the truth."

FROM CROSS-EXAMINATION OF SCHACHT

Hjalmar Schacht, a defendant, who became a witness in his own behalf was cross-examined for the United States by Mr. Justice Jackson:

Q. Yesterday, I think it was, you testified you had made public statements against the terror policy of the regime, and in evidence you quoted from your Königsberg speech.

A. Yes.

Q. Unfortunately, Dr. Schacht, you stopped just at the point where I got interested in it.

A. Yes, that is true, isn't it? (laughing)

Q. Yes. This is what you quoted:

Those are the people who heroically smear window panes in the middle of the night, who brand every German who trades in a Jewish store as a traitor, who condemn every former Freemason as a bum, and who, in the just fight against priests and ministers who talk politics from the pulpit, cannot themselves distinguish between religion and misuse of the pulpit.

A. Yes.

Q. Now let us go on:

The goal at which these people aim is generally correct and good. There is no place in the Third Reich for secret societies, regardless how harmless they are. The priests and preachers should take care of the souls, and not meddle in politics. The Jew must realize that their influence is gone for all times.

That was also a part of that speech, was it not?

A. Yes.

* * *

Q. You gave to the Tribunal your reasons, which you said were reasons of principle, for not becoming a [Nazi] Party member?

A. Yes.

Q. Isn't it a fact that you have told the United States prosecution staff that you asked Hitler whether to join the Party, and that to your great relief Hitler told you not to?

A. Yes. I wanted to ascertain that before I participated in his actions in any way or co-operated with him—whether he demanded that from me namely, that I should become a member of the Party. He said No, and I was most relieved.

Q. So you remained out of the Party with Hitler's consent and approval?

A. Yes, of course. I think that is just another reason which will prove I have never been a member of the Party.

Q. When you received the Party Golden Swastika you stated that it was the greatest honor that could be conferred by the Third Reich?

A. It was, yes.

Q. And while you didn't wear it in your daily life, you did wear it on official occasions?

A. Yes. It allowed one great comforts during railroad journeys and rides in autobusses.

Q. From 1933 to 1942 you contributed a thousand Reichsmarks a year to the Nazi Party?

A. No. Yes, I beg your pardon; from 1937 to 1942.

Q. Didn't you say in an interrogation that it was from 1933 to 1942?

A. No, that is an error. From 1937, after I had received the Swastika. That is a misunderstanding, but after I had received it I said to myself, "It is decent that I will give them a thousand marks, and that is that."

Q. For upwards of ten years—not quite ten years—you accepted and held office of one kind or another under this regime, did you not?

A. From March 17, 1933 to January 21, 1943.

Q. And as I understand you, at least a part of the time Hitler deceived you and all the time you deceived Hitler?

A. No, oh no.

Q. I have misunderstood you?

A. Yes.

Q. Well now—

A. I think that in the first years, at least, I didn't deceive Hitler. I not only believe so, I know it. I only started deceiving him beginning in 1938. Until then, I was always telling him my honest opinion. I didn't cheat him at all; the contrary.

Q. What becomes, then, of your explanation that you entered his government in order to put brakes on his program? Did you tell him that?

A. Oh, no. I should hardly do a thing like that. He wouldn't have let me in then. But I didn't deceive him about that.

Q. Did he know your purpose in joining his government was to defeat his program by sabotage?

A. I didn't say that I wanted to defeat his program. I said that I wanted to direct it into orderly channels.

Q. Well, you have said that you wanted "to put brakes" on it. You used that expression?

A. Yes.

Q. To slow it down?

A. Yes.

Q. And he wanted to speed it up, isn't that right?

A. Yes, perhaps.

Q. You never allowed him to know that you had entered his government for the purpose of slowing down his rearmament program, did you?

A. I didn't have to tell him what I was thinking. I wasn't deceiving him. I wasn't telling anything wrong. I would hardly tell him what I was thinking inside me. He didn't tell me either, and you don't tell your political opponents either, but I never deceived him except after 1938.

Q. I am not asking you about a political opponent. I am asking you about the man in whose government you entered and became a part.

A. Yes.

Q. You used the words "sabotaging his rearmament program" yourself in describing your activities, did you not?

A. Yes, yes I did so, shall we say, after 1936. But then he noticed that. That wasn't deceit.

Q. When did your doubts about Hitler as a man, his integrity, first arise?

A. I have explained that in so much detail during the entire examination that I don't believe you want me to repeat it again.

Q. Did that occur?—I'll put it in the terms of your interrogation, since your interrogation is a little clearer.

In 1934 [so your interrogation runs] he killed or let be killed lots of people without their having any juristical substance, and a few days after, in the Reichstag, he said he was the highest judge in

Germany. He was certainly not, and for the first time I was shaken by his conception. It seemed to me absolutely immoral and un-human.

Is that correct?

A. I said the same here yesterday before the Tribunal, and the day before, exactly the same.

Q. Well, I want to fix these dates, Dr. Schacht. You see, your purpose in this trial and mine aren't exactly the same.

A. No, no, I know that.

Q. Now, you also received full information about the operation of the Gestapo from Gisevius in 1934 or 35 as he testified, did you not?

A. No, he did not say that. He said that he knew about these matters. He didn't tell me everything, but I said earlier today, this morning, that I admit that certain matters were communicated to me by him, and that I could and did draw my conclusions from that. At the beginning of May 1935 I had already discussed that matter with Hitler.

Q. You were informed about the Gestapo terrorism, Reichstag fire—

A. The Reichstag fire.

Q. —the falsity of the purge claim—

A. Just one moment. May I go in the right order? The Reichstag fire was something that I was told years later by the late Count Helldorf who has been mentioned by Gisevius.

Q. You mean Gisevius never told you about that?

A. I think I heard it from Helldorf. I may have heard it from Gisevius but I think it was Helldorf. But at any rate, it was after 1935 that I heard about it. Until then, I didn't think it was possible.

Q. You never doubted Gisevius's word when he told you in 1934 or 35 as he testified, did you?

A. Just a moment. He told me either in 1934 or 35, but not 1934 and 35, and when he did tell me—well if Gisevius said so—I assume that it is true.

Q. It was then that you knew about the persecution of the churches and the destruction of the labor unions, wasn't it?

A. The destruction of the labor unions took place as early as May 1933.

Q. You knew all about that, didn't you?

A. I didn't know all about it, but it became known to me. I knew just that, what every other German knew about it, and what the labor unions knew themselves.

Q. As a matter of fact, that was one of the reasons for the contributions by yourself and other industrialists to the Nazi Party, wasn't it?

A. Oh, no; oh, no. That was never mentioned.

Q. You mean that meetings of industrialists were held and as important a thing to industry as the destruction of the labor unions was never mentioned in your conferences?

A. I don't know about it. Please, will you remind me of anything in particular?

Q. Confiscation of the properties, the putting of labor union leaders into concentration camps?

A. I heard about it. Just a minute. Just who went to concentration camps—that I don't know. Regarding the confiscation of the property, I was informed because that was publicly announced. But as far as industrial meetings are concerned, if I understand you correctly, that is something I don't know.

Q. Now, you also knew very early about the persecution of the Jews, didn't you?

A. I have explained with great exactness here today just what I did know about the persecution of the Jews, how I acted in connection with the persecution of the Jews, and that as long as I was Minister I did everything to prevent these things.

Q. I understood your generalities and I am trying to get a little more detail about it, Dr. Schacht. Did you not testify as follows, on your interrogation on October 17, 1945?

Q. The National Socialists, as I took it from the program, intended not to have such a great percentage of Jews in the governmental and cultural positions of Germany, with which I agreed.

A. Yes.
Q.

Q. Well now, you had read *Mein Kampf*, had you not?
A. Yes.
Q. And you knew the views of Hitler on the Jewish question did you not?
A. Yes.

You so testified, did you not?
A. Yes.
Q.

Well now, during your time as Reichsminister, statutes were passed, were they not, prohibiting all Jewish lawyers, for example, from practicing in the courts?
A. Yes, that is what I said.
Q. Did you agree with that?
A. Yes.

Did you say that?
A. Yes.
Q. And you did agree?
A. Yes, I always agreed with the principle.
Q. Yes. And you also agreed with the principle of excluding all Jews from civil service positions, did you not?
A. No. I want to emphasize in this connection that I agreed with the principle about the dominating Jewish influence in the legal government circles; or rather, I always said that I did not consider that the dominating influence was favorable and was neither in the interest of Germany nor the German people, because that was a Christian state and based on Christian conceptions; nor was it in the interest of the Jews since it would increase animosity against the Jews, or rather, awaken it. I was always for a limiting of the Jewish participation, limiting of figures in this connection, not actually based on the population figures, but perhaps on a certain percentage.
Q. Well, let's go on with the interrogation. The interrogations are always so much briefer than the answers made in court where the press is present, if I may say so.
Did you give these answers?

Q. Now, with respect to civil service, there was this Aryanization clause that was put in. Did you agree with that legislation?
A. With the same limitation.
Q. Now, did you ever express yourself in the Cabinet or elsewhere to the point that you wanted these restrictions put in—restrictions you have been talking about?
A. I don't think so; useless to do it.
Q. You say "useless to do it"?

A. Yes.

Q. I thought you said at one time or another that the reason you stayed in is because you thought you might have some influence on policy.

A. Yes.

Q. You didn't consider this as important enough a matter to take a position on it?

A. Not important enough matter to break.

A. That's right.

Q. Then, you were asked this:

You certainly signed a law with respect to the prohibition against Jews receiving licenses to deal in foreign currencies.

Do you remember that?

A. Yes.

Q.

A. Yes, it may be.

Q. You were in favor of that?

A. I don't remember what the details were of that question.

Q. Well, it is not a matter of details. The question is a matter of discrimination.

A. Yes.

You said that?

A. Yes, certainly.

       ✿   ✿   ✿

Q. You also favored the law and signed the law prohibiting all Jews from being admitted to examinations for public economic advisors for co-operatives, for example?

A. Yes, possibly. I don't remember. Probably it is right.

Q. And you also approved a law imposing the death penalty on German subjects who transferred German property abroad or left German property abroad?

A. Yes.

Q. And of course you knew that that affected, chiefly and most seriously the Jews who were moving abroad?

A. I hope that the Jews weren't deceiving or cheating any more than the Christians. I hope the Jews didn't cheat any more than the Christians.

Q. The question was asked of you:

Well, now, was there a matter of conscience involved, or was there not?

And you answered:

To some extent, yes, but not important enough to risk a break.

A. Yes.

Q. And the question:

Yes. In other words, you had quite another objective which was more important.

A. That's right.

Q. Well, what was that objective, Dr. Schacht?

A. Well, the objective was to stay in power and to help carry this through in an ordinary and reasonable way.

Q. That is to say, the restoration of the German economy.

A. Quite.

Q. And the completion of the armament program.

A. The completion of the international equality, political equality of Germany.

Q. By means of armament, as you yourself have said.

A. Also by means of armament.

A. All correct, and I stand by that today.

*   *   *

Q. Now, as to the rearmament program, you participated in that from three separate offices?

A. Yes. I don't know which ones you mean, but please go ahead. Please assume so.

Q. I will list them. In the first place, you were Plenipotentiary for War?

A. Yes.

Q. You were President of the Reichsbank? That was the financial end of it?

A. Yes, yes.

Q. And you were Minister of Economics, in which position you had control of the general economic situation?

A. Yes. They weren't controls so general that I can confirm your statement just like that, but I was Minister of Economy.

Q. Now, let us take up first this position of Plenipotentiary for War. You have testified that this position was created for two purposes: (a) preparation for war, (b) control of the economy in the event of war. Is that correct?

A. That means preliminary planning in the event that a war should happen, and the direction of economy in the event of the outbreak of war having taken place, that preliminary period and the later period during war.

Q. You were asked about your functions and answered that "As the Chief of Staff worries in advance about mobilization from the military point of view"—so you were concerned with it from the economic point of view?

A. Yes.

Q. And your position as Plenipotentiary for War was of equal rank with the War Ministry? As you told us, those charged with responsibility in event of war were, first, the Minister of War and the Chief of the General Staff of the Wehrmacht; and, secondly, on an equal footing, Dr. Schacht, as Plenipotentiary for Economics. Is that correct?

A. I assume so, yes.

Q. And in January 1937 you wrote this, did you not?

I am engaged in the preparation of the war economy, according to the principle that our economic war organization must be so organized in time of peace that the war economy can be directly diverted in case of emergency from this peace-time organization, and has not to be newly created at the outbreak of war.

A. I assume that that is correct.

Q. Those being your functions as Plenipotentiary for the War Economy, let's turn to your functions as President of the Reichsbank. You have said that the carrying out of the armament program was the principal task of the German policy in 1935, did you not?

A. No doubt.

Q. There is no doubt that you voluntarily assumed the responsibility for finding financial and economic means for doing that?

A. Indubitably.

Q. And you were the financial and economic administrator in charge of developing the armament industry of Germany?

A. Oh, no; no, in no way.

Q. Well, I may have misunderstood your interrogation. I will ask the whole question so you will get it.

A. Yes.

Q.

Now, in connection with this development of the armament industry, you charged yourself as the financial and economic administrator of it.

The record says that you nodded your head.
The next question was:

Q. And in that connection you took various steps. Would you be good enough to describe for us the larger steps which you took with reference to this goal of rearmament, first, internally, and, secondly, with respect to foreign nations?

A. Internally I tried to collect every money available for financing the MEFO bills. Externally I tried to maintain foreign commerce as much as possible.

Did you make those answers, and are they correct?

A. I am sure that you are correct.

Q. And your purpose in maintaining foreign trade was to obtain enough foreign exchange to permit the imports of raw materials, not manufactured, which were required for the rearmament program. Is that not correct?

A. That is the question that was put to me. Now comes the answer. Please, will you look at the answer?

Q. What is your answer now?

A. My answer today is that that was not the only aim.

Q. But that was the primary aim, was it not?

A. No, not at all.

Q. All right, what was the other aim?

A. To keep Germany alive, to assure Germany being at work, to obtain sufficient food for Germany.

Q. What was the dominant aim?

A. The food supply in Germany and the occupation for the export industry.

Q. Well, I should like to go over one or two of these documents with you as to your aim. I quote Document 1168–PS, of May 3, 1935, entitled "Financing of Armament," Exhibit 37:

The following comments are based on the assumption that the accomplishment of the armament program in regard to speed and extent is the task of German policy, and that therefore everything else must be subordinated to this aim, although the reaching of this main goal must not be imperiled by neglecting other questions.

Did you write that?

A. Not only did I write it, but I handed it to Hitler personally. It is one of twin documents, one of which has already been submitted as an exhibit by the prosecution; it has been treated quite in detail by the prosecution. I did not receive the second document. When my defense counsel examined me I stated here that I was keen that Party collections and Party money, which was drawn from all sources of the German Reich, should be stopped, because the difficulty for me was to get the money to finance rearmament and the cashing of MEFO bills. It was extremely difficult. I could only get that point across before Hitler if I told him that it was a matter of course that this was being done in the interests of rearmament, and I told him that this was done—

Q. Yes, but—

A. Please let me finish; please don't interrupt me—I want to finish. If I had told him that this was done in the interest of building a theater, or something like that, that would not have pleased him. However, if I told him it must be done because otherwise we couldn't rearm, then that was the very point where I could touch Hitler, and that is why I said so, as I admitted during the examination by my solicitor.

Q. And you didn't call that misleading him?

A. I wouldn't call it misleading; I would call it leading.

Q. But leading, without telling him the true motive by which you were actuated at least.

A. I think you can score many more successes when you want to lead someone if you don't tell them the truth than if you tell them the truth.

Q. I am very glad to have that frank statement of your philosophy, Dr. Schacht. I am greatly indebted to you.

* * *

Q. At the time when you started the MEFO bills, there were no ready means available for financing the rearmament?

A. Quite.

Q. That is to say, through normal budget finance methods?

A. Not enough.

Q. Also, you were limited at that time by the statute of the Reichsbank?

A. Quite.

Q. And you found a way?

A. Yes.

Q. And the way you found was by creating a device in effect which enabled the Reichsbank to lend, by a subterfuge, to the Government what it normally or legally could not do?

A. Right.

Q. Is that true?

A. Yes, of course.

Q. The following questions were asked of you:

> Q. I understand that basically what was built up in Germany in the way of an armaments industry, a domestic economy that was sound, and a Wehrmacht, the efforts that you put in from 1934 to the spring of 1939, when MEFO financing stopped, were responsible in large part for the success of the whole program.
>
> A. I don't know whether they were responsible for it, but I helped a great deal to achieve that.

A. Yes.

Q. And you were asked as follows, on October 17, 1945:

> Q. In other words, in effect you are not taking the position that you are not largely responsible for the rearming of the German Army.
>
> A. Oh no, I never did.
>
> Q. You have always been proud of that fact, I take it.
>
> A. I wouldn't say proud, but satisfied.

Q. Is that still your position?

A. To that I should like to say this: the question of MEFO bills is quite certainly a system of financing which normally would never have happened. During my examination by my solicitor I have since made a statement on the subject. But, on the other hand, I can say that this question was dealt with by all legal experts in the Reichsbank and by that means of this subterfuge, as you put it, means were found, which was legally possible.

Q. No, I didn't put it; you put it to be a subterfuge.

A. All right, I beg your pardon; what you quoted was my answer. I beg your pardon. The matter was legally investigated, and we told ourselves: "That is the way we can work it". Apart from that, I am still satisfied today that I contributed to rearmament—only I wish that Hitler had used it differently.

Q. Well, on your sixtieth birthday Minister of War Blomberg said, "Without your help, my dear Mr. Schacht, none of this armament could have taken place," did he not?

A. Yes, those are the sort of polite words one says on such occasions. But there is quite a bit of truth in it too; I have never denied it.

Q. That is the way it looks to me.

✿   ✿   ✿

Q. Well, on December 24, 1935, you wrote EC–293, which is United States Exhibit 834, and used this language, did you not?

If a degree of armament going beyond these is now demanded, it is, of course, quite far from me to deny or change my advocacy of the greatest possible armament, expressed for years, both before and since the seizure of power; but it is my duty to point out the economic limitations of this policy.

A. That is pretty good.
Q. And that is true?
A. Yes.
Q. Then there came the Four Year Plan in 1936?
A. Yes.
Q. You did not like the appointment of Göring to that position?
A. I thought he was unsuited. Apart from that, of course, it gave on opening for a policy which was opposed to mine. I knew perfectly well that now the exaggerated rearmament was starting, whereas I was for restricted rearmament.

✿   ✿   ✿

Q. I turn to your interrogation of October 16, 1945, United States Exhibit 636, and ask if you did not give the following testimony:

By Schacht:
After Göring had taken over the Four Year Plan, and I must say after he had taken over the control of foreign exchange since April

1936, but still more after the Four Year Plan, September 1936, he has always tried to get control of the whole economic policy. One of the objects, of course, was that as Plenipotentiary for War Economy in case of war, and he being only too anxious to get everything into his hands, he tried to get that away from me. Certainly as long as I had the position of Minister of Economics I certainly objected to that.

You made that statement?
A. I believe that is correct.
Q. And then you describe your last visit with him after Hitler, for two months, had endeavored to unite Göring and yourself. You described it as follows:

Then I had a last talk with Göring, and at the end of that talk Göring said, "But I must have the right to give orders to you." Then I said, "Not to me, but to my successor." I have never taken orders from Göring, and I would never have done it because he was a fool in economics and I knew something about it, at least.

Q. Well, I gather that was a culminating, progressive, personal business between you and Göring. That seems perfectly obvious.
A. Certainly.

Is that correct?
A. Yes, certainly.
Q. In fact you told Major Tilley this:

Hitler I called an amoral type, but Göring I can only regard as immoral and criminal. By nature endowed with a certain bonhomie which he managed to exploit for his popularity, he was the most egocentric being imaginable. The assumption of political power was for him only a means for personal enrichment and personal good living. The success of others filled him with envy. His greed knew no bounds. His predilection for jewels, gold, and finery was unimaginable. He knew no comradeship. Only so long as someone was useful to him was he friends with him, but only on the surface.

Göring's knowledge in all fields equaled zero, especially in the economic field. Of all the economic matters which Hitler entrusted to him in the autumn of 1936, he had not the faintest notion, though he created an immense official apparatus and misused his powers as lord of all economy most outrageously. In his personal appearance he was so theatrical that you could only compare him with

Nero. A lady who had tea with his second wife reported that he appeared at this tea in a sort of Roman toga and sandals studded with jewels, his fingers bedecked with innumerable jeweled rings and generally covered with ornaments, his face painted and his lips rouged.

Did you give that statement to Major Tilley?
A. Yes.

*　　*　　*

Q. I refer to your interrogation of October 16, 1945, and ask whether you gave these answers to these questions:

Q. Let me ask you, then, in 1937, what kind of war did you envisage?
A. Never. We might have been attacked, invaded by somebody, but even that I had not expected.
Q. You had not expected? Did you expect a possibility of a mobilization and concentration of economic forces in the event of war?
A. In the event of an attack against Germany, certainly.
Q. Now, putting your mind back to 1937, are you able to say what sort of an attack you were concerned with?
A. I don't know, sir.
Q. Did you have thoughts on that at the time?
A. No, never.
Q. Did you then consider that the contingency of war in 1937 was so remote as to be negligible?
A. Yes.
Q. You did?
A. Yes, I have never thought of a conflict with Russia.

Did you give those answers?
A. Exactly the same that you find in this interrogation, I have said here before this Tribunal.
Q. Now, you testified that you tried to divert Hitler's plan which was to move and expand to the east—you tried to divert his attention to colonies instead?
A. Yes.

*　　*　　*

Q. You considered that the possession and exploitation of colonies was necessary for the sort of Germany you had in mind creating?

A. If you would like to replace the word "exploitation" by "development" I believe there will be no misunderstanding, and so far I agree with you.

Q. Well, by "development" you mean trading, and I suppose you expected to make a profit out of trade?

A. No, not only trade but developing the natural resources, that is to say, the natural existing economic possibilities of the colonies—to have those developed.

Q. And it was your proposal that Germany should become reliant on those colonies instead of relying on expansion to the east?

A. Every move of expansion within the European continent was viewed by me as complete nonsense.

Q. But you agreed with Hitler that expansion, either colonial or to the east, was a necessary condition of the kind of Germany you wanted to create.

A. No, that I have never said; I told him it was insanity to undertake anything toward the east; only colonial development was the solution.

* * *

Q. After the Fritzsche affair, at least, you knew that Hitler was not intent upon preserving the peace of Europe by all possible means.

A. Yes, I had my doubts.

Q. And after the Austrian *Anschluss* you knew that the Wehrmacht was an important factor in his Eastern policy.

A. Well, one may express it that way. I don't know exactly what you mean by it.

Q. Now, as to the move into Austria, I think you gave these answers:

Q. Actually Hitler did not use the precise method that you say you favored?

A. Not at all.

Q. Did you favor the method that he did employ?

A. Not at all, sir.

Q. What was there in his method that you didn't like?

A. Oh, it was simply overrunning, just taking, the Austrians over the head—or what do you call it? It was force, and I have never been in favor of such force.

Did you give those answers?

A. Yes.

Q. Now you have made considerable complaint here that foreigners didn't come to your support at various times in your efforts to block Hitler, have you not?

A. Certainly.

＊　＊　＊

Q. As a matter of fact, at the time of the *Anschluss* you joined in the attack on foreigners who were criticizing the methods, didn't you?

A. When and where? Which attack?

Q. All right. After the Austrian *Anschluss*, when force was used, with your disapproval, you immediately went in and took over the Austrian National Bank, didn't you?

A. That was my duty.

Q. And you liquidated it for the account of the Reich.

A. Not liquidated; I merged it.

Q. All right.

A. Amalgamated.

Q. Amalagamated it. And you took over the personnel.

A. Everything.

Q. Yes. And the decree doing so was signed by you.

A. Certainly.

Q. You called the employees together on March 21, 1938.

A. Yes.

Q. And you made a speech to them.

A. Yes.

Q. Well, I would like to quote some of it to you.

I think it is quite useful if we recall these things to our mind in order to expose all the sanctimonious hypocrisy exuding from the foreign press. Thank God, these things could after all not hinder the great German people on their way, for Adolf Hitler has created a communion of German will and German thought; he bolstered it up with the newly strengthened Wehrmacht, and he then finally gave the external form to the inner union between Germany and Austria.

I am known for sometimes expressing thoughts which give offense and there I would not like to depart from this custom.

Hilarity is noted at that point in your speech.

I know that there are even here in this country a few people—I believe they are not too numerous—who find fault with the events of the last few days. But nobody, I believe, doubts the goal and it should be said to all grumblers that you can't satisfy everybody. One person says he would have done it maybe in one way, but the remarkable thing is that they did not do it

—and in parentheses there appears the word "hilarity". Continuing with your speech—

that it was only done by our Adolf Hitler [long continued applause] and if there is still something left to be improved, then these grumblers should try to bring about these improvements from the German Reich and within the German community, but not to disturb it from without.

Did you use that language?
A. Yes.
Q. In other words, you publicly ridiculed those who were complaining of the methods, didn't you?
A. If that's the way you see it.
Q. Then, you also, in addressing the personnel of the Austrian National Bank which you were taking over, said this:

I consider it completely impossible that even a single person will find his future with us who is not wholeheartedly for Adolf Hitler. [Strong continued applause; shouts of "Sieg heil."]

Continuing with the speech:

Whoever does not do so had better withdraw from our circle of his own accord. [Stormy applause.]

Is that what happened?
A. Yes, they all agreed.
Q. Now, had the Reichsbank, before 1933 and 1934, been a political institution?
A. No.
Q. Had politics been in the Reichsbank?
A. Never.
Q. Well, on this day, speaking to its employees, you said this, did you not:

The Reichsbank will always be nothing but National Socialist, or I shall cease to be its manager. [Heavy, protracted applause.]

Did that happen?

A. Yes.

Q. Now, sir, you have said that you never took the oath to Hitler.

A. Yes.

Q. I ask you if this is what you, as head of the Reichsbank, required of your employees who were taken over in Austria, and I quote:

> Now I shall ask you to rise. [The audience rises.] Today we pledge allegiance to the great Reichsbank family, to the great German community; we pledge allegiance to our newly arisen, powerful Greater German Reich, and we sum up all these sentiments in the allegiance to the man who has brought about all this transformation. I ask you to raise your hands and to repeat after me:
>
> "I swear that I will be faithful and obedient to the Führer of the German Reich and the German people, Adolf Hitler, and will perform my duties conscientiously and selflessly." [The audience takes the pledge with uplifted hands.]
>
> You have taken this pledge. A scoundrel he who breaks it. To our Führer a triple "Sieg heil."

Is that a correct representation of what took place?

A. The oath was the required civil service oath and it was quite according to that which I said yesterday, that the oath was given to the head of the state, as I explained before. "We stand united for the German people"—I don't know exactly what the expression was—just the same thing you said in that oath.

❋　❋　❋

Q. You say you never broke the oath?

A. I don't know what you want to express by that. Certainly I did not keep the oath which I took to Hitler, because Hitler himself was a criminal who did not keep his word, and there was no other head of state. I don't know what you want to say, but I did not keep my oath to him and I am proud of it.

Q. So you were administering to your employees an oath which at that moment you were breaking and intending to break?

A. Again you confuse different periods of time. That was during a time in March 1938 when, as you have heard before, I still had my doubts, and therefore it was not clear in my mind just exactly what kind of a man Hitler was. Only when in the course of 1938 I found out that Hitler was eventually walking into a war, did I break the oath.

Q. When did you find him walking into a war?

A. When, in the course of the year 1938, by and by, judging from the events, I could assume that eventually Hitler would steer into a war, that is to say, intentionally. Then only did I break my oath.

Q. Well, you stated yesterday that you started to sabotage the government in 1936 and 37.

A. Yes, because I did not want excessive armament.

※　※　※

Q. Now, we come to Czechoslovakia. Did you favor the policy of acquiring the Sudetenland by threat of resort to arms?

A. No.

Q. I think you characterized the manner in which the Sudetenland was acquired as wrong and reprehensible.

A. I don't know when I could have done that. I said that the Allied politics made the donation of the Sudetenland to Hitler, whereas I always had expected that the Sudeten Germans would get autonomy.

Q. Well, on October 16, 1945, in United States Exhibit 636, I ask if you didn't make these replies to questions:

Q. Now, I am coming back to the march against Czechoslovakia which resulted in the appeasement policy in Munich and the cession of the Sudetenland to the Reich.

A. Yes.

Q. Did you at that time favor the policy of acquiring the Sudetenland?

A. No.

Q. Did you favor at that time the policy of threatening or menacing the Czechs by force of arms, so as to acquire the Sudetenland?

A. No, certainly not.

Q. Then I ask you, did it strike you at that time or did it come to your consciousness that the means which Hitler was using for threatening the Czechs, was the Wehrmacht and the armament industry?

A. He could not have done it without the Wehrmacht.

Did you give those answers?

A. Yes.

Q. Continuing:

Q. Did you consider the manner in which he handled the Sudeten question wrong or reprehensible?

A. Yes.

Q. You did?

A. Yes, sir.

Q. And did you have a feeling at that time, looking back on the events that had proceeded and in your own participation in them, that this army which he was using as a threat against Czechoslovakia was at least in part an army of your own creation? Did that ever strike you?

A. I cannot deny that, sir.

A. Certainly not.

Q. But here again, you turned to help Hitler once he had been successful with it, didn't you?

A. How can you say such a thing? I could not know, I did not know that Hitler would need the army in order to threaten other nations.

Q. After he had done it, you turned in and took over the Czech bank, didn't you?

A. Of course.

Q. You followed to clean up economically just so far as Hitler got the territory, didn't you?

A. But excuse me. He did not take it with violence. The Allies had given it to him. That had all been settled peacefully.

Q. Well, we have your testimony on the part the Wehrmacht played in it and what part you played in the Wehrmacht.

A. Yes, of course, I never disputed that.

Q. No. What I mean is this, referring to your interrogation of the 17th of October:

Q. Now, after the Sudetenland was taken over by the Munich agreement, did you as president of the Reichsbank do anything about the Sudeten territory?

A. I think we took over the affiliations of the Czech bank of issue.

And you also arranged for the currency conversion, did you not?

A. Yes.

Q. That is what you did after this "wrong and reprehensible" act had been committed by Hitler, didn't you?

A. It was not a wrong and reprehensible act of Hitler. He didn't commit any such act, but Hitler, in the way of contract, has received the Sudeten German area and, of course, the currency and the institute which issued the currency had to be amalgamated with German institutions. There is no possibility to speak of injustice. I cannot believe that the Allies would have put their signature to an injustice.

Q. So you think that everything up to Munich was all right?

A. No. I am certainly of different opinions; there was much injustice.

Q. Were you in the Court when Göring testified as to his threat to bomb Prague—"the beautiful city of Prague"?

A. Thanks to your invitation, I was here.

Q. I suppose you approved that use of the force which you created in the Wehrmacht?

A. I disapproved—disapproved under all circumstances.

Q. You didn't think that was right dealing, then?

A. No, no, that was an atrocious thing.

Q. Well, we found something we agree on, Doctor. You knew of the invasion of Poland?

A. Yes.

Q. As an unqualified act of aggression on Hitler's part?

A. Absolutely.

Q. The same was true of the invasion of Luxembourg.

A. Absolutely.

Q. And of Holland?

A. Absolutely.

Q. And of Denmark?

A. Absolutely.

Q. And of Norway?

A. Absolutely.

Q. And of Yugoslavia?

A. Absolutely.

Q. And of Russia?

A. Absolutely, sir; and Norway and Belgium, which you left out.

Q. Yes; well the entire course was a course of aggression?

A. Absolutely, to be condemned.

Q. And the success of that aggression at every step was due to the Wehrmacht which you had so much to do with creating?

          *   *   *

Q. As Minister without Portfolio, what did your Ministry consist of?

A. Nothing.

Q. What employees did you have?

A. One female secretary.

Q. What space did you occupy?

A. Two or three rooms in my own apartment, which I had furnished as office rooms.

Q. So the government did not even furnish you an office?

A. Yes, they paid me a rental for those rooms.

Q. Oh, and whom did you meet with as Minister without Portfolio?

A. I do not understand. Whom was I supposed to have met?

Q. Did you have any meetings? Did you have any official meetings to attend?

A. I have stated here repeatedly that after my retirement from the Reichsbank I never had a single meeting or conference at all, official or otherwise.

Q. Did anybody report to you, or did you report to anybody?

A. No, nobody reported to me, and I did not have to report to anybody else.

Q. Then I take it that you had no duties whatever in this position?

A. Absolutely correct.

Q. And you were Minister without Portfolio, however, at the time that Hitler came back from France, and you attended the reception for him at the railway station?

A. Right.

Q. And went to the Reichstag to hear his speech?

A. Yes.

Q. Now, notwithstanding your removal as President of the Reichsbank, the government continued to pay you your full salary until the end of 1942, did it not?

A. I stated yesterday that that is not correct. I received my salary from the Reichsbank, which was due to me by contract. A ministerial salary was not paid to me. I believe that as Minister I received certain representative funds. However, I did not receive a salary as Minister.

* * *

Q. Did it ever occur to you that a resignation would be the appropriate way of expressing your protest against these things which you now say you disapproved?

A. No, I assume that a resignation would not have been the means to put through those things which have to be done; and I regretted it very much that Beck retired. Those things which happened were caused by an entirely false policy. This policy was partly forced upon us. We did not handle it properly. In February Neurath was dismissed. In the fall Beck stepped out. In January 1939, I was dismissed. It was always one after the other who was thrown out, if it had been possible. In our group —if I may speak of a group—what we had hoped for and expected—that is to undertake a common action—would have been an excellent thing. However, these individual retirements had no use whatsoever; at least they had no success.

Q. You felt that Beck should have stayed at his post and been disloyal to the head of state?

A. Absolutely.

* * *

Q. And all of these events of which you disapproved never were of sufficient consequence to cause you to resign and withhold a further use of your name from this regime?

A. Until then I had still maintained the hope that things would turn towards the better and, consequently, I accepted all the disadvantages which were connected with my remaining in office, even the danger that some day I would be judged, as it is happening today.

Q. You continued to allow your name to be used at home and abroad despite your disapproval, as you say, of the invasion of Poland?

A. I have never been asked whether I permitted this, and I have never given that permission.

Q. You knew perfectly well, did you not, that your name meant a great deal to this group at any time, and that you were one of the only men in that group who had any standing abroad?

A. The first which you mentioned I already accepted yesterday from you as a compliment. The second, I believe, is not correct. I believe that several other members of the regime also had a standing in foreign countries, among whom also were a few who are sitting with me in the prisoner's dock.

* * *

Q. Now, Dr. Schacht, while you were Minister without Portfolio aggressive wars were instituted, according to your testimony, against Poland in September 1939, against Denmark and Norway in April 1940, against Holland and Belgium in May 1940; in June there was the French armistice and surrender; in September 1940, there was the German-Japanese-Italian Tripartite Pact; in April 1941, there was an attack on Yugoslavia and Greece, which you say was aggressive; in June 1940 there was the invasion of Soviet Russia, which you say was aggressive; on December 7, 1941, Japan attacked Pearl Harbor, and after the attack declared war on the United States; on December 8, 1941, the United States declared war on Japan, but not on Germany; on December 11, 1941, Germany and Italy declared war on the United States; and all these things happened in the foreign field and you kept your position as Minister without Portfolio under the Hitler Government, didn't you?

A. Mr. Justice—

Q. Isn't that a fact?

A. Yes, and I wish to add something to this. Dozens of witnesses who have testified here, and from myself you have heard again and again that it was absolutely impossible unilaterally to retire from an office because, if I have been put in as a minister by the head of a government, I can only retire over his signature. You have also heard that at various times I attempted

251

to rid myself of this ministerial office. Besides the witnesses' testimony, I can bring you testimony from others, including Americans, that it was well known that Hitler did not permit anyone to retire from an office without his permission. And now you accuse me that I remained. I did not remain for my pleasure. I remained because there was no other possibility for me than with a tremendous crash to retire from the Ministry, and this crash I tried to bring about almost every day until finally in January 1943 I succeeded in doing that and then disappearing from my office under certain danger to my life.

Q. Well, I'll deal with your explanation later. I am now getting the facts. You didn't have an open break with Hitler; you were not entirely out of office until after the German offensive broke down in Russia and the German armies were in retreat, and after the Allies landed in Africa, did you?

A. A letter by which I brought about the last successful crash is dated November 30, 1942. The crash and its success is dated January 21, 1943, because Hitler and Göring and some other people who had to deal with it needed seven weeks to make up their minds about the consequence of my actions.

Q. Then, by your letter, it plainly shows that you thought the ship was sinking, wasn't it?

A. My oral and written declarations from many previous times have already shown this. You have also already spoken about this. I had mentioned my doubts to Ribbentrop and Funk. I have given a number of descriptions here which prove that I never believed in the possibility of a German victory at any time. My disappearance from my office has nothing to do with these questions at all.

Q. Now, while you were remaining as Minister without Port-folio because you thought it might be dangerous to resign, you were also encouraging the general in the Army to commit treason against the head of the state, were you not?

A. Yes, and I would like to make an additional explanation to this. It was not because of the threatening danger to my life. For myself I was not afraid of danger to my life because my life had been endangered from 1937 on. I had been in constant danger of my life and I was exposed to the whim of the Party and of the head of the Party. Your question that I tried to turn a number of generals to treason against the head of the state I answer with the word yes.

Q. And you also tried to get assassins to assassinate Hitler, did you not?

A. In the year of 1938 when the first attempt was made by me, I did not think of an assassination of Hitler. However, I must admit that later I said if it could not be done any other way, we will have to kill him.

Q. Did you say "We will have to kill him," or did you say "Somebody else will have to kill him"?

A. If I had had the opportunity I would have killed him myself. Yes. But, please don't accuse—don't put me before a German court for attempted murder, because in that case I am guilty.

Q. Now, whatever your activities, they were never sufficiently open so that the Foreign Office files in France, which you say were searched by the Gestapo, had a single bit of it?

A. Yes, I couldn't announce it or it would have been in the newspapers.

Q. And the Gestapo, with all its spying on you, never put you under arrest until the July 20, 1944 attack on Hitler's life?

A. They could have put me under arrest earlier than that if they had been a little smarter, but that seems to be a strange attribute of any police force.

Q. And it was not until 1943 that the Hitler regime dismissed you? Until that time they apparently were in the belief that you were doing them more good than harm?

A. The thoughts which they had at that time I don't know. Please don't question me about that. You will have to ask somebody from the regime, and you have plenty of those right here.

* * *

Q. And so, Dr. Schacht, we are to appraise your testimony in the light of the fact that you personally, over a long period of time, pursued a course of sabotage of your government's policies, and preferred treason against the head of the state rather than openly resign your office?

A. You constantly refer to my resignation. I have told you and proven to you that a resignation was not possible. Consequently your conclusion is a wrong one.

Q. Let's see. In your interrogation on October 16, 1945, United States Exhibit 636, some questions were asked you about the generals of the Army, and I ask you if you didn't—if you weren't asked these questions and if you didn't give these answers:

> Q. I say, suppose you were chief of the general staff, and Hitler decided to attack Austria, would you say you had the right to withdraw?
> A. I would have said, "Withdraw me, sir."
> Q. You would have said that?
> A. Yes.
> Q. So you take the position that any officer could at any time, withdraw if he thought that the moral obligation was such that he felt that he could not go on?
> A. Quite.
> Q. In other words, you feel that the members of the general staff of the Wehrmacht who were responsible for carrying into execution Hitler's plan are actually guilty with him?
> A. That is a very difficult question you put to me, sir, and I answer yes.

You gave those answers, didn't you?
A. Yes, and I shall have to ask permission from the court to give an explanation. If Hitler—if Hitler, I say, ever had given me an immoral order, I would have refused to execute it. That is what I said about the generals also, and I stand to this testimony which you have just read.

❖ ❖ ❖

ALBERT SPEER

Albert Speer is by profession an architect who designed and supervised the building of many of the structures which were put up by the Nazi regime. After 1943 he was Reich Minister for Armament and Munitions, generally charged with maintenance of production. The principal accusation of personal participation in the Nazi crimes was his part in using slave labor and prisoners of war in production. He was a Party member and had served in the Reichstag and was a member of the Hitler cabinet. He remained until the end, but after the war became hopeless for Germany, he opposed its continuance and particularly opposed Hitler's plan to demolish bridges, highways, and

ALBERT SPEER TESTIFYING

"... the tremendous danger, however, contained in this totalitarian system only became abundantly clear at the moment when we were approaching the end.... The combination of Hitler and this system brought about this tremendous catastrophe to the world."

factories to prevent their falling into Allied hands. Speer's contention was that such facilities would be needed by any society that survived the war and that Germans no less than others would suffer from their destruction. He was overruled, but continued to resist the destruction as much as possible. As he saw no other way to bring a halt to the destruction and bloodshed he became a party to several plots against the life of Hitler and other high-ranking Nazis. His testimony as to the attitude of Hitler toward the German people in defeat should be one of the most effective preventions of the revival of a Hitler tradition in Germany.

꙳ ꙳ ꙳

Albert Speer, defendant, appearing as a witness on his own behalf cross examined for the United States by Mr. Justice Jackson:

Q. Coming to the questions dealt with in the second part of your examination, I want to ask you concerning the proposal to denounce the Geneva Convention.

You testified yesterday that it was proposed to withdraw from the Geneva Convention. Will you tell us who made those proposals?

A. This proposal, as I have already testified yesterday, came from Dr. Goebbels. It happened after the air attack on Dresden but Goebbels and Ley had earlier—that is, as early as April 1944 —had frequent conversations to the effect that the war effort should be increased with every means, so that I had the impression that Goebbels was merely making the Dresden attack the cause for a suggestion to renounce the Geneva Convention.

Q. Was the proposal at that time to resort to poison gas warfare?

A. I couldn't ascertain by my own direct observation that gas warfare was to be started, but I knew from Ley, Goebbels, from various associates of Ley, and Goebbels that they were discussing the question of using our two gases, Tabun and Sarin, and they desired to have it used. They believed that these two gases would have a particular effect and they did in fact produce the most frightful results. We made these observations as early as the autumn of 1944 when the situation was deteriorating considerably and quite a number of people were very worried about it.

Q. Will you tell us about these two gases, their production, their effects, their qualities, and the preparations that were made for gas warfare?

A. That, I could not tell in detail. I am not enough of an expert. All I know is that these two gases had the most unusually outstanding effects and that no respirator, no protection would be of any use against them as far as they go, so that the soldiers would therefore have been unable to protect themselves against this gas in any way. For the manufacture of this gas we had approximately three factories all of which were undestroyed and which, until November 1944, were working at full speed. When rumors regarding the possibility of the employment of gas reached us, I stopped gas production in November 1944. I stopped it by the following means: I blocked the supplies for the component parts and components of the gases; according to evidence before the Allied authorities, the gas production was in fact stopped—came to an end by January 1945. First of all, I tried to write Hitler a letter, which is available and which is dated October 1944, to use legal means to obtain his permission that these gas factories should stop producing. The reason I gave him was that the component products, mostly sozian, were needed urgently for other purposes because of air attacks. Hitler informed me right away that the gas production would have to continue under all circumstances, but I gave the instruction that the component products should no longer be supplied.

Q. Can you identify others of the group that were advocating gas warfare?

A. As far as the military were concerned, they—certainly not one of them—were in favor of gas warfare. All the reasonable militarists turned the gas warfare down as being utterly insane because, considering your superiority in the air, it would merely mean that the unprotected German cities would suffer the most tremendous catastrophe in no time at all.

* * *

Q. And your reasons, I take it, were the same as the military's; that is to say, it was certain Germany would get the worst of it if Germany started that kind of warfare. That was what was worrying the military, wasn't it?

A. No, not only that. At that stage of the war, it was perfectly clear that under no circumstances should there be the committing of international crimes which would then be held against the German people after the war was lost. That was the decisive reason for me.

Q. Now, what about the bombs, after the war was plainly lost, aimed at England day after day; who favored that?

A. You mean the rockets?

Q. Yes.

A. For us, as far as production was concerned, these rockets were the most expensive affair. Their effect compared to the output was negligible. We did not, therefore, find ourselves particularly interested in producing this affair to a very considerable degree. The person who was advancing this most was Himmler in this case. He gave *Obergruppenführer* Kammler the task of supervising and carrying out the firing of the rockets against England. In army circles, they were of the same opinion that I was, namely, that these rockets would be, or were, too expensive; and in air-force circles, the impression was similar because at the expense of one rocket one could build a fighter. It is quite clear that it would have been so much better for us if we hadn't permitted this nonsense.

❄   ❄   ❄

Q. And certain experiments were also conducted and research conducted in atomic energy, were they not?

A. Unfortunately, because our best experts we had in atom research had gone to America, we hadn't advanced as far as we wanted to. We suffered setbacks in atom research and actually we were about one to two years from achieving results—the results of splitting the atom.

Q. The policy of driving people out who didn't agree with Germany hasn't produced very good dividends, has it?

A. That, as far as we were concerned, had a very decisive disadvantage particularly in this sector.

❄   ❄   ❄

Q. The reports, then, of a new and secret weapon were exaggerated for the purpose of keeping the German people in the war?

A. That was the case mostly during the last phase of the war. Beginning with June or July 1944, I went to the Front very often. I visited about forty frontal divisions in their sectors, and I had to find out on those occasions that the troops, just as much as the Germans—the German nation—were given hopes regarding a new weapon which was due to come, that there should be a miraculous weapon which, without requiring the use of a man and soldier, would then guarantee victory. It was due to this belief that many people in Germany lost their lives, although due to reasons in their own thought they must have realized the war was finished. They believed that within the near future this new weapon would arrive. I wrote about this to Hitler and in various speeches, even before Goebbels's propaganda leaders, I tried to work against this conviction or belief. Both Hitler and Goebbels told me, however, that this wasn't propaganda which they were making but that this was a belief which had arisen from the people. Only in the dock here in Nürnberg, was I told by Fritzsche that this propaganda was made systematically through some channels.

※　　※　　※

Q. When did it become apparent that the war was lost? I take it that your attitude was that you felt some responsibility for getting the German people out of it with as little destruction as possible. Is that a fair statement of your position?

A. Yes, but I had that feeling not only with reference to the German nation. I was aware of the fact that one should equally avoid that destruction should take place in the occupied territories. That was as important to me as the other for a very realistic reason. I considered that all this destruction would no longer be limited to us after the war, but to the following German government and coming German generations.

Q. Where you differed with the people who wanted to continue the war to the bitter end, was that you wanted to see Germany have a chance to restore her life. Is that not a fact? Whereas, Hitler took the position that if he couldn't survive, he didn't care whether Germany survived or not?

A. That is true, and I would never have had the courage to make this statement before this Tribunal if I hadn't been able to prove it by the means of my documents, because such a statement is so incredible. The letter, however, which I wrote to Hitler on March 29 and in which I confirmed this, shows that he said so himself.

Q. Were you present with Hitler at the time he received the telegram from Göring, suggesting that Göring take over power?

A. On April 23 I flew to Berlin in order to take leave of several of my associates, and, as I want to tell you quite openly, also in order to place myself at Hitler's disposal after everything that had happened. Perhaps this will sound peculiar to you, but the conflicting feelings, which I had with reference to what I was trying to do against him and all the actions which he had committed, still didn't give me a clear basis inside me for my relationship to him, so I flew to see him. I didn't know whether he would order me to remain in Berlin. It was my impression, however, that it would be my duty not to run away like a coward but once again to appear on the scene. It was on that day that Göring's telegram arrived—Göring's telegram to Hitler, the telegram to Ribbentrop, I mean—arrived, and Bormann submitted the telegram to him.

Q. Submitted it to Hitler?

A. Yes, to Hitler.

Q. What did Hitler say upon that occasion?

A. Hitler was most excited about the contents of the telegram, and he expressed himself in a very clear manner about Göring. He said that he knew for some time that Göring had failed, that he was corrupt, that he was a drug addict. I was very shaken by this, because it occurred to me that if the head of the state had had such knowledge for some considerable time, then it was irresponsible on the part of the head of the state to have left this man in office—this man on whom depended the lives of huge numbers of people. It was typical of Hitler's attitude towards the entire problem, however, that he followed his statement up by saying: "But he can, nevertheless, negotiate the capitulation."

Q. Did he say why he was willing to let Göring negotiate the capitulation?

A. No. He stated in an offhand manner: "It doesn't matter anyway who does it." His disregard for the German nation was expressed in the way he said this.

Q. That is, his attitude was that there was nothing left worth saving, so let Göring work it out. Is that a fair statement of his position?

A. That was my impression, yes.

Q. Now, this policy of driving Germany to destruction after the war was lost had come to weigh on you to such a point that you were a party to several plots, were you not, in an attempt to remove the people who were responsible for the destruction, as you saw it, of your country?

A. Yes. But I want to add—

Q. There were more plots than you have told us about, weren't there?

A. During that time it was awfully easy to start a plot, because you could talk to practically anybody in the street and tell him what the situation was, and then he would say, "That is insanity"; and if he had any courage he placed himself at your disposal. Unfortunately, I didn't have an organization at my disposal which I might have commanded and with the help of which I could have done anything. That is why I had to depend on my personal conversations by which I remained in contact with various people. But I do want to say that it wasn't as dangerous as it looks here because, actually, the few unreasonable ones who remained were perhaps a few dozen. The other eighty million were perfectly reasonable when they knew what this was all about.

* * *

Q. You have eighty million sane and sensible people facing destruction; you have a dozen people driving them on to destruction and they are unable to stop it. I ask you if you have a feeling of responsibility for having established the Führer principle, which Göring has so well described for us, in Germany?

A. I, personally, by becoming minister in February 1942, had placed myself at the disposal of this Führer principle, this leadership principle. But in my organization I recognized that this principle of leadership was full of tremendous mistakes and therefore I tried to weaken its effect. The tremendous danger, however, contained in this totalitarian system only became abundantly clear at the moment when we were approaching the end.

It was then that one could see what the meaning of the principle was—namely, that every order should be carried out without any criticism. Everything that has happened during this trial, everything you have seen in the way of orders which were carried out without any consideration, did after all turn out to be mistakes; and there was the final result of the order to destroy bridges and carry out the destruction—all the outcome of that totalitarian system. This system—let me put it like this: at the end of the system it has become clear what tremendous dangers are contained in any such system, as such, quite apart from Hitler's principle. The combination of Hitler and this system then brought about this tremendous catastrophe to the world.

Q. Well, Hitler is dead—I assume you accept that?—and we ought to give the devil his due. Isn't it a fact that in the circle around Hitler there was almost no one who would stand up and tell him that the war was lost, except yourself?

A. That is correct with certain limitations. Amongst the military leaders there were many who, with reference to their own sphere, explained to Hitler very clearly what the situation was. Many army group commanders, for instance, made it clear to him how catastrophic developments were and that there were often serious arguments concerning the situation. Men like Guderian and Jodl, for instance, talked about their own sector very clearly quite often in my presence, and Hitler had to know from what they told him what the entire situation was. I have not been able to ascertain, however, that those who are actually responsible were around Hitler to tell him the war was lost; nor did I experience that these responsible people attempted to establish communications among themselves to come to some joint step against Hitler. With a few exceptions, I didn't attempt that on my part either because it would have been useless. Hitler, during that phase, had frightened all these close associates to such an extent that they were without any will of their own.

Q. Well, let us take the number two man who has told us that he was in favor of fighting to the very end. Were you present at a conversation between Göring and General Gallant in which Göring, in substance, forbade Gallant to report the disaster that was overtaking Germany?

A. No; in that form, that isn't correct. That was another conference.

Q. Well, tell us what there is about General Gallant's conversation with Göring as far as you know it.

A. This was at the Führer's headquarters in East Prussia outside Göring's train. Gallant had reported to Hitler that the enemy fighter planes had accompanied bombing squadrons as far as Lüttich and that it was to be expected, therefore, that the bombing units would, in the future, appear much farther from their bases, still accompanied by fighters. After the discussion on the military situation Göring got hold of Gallant before Hitler and, first of all, in an excited manner told him that this couldn't possibly be true, that this couldn't be the facts, that they couldn't go as far as Lüttich, these fighters. He said, in this connection, based on his experience as an old fighter pilot, that he knew that that was certainly so. Thereupon, Gallant replied that, after all, the fighters had been shot down and they were lying on the ground burning, and Göring wouldn't believe that was true. Gallant was a very outspoken man who told Göring his opinion most clearly and he wouldn't allow Göring's excitement to influence him. Finally, Göring, as Supreme Commander of the Air Force, prohibited Gallant expressly from making any further reports about this matter. It was impossible, he said, that enemy fighters could penetrate so deeply into Germany, and he was giving the order, therefore, that that was the opinion which he would have to accept as being correct. I continued to discuss the matter afterwards with Gallant and, as a matter of fact, Gallant, as the General of the Fighter Command, was relieved of his duty by Göring. At this point, Gallant had been in charge of all fighter units in Germany. He was in supreme command of the Air Force.

✽   ✽   ✽

Q. Your statement some time ago that you had a certain responsibility as a minister of the government for conditions—I should like to have you explain a little further what responsibility you refer to when you say you "assume responsibility" as a member of the government.

A. Oh, yes. In my opinion, in the life of the state, there are two types of responsibility. One is the responsibility one has for one's own sector and for that, of course, one is fully responsible. Over and above that, it is my own personal opinion that with reference to utterly decisive matters, there is total responsibility. There must be total responsibility in so far as a person is one of the leaders, because who else could assume responsibility for the development of events if not the immediate associates who work with and around the head of the state? This total responsibility, however, can only be applied to principal affairs. It cannot be applied to the handling of details which have occurred in the spheres of influence of other ministries or other responsible sources, because otherwise the entire discipline of the state would be completely muddled up, and no one would ever know who is individually responsible in his sphere of influence. These spheres must be cleanly divided.

Q. Your point is, I take it, that you, as a member of the government and a leader in this period of time, acknowledge a responsibility for its large policies, but not for all the details that occurred in their execution. Is that a fair statement of your position?

A. Yes.

* * *

ERHARD MILCH

Erhard Milch was a Captain of Fliers in the first World War. He was engaged in civil aviation at the time of the Nazi seizure of power. Göring at once sought him out to aid in building the air power of Germany. He joined the Hitler government in 1933 and held the rank of Field Marshal after 1940. Some of the incidents he relates throw light on the functioning of a totalitarian system.

* * *

Erhard Milch, called as a witness on behalf of Hermann Göring, was cross-examined for the United States by Mr. Justice Jackson:

Q. You occupied a very high position in the German Air Force?
A. I was General Inspector.
Q. You had a very large part in building up the Luftwaffe?
A. Yes.

Q. And you were honored for that in 1941 by the Hitler regime?

A. You mean the promotion to Field Marshal?

Q. When was your promotion to Field Marshal?

A. On July 19, 1940.

Q. And did you not receive a gift from the Hitler regime in recognition of your services?

A. In 1942 at the event of my fiftieth birthday I received a recognition.

Q. And the recognition was in the form of cash, wasn't it?

A. Yes, it was a cash recognition out of which I could buy an estate.

Q. And what did it consist of?

A. The money amounted to 250,000 marks.

❖ ❖ ❖

Q. There came a time when some engineers were sent to Russia, were they not, to inspect the air construction there, factories, facilities, and that sort of thing?

A. Yes, that is correct.

Q. When they came back, you learned that they had reported that Russia had greater capacity for building airplane engines than all six of the German factories, did you not?

A. Yes, that is correct.

Q. What order did Göring give about that information being made available, even to the Führer?

A. Göring did not believe that information at that time. I know that from the words of Colonel General Udet.

Q. Is it not a fact that you stated to the interrogators before that Göring called them defeatists and forbade them to repeat that information to any person, and threatened them with concentration camp if they repeated that information?

A. No, I cannot say that it was so far-reaching.

Q. You put it in your form now and tell us just what was said by Göring on that subject.

A. At a considerably later date, when it was the question of American armament figures, the Reichsmarshal told me once, "Now, you also are going to be a defeatist and believe these large figures." I told him then that I did indeed believe these figures, but at that time that had nothing to do with the Russian affair.

Q. Were those Russian figures ever reported to Hitler, or to the Reichstag or in any way made public to the German people?

A. The Russian figures? That I could not say. I had nothing to do with that question. The American figures were presented to Hitler, I am sure, but Hitler did not believe them.

Q. You testified on Friday, I believe, that you knew at the commencement of the war with Russia that it would end with the annihilation of Germany. I remind you of that, and that is correct, is it not?

A. Not with the destruction—the annihilation—but with defeat.

Q. Well, you went to Reichsmarshal Göring to protest against the entrance into the Russian war, is that right?

A. Yes.

Q. And did Göring agree with you that it would end with the defeat of Germany?

A. No, he did not agree. With respect to his relation to Hitler, he had to be very cautious in his statements. I told him about the reasons, the difficulties for Germany, and he nodded; and I had the impression from his words that he had tried the same objections with Hitler—that he had presented the same arguments to Hitler without success.

Q. In other words, he agreed with you that it would end in the defeat of Germany, but he didn't want it said to Hitler, is that right?

A. No, I cannot say that that is so. That was my conclusion—that it would end in defeat for Germany. He just agreed that this war had to be avoided at any rate, and that it would be a misfortune for Germany. In that connection, the word "defeat" was not mentioned by him.

Q. Was it mentioned by you?

A. I mentioned that that would be the defeat of Germany—to start a two-front war with an adversary as strong as Russia.

Q. And did he disagree with you about that? Did he take issue with you about that?

A. No, we did not argue about it. He only declared himself opposed to undertaking any further step because he considered it impossible, and it would only create the impression with Hitler that the Air Force were defeatists.

Q. And you didn't attempt any further to convey the information, on which you thought Germany would be defeated if she entered war with Russia, to Hitler or to any other officer of the High Command?

A. That was impossible for me. I could not do anything against the order of my superior.

Q. The Reichsmarshal?

A. The Reichsmarshal, yes.

* * *

Q. Now I want to ask you some questions about certain exhibits. I refer to number 343–PS, United States Exhibit 463. I would like to have that exhibit shown to you.

(*A document was submitted to the witness*)

A. These letters are signed by myself and they are on my stationery. They must have been drafted by the *Sanitaetsinspektion*, Medical Inspection. I do not remember the contents any more, as I said a few days ago.

Q. I understand from your interrogation that you gave as the reason why these letters were brought to you for signature, that your office was in fear of Himmler and didn't want to take the responsibility of writing a letter to him, is that right?

A. Not my office, but I believe the medical inspection did not want to get into a bad position with Himmler.

Q. I think you also said that the officials of that department were afraid of the SS.

A. Yes, that is what I wanted to say.

Q. Were they engaged in any illegal conduct or any activity against the government?

A. I did not quite get that.

Q. They were responsible officials doing their duty, as far as you know, is that right?

A. Yes, Mr. Justice. There one has to think about the conditions as they developed during the war.

Q. That is exactly what I want you to think about, and tell me about. Why were these people, performing their duty in a government office, afraid of Himmler or the SS? Explain that to us.

A. Not of the SS as such, but of the Secret Police. For none of us was the position an easy one. We were all convinced that we were under surveillance regardless of what rank we had. I believe there was nobody about whom there were not files kept, and hence many people, for that reason, were brought to trial. And the difficulties which arose from this fact did not touch only these people or myself, but went all the way up to the Reichsmarshal, who was also affected by it.

Q. I take it from your testimony that the reputation of the Gestapo was pretty well understood in Germany.

A. The last years of the war particularly so, yes. I could not say how far this was based on facts, but there was that feeling.

Q. Now, I think you also testified that some high military authorities did resign. I call your attention to your testimony in your interrogation by us, about von Fritsch and Beck. They resigned, didn't they?

A. No, they did not resign. They were already out.

Q. They were thrown out, is that it?

A. Yes, they were told they were not needed any more.

Q. I understood you to say that even the generals did not dare utter an opinion after those two left.

A. No, I never said that. I cannot remember that. I will be grateful if I could see the minutes.

Q. Well, I have them. I will ask you if you were not asked these questions and gave these answers:

Q. From your knowledge of conditions in army circles, among the air force, and among the general staff people who would have any opinion as to beginning a war, would they share your view?

The minutes show that you answered:

A. All of them unanimously—all officers—agreed with me. All higher officers agreed with me. A long time ago I had talked to Field Marshal von Blomberg, in 1937, about the danger of war on account of the careless policy of our politicians and we feared at that time that England or France wouldn't tolerate that policy in the long run. November 1, 1937, I had a long discussion with von Blomberg about this matter, and he was of the same opinion.

A. Yes, I remember.

Q. That is true, isn't it? You were then asked this:

Is it true that after General Fritsch and General Beck left their offices the position of the army was subordinated to the position of the political personality?

A. No, not subordinate. The army was always directly subordinate to the Führer or the Reich President. Nothing was changed. In that, the Chief of State was at the same time the Supreme Commander.

Q. At the time you were interrogated, your answer, which I will now read, was this:

Yes, because Hitler took over the High Command personally of the Army and the Navy and the Air Force. That was the position that was held by von Blomberg before, and Blomberg was in a position to resist Hitler, which he had done very often, and Hitler respected and feared and listened to his advice. Blomberg was the only elder soldier who was clever enough to reconcile military and political questions. This resistance—

A. Yes, it was my conviction.
Q. (continuing)

This resistance could not be kept up by the men near Hitler later on. They were too weak for that. For that reason he probably chose them.

Is that true?
A. My opinion.
Q.

Q. Did the generals with whom you associated even before 1939 not feel that the course of action which was being taken by Hitler would be likely to result in a war?
A. Those who were able to think in foreign political terms, yes; but they had to be very cautious about it, because they could not utter any opinion, they dared not utter—any opinion or writing.

Is that right?
A. Right.
Q. And what were the high generals in command afraid of that they didn't utter an opinion?
A. That general wouldn't have had a chance if it was reported to Hitler.
Q. Who would have done anything about it? There were many

generals and only one Hitler. Who was going to carry out any orders against them?

A. It was just not possible. Hitler was so powerful that the counterarguments of others—well, he just refused; he never let them utter any.

Q. And Hitler had the SS, didn't he, and Himmler, and Kaltenbrunner?

A. Yes, he had that also. Besides, he had the entire Wehrmacht, which had sworn an oath on him.

Q. I think you said that after March 5, 1943—in your interrogation—that Hitler was no longer normal. Did you make that statement?

A. I said that in my opinion Hitler during the last years was not the same as he was in the beginning, from 1933 until the war. I said that after the campaign against France there had been some change in him. That was my personal, private opinion, because what he did afterwards contradicted what he had taught before himself—contradicted it by 180 degrees. I could not consider that normal.

Q. And you want us to understand that Göring continued to act as number two man and took the orders from an abnormal man? Is that your story?

A. That abnormality was not so recognizable that one could think this man sick of mind; it did not have to go so far; the abnormality could be invisible to the masses. I believe that a doctor could say more about that than I. I talked to such gentlemen about it at that time.

Q. It was their opinion that he was abnormal?

A. That there was a possibility of an abnormality. That was affirmed by a doctor who knew him.

Q. A doctor of repute in Germany?

A. No, he is not very well known. He hadn't told it to anybody else, because that was not visible.

Q. He is in a concentration camp, I suppose?

A. Or worse.

Q. And if you had expressed your opinion that Hitler was abnormal, you probably also would have been there, would you not?

A. I would have been shot immediately.